REA

FRIENDS
OF ACPL

Lend Me Your Ear

Lend Me Your Ear

RHETORICAL CONSTRUCTIONS OF DEAFNESS

~

Brenda Jo Brueggemann

Gallaudet University Press
Washington, D.C.

Gallaudet University Press
Washington, DC 20002

The poem "Deafness" on page 102 is reprinted by permission of the editor from *Poetry* 167.1-2 (October/November 1995): 30. © 1995 by The Modern Poetry Association.

All efforts have been made to obtain permission to reprint copyrighted material.

Library of Congress Cataloging-in-Publication Data

Brueggemann, Brenda Jo, 1958–
    Lend me your ear : rhetorical constructions of deafness / Brenda
Jo Brueggemann
       p.   cm.
    Includes bibliographical references (p.) and index.
    ISBN 1–56368–079–3 (hc. : alk. paper)
    1. Deafness—Social Aspects. 2. Deaf—Social conditions.
3. Deaf—Means of communication. 4. Deaf—Education. 5. Sociology
of disability. I. Title.
HV2380.B69   1999
362.4'2—dc21   99–20807
                                                            CIP

for Jim

Contents

Acknowledgments

I can hardly begin to acknowledge the support it has taken to make this book. The listening, giving, sharing, enabling, questioning, caring, cheerleading, patience, attentiveness, and willingness that these institutions, organizations, and individuals have offered me has meant and still means much.

Really, this began with my dissertation research, aided by a grant from the National Council of Teachers of English in 1991. An Ohio State University Seed Grant and two quarters of release time from my department made all the difference for completing the bulk of the interviews, traveling numerous times to Gallaudet University, and completing most of the background research. Toward the end, a Coca-Cola Foundation for Research on Women grant helped me complete chapter 4, "Diagnosing Deafness: The Audiologist's Authority," and remarkable grant support from the Gallaudet University Press did much to bring the manuscript to print.

The "subjects" of the study deserve far more than just their bibliographical entry. For their time, wisdom, sometimes continued conversations over these seven years, I thank all those "hidden" pseudonymously as my "sources." I know their names. I know, too, how much they have mattered in making this the book I always wanted it to be.

Flying Words Project—the two-man team of Kenny Lerner and Peter Cook—were also oddly research subjects (though named) even as they were sheer inspiration. I watched a colleague, Susan Burch, deliver a paper on their work (and show a video clip) at MLA a number of years ago. Together, she and I have become surely their strongest fans, intent on seeing their work get the recognition it deserves. What's more, watching their work—seeing their own words fly, and their hands, bodies, and faces, too—has somehow given me all the more incentive to do just what Hélène Cixous encouraged me, as a woman and with my whole body, to do: to "write!" and to "fly—flying in language and make it fly."

Research assistants, usually Ohio State undergraduate and graduate students, made possible both by my department's generosity and by several of the grant awards I received, helped me fly, and led me to writing as well. Christian Zawodniak and Travis Barrett learned much about deafness and "the deaf world" as they interviewed deaf and hard-of-hearing students around the Columbus and Ohio State area and worked with me on parts of this project; and through their learning, I too learned anew. Vic Mortimer and Melissa Goldthwaite often gave more than their fair share of research assistance. Transcribing difficult interviews, tracking down sources, reading drafts, even completing an audiological evaluation at our local clinic—their hands are everywhere in this project. And this, too: Melissa Goldthwaite read every chapter with care, offering the gentlest but firmest of encouragement and fine-tuning my style, asking simple but important questions in the margins. This is good, since I have always wanted to write just like her.

The baby-sitters it took to see this book through are another kind of assistance that counts here—really counts. With a husband also teaching and completing a Ph.D., and two preschool children at home throughout most of the work, I could not have done it without them (and that is no mere phrase in this instance). Rob Stacy, Lisa Tatonetti, Melissa Goldthwaite, and Elizabeth Hamilton helped keep home the best place for my return.

Friends and colleagues to work (and play) with who encourage, engage, push us farther, feed us, respond in depth to the needs of our prose and our person—these are the dreams of any scholar. I live in that dream. Lee Abbott, Nick Howe, Nan Johnson, Georgina Kleege, Andrea Lunsford, Jeredith Merrin, Debra Moddelmog, Beverly Moss, Jim Phelan, Jackie Jones-Royster, and Melanie Rae Thon are my home colleagues here at OSU who have most helped build the dream. Their attention to my career, my voice, and my work on this project echoes in each and every page. And I owe a special acknowledgment to Andrea Lunsford and Jim Phelan, my senior colleagues, who had the vision at one crucial point to help me turn what was almost the end of my career into what has become a beginning. In a different way, Georgina Kleege's vision, too, is on every page here: as a pal, a lunch date, a tai chi partner, a colleague in disability studies, and a writer whose gifts and guts I never tire of ooohing and aaahing over, learning from, sharing with others, copying.

Lives and knowledge are rarely only local. And I am no exception. The cast of colleague-friends beyond "the heart of it all" here in Columbus, Ohio, who have offered ears, wisdom, time, questions, and continued conversations (call it support, in general) have credits spanning many years and numerous places. Mike Rose, Jim Raymond, and Gesa Kirsch got me going in graduate school. And they've stayed with me since. Lisa Ede and Cheryl Glenn have lately become the picture in my head when I think of "ideal audience"—tough, giving, so very engaged, eager to learn, not afraid to question, sharp as tacks, and funny, too. Lennard Davis's own "deafness as insight"—both professionally and personally—has been a beacon for me to follow. Susan Burch and Kathy Wood, my Gallaudet goddesses, have lead me through the hardest parts here about literacy and sign language poetry. They held my hand some, tugged me on when I got stubborn, stood near the finish with a big smile and hug—and shared their own brilliant projects, their homes and food, as well. Who could ask for more? Jane Detweiler was there when I began "coming out"—she was probably even part of the reason I did it—and I learned more than I could ever let her know from her grace, her sensitivity, her anchored presence in my personal and professional life these past ten years.

My newfound colleagues in "disability studies in the humanities" brought much enrichment and certainly renewed vigor toward the completion of this book—and just when it was most needed. One of the greatest sources of pride in my professional life is to be associated with Johnson Cheu, Patricia Dunn, Tammy Gravenhorst, Mark Jeffreys, Tonya Johnson, Georgina Kleege, Simi Linton, Nancy Mairs, David Mitchell, Sharon Snyder, Ellen Stekert, and Mark Willis in building courses, task forces, colloquiums, resolutions, initiatives, and even major organizational committees that further the intersection of disability studies in the humanities. And they are good to share meals with, too. In some of the same senses, my late (in the scope of this project) association with Vic Van Cleve, Gallaudet University Press director (and eminent scholar of Deaf history), came along at just the right time. Vic Van Cleve's passion yet sensibility for nurturing this work, for wringing more out of me when it needed wringing, for leading me through smart revisions, and even for sharing bike stories and witticisms over e-mail, genuinely made this publication pure joy. So too has Ivey Pittle Wallace's editing and encouragement made this manuscript whole.

There are also colleagues, from the past, whose work and lives have intersected mine in significant ways that eventually affected this book. They, too, deserve note: Lois Bragg, Amy Devitt, and Debra Journet.

It is my family, though, that this is written for, with, beside. My grandmother, Esther Koehn, who has believed in me so much—and right from the beginning—that sometimes it still makes my heart ache, my soul soar. (Someday I'll write that romance novel just for her.) My mother and father, Joyce and Roy, who let me be Brenda, neither deaf nor hearing, and a lover of language. My sisters, Barbara and Beverly, who just listen, have always listened, even when I thought they were ignoring me. And the family I live with now—who let me go away for periods of time to interview, research, write and still loved me mightily when I came back (with presents), who have taught me most and best that I don't have to be either-or, but can certainly be both-and: hearing and deaf, mother and scholar, motivated and tired, good and bad. But on whichever end of the hyphen I am ever standing, I am always, always blessed to be a part of their family, this family, my family. Thank you: Jim, Karl, Esther.

CHAPTER 1

*R*hetorical Constructions of Deafness: Discovering All the Available Means of Persuasion

A rhetorical culture is an institutional formation in which motives of competing parties are intelligible, audiences available, expressions reciprocal, norms translatable, and silences noticeable[;] . . . regardless of circumstances, a rhetorical culture is first and foremost an idea.

—THOMAS FARRELL, *Norms of Rhetorical Culture*

About deafness, I know everything and nothing. Everything, if forty years firsthand experience is to count. Nothing, when I realize the little I have had to do with the converse aspects of deafness—the other half of the dialogue. Of that side my wife knows more than I. So do teachers of the deaf and those who work among them; not least, people involuntarily but intensely involved—ordinary men and women who find themselves, from one cause or another, parents of a deaf child. For it is the non-deaf who absorb a large part of the impact of the disability. The limitations imposed by deafness are often less noticed by its victims than by those with whom they have to do.

—DAVID WRIGHT, *Deafness: A Personal Account*

As far as anyone knows, I have been deaf from birth; I have been a rhetorician about that long, too. Some days I do not call myself "deaf"—some days I'm "just hard-of-hearing," the term I grew up with, and other days I'm quite "hearing." The decisions I (and others) make about naming myself from day to day, from situation to situation, are rhetorical ones; in fact, I hardly know of a more significant way that rhetoric intersects my daily

1

life than in the debates—both within myself and the culture at large—about *deafness,* its literal and figurative meanings. Moreover, because deafness so often translates into vast communication difficulties in our culture—because it creates problems with listening, as well as speaking, writing, and reading—it stands, too, at the center and peripheries of the very rhetorical tradition. Deafness is a thorn in rhetoric's side, a spot in its eye, a buzz in its ear.

That is to say that deafness disrupts the institutional formations of our first and foremost ideas of a "rhetorical culture" at large. To unravel Thomas Farrell's definition of a rhetorical culture, when deaf ears are literal—not just figurative—the motives of competing parties are often *not* intelligible, audiences are usually *not* available, expressions are anything *but* reciprocal, and norms remain *un*translatable. Only the silences stand noticeable. In this book I want to listen to those silences, to lend my ear to the rhetorical constructions of deafness, to attend to key arguments as I explore the various institutional formations of deafness as an idea in contemporary culture. This book is both about rhetoric and about deafness.

The Good Woman Writing Well? or, Notes on a Rhetorical Method

This is a book about rhetoric because, like David Wright in my epigraph, I know everything and nothing about deafness. So, I have had to go lending my ear, listening to others in order to explore the "converse aspects of deafness" and to uncover, as Aristotle always encouraged me to, "all the available means of persuasion" in constructing the idea and the culture of deafness. In doing so, I probably have not now or ever, literally or figuratively, fit the classic notion of the rhetorician, Quintilian's *vir bonus dicendi peritus* ("good man speaking well"). But I have done the best I could.

Rhetoric, I have long contended, is not just the art of "see[ing] all the available means of persuasion in each case" but is, moreover, the use of those available means to construct the boundaries between cultures, communities, and disciplines and thereby between selves.[1] *What* we argue and persuade about (product), *how* we argue about it (process), and *why* we are arguing and persuading in the first place (purpose) are primary in forming the boundaries of our selves and our communities, cultures, and disciplines of knowledge. Whether we argue about ideas (ideological constructs) or about material circumstances, we use language. In using language, we enter the realm of rhetoric, where individuals and cultures construct and are constructed.

Take, for example, the case of *disability* itself. Disability is not an absolute, not the (im)pure and physically evident "other" to ability, normalcy, completion. We have constructed the binary between *disability* and *ability/normalcy.* The construction, as all cultural and categorical constructions are, is rhetorical; and here, I mean rhetoric as something more than just a critical tool. It is also something generative and epistemic—something capable of creating knowledge, too. In the way that Derrida has taught us, the concepts of the "normal" body and the "disabled" body variously supplement, contradict, hold up, and cancel out each other. One simply does not exist without the other. It is not so much that people are disabled—a passive portrayal of some "others" out there beyond our own bodies—but that they are us; moreover, they/us, quite actively, are involved in what Michael Oliver has aptly called a "politics of disablement."[2]

This is not just local politics either; it is a global and historical constant (even as it is ever-shifting). As Lennard Davis stakes out its territory, the "politics of disablement," the false binary between "normalcy" and "disability," "is not a minor issue that relates to a relatively small number of unfortunate people; it is a part of a historically constructed discourse, an ideology or thinking about the body under certain historical circumstances. Disability is not an object—a woman with a cane—but a social process that intimately involves everyone who has a body and lives in the world of the senses."[3]

How subtly the politics of disablement plays out might be illustrated in a number of ways. The available stories reverberate endlessly, and while the scenarios might shift, the screen never goes blank. We might stop the audio loop for but a moment—freeze the frame—and we would see Bob Dole, former Senate majority leader, 1996 Republican presidential candidate. But the Bob Dole we see would depend, say, on whether we looked at the daily photographs of Dole on the campaign trail in the month of July 1996—shortly before the Republican National Convention—or whether we looked at the Dole of the convention itself.

The Bob Dole in the early months of the campaign, the preconvention months, appears in my hometown newspaper daily. He is a Bob Dole entirely able, fit as a fiddle, dancing with some of the locals at a Polish festival in small-town Ohio, visiting with former President Reagan (not so entirely fit and able), engaging in the usual candidate capers. Yet I am suspicious here of the "usual." I peer hard at each photograph, looking for that hand they won't show. The invisible hand, the disabled hand on the disabled arm. Dole usually manages to hold his body in such a way, or to be hidden behind others in such a way, that the hand and its stiff-by-his-side arm do not show. The shoulder and part of the upper arm are there—surely to assure us that he does indeed have a body intact. But when he dances, the arm that can't encircle the Polish woman's waist is cleverly turned away from the photographers. He's no "cripple"! The man can dance! And when he visits with Reagan, the photo taken of the two of them literally fades his right arm out—as if the photographers are at fault for his lack of clarity, for the man not quite "whole" in the picture. (Indeed, *both* Dole and the quite aged Reagan look remarkably fit, young, happy.)

So, the "handlers," those political elusives we all whisper about, have determined, for whatever reasons, that Bob Dole's arm will not be part of the picture in this presidential campaign. I could handle that.[4] It is certainly part of the Bob Dole I've come to recognize—the one who entirely forgot to mention his own "disability" in a graduation speech he gave at Gallaudet University as he applauded the deaf students there for their struggles over adversity.

But then I shift a few frames forward, and things begin to sound and look quite different. Now the Republican National Convention is under way. The newspapers run stories of Bob Dole's "badge of honor"—the arm wounded in World War II action—and do a feature on the "Republican fervor" of the citizens in the small Italian town where he was wounded. The newscasters make patriotic plays out of what was, just last month, faded out of photographs. The cameras even follow Mrs. Dole out to the convention floor and pan on her stopping to talk with a citizen in a wheelchair.[5]

The frame moves forward a space or two: a week after the convention (while the Democratic convention is underway), Dole's disability has been claimed and he has made a remarkable jump in the polls since before the convention. A photograph appears one morning in my newspaper, several pages back. It haunts me. Taken from the ground up, it looks up into a sort of fuzzy circle of hands, almost as if they were meeting in a football huddle. Everything is a bit unclear. One hand in that circle, a right one—and the most distinct in the picture—is balled in a fist with a pen sticking out from it. Another hand, a left one, reaches out to the other hands in the circle. Above the circle of hands is Bob Dole's face—interestingly, with another pen in his mouth. Presumably, he had to give up his writing hand, his left hand, to greet his constituents. Presumably, too, we can deduce from this photo Dole's still-intact political abilities—he can still shake hands, he can still write, he can still sign bills. His disabled hand is no hindrance; it does not hamper his ability.

But there is even more to this construction of disability than this effective photo: the caption beneath it tells us that "Dole, whose right arm was disabled in World War II, must shake his left hand, of which he has limited use." This is, to my knowledge, the first blatant declaration of Dole's "disability" and "limited use" in print.[6] And it doesn't stop there. Beneath that Associated Press photo with the telling caption is, placed rather strategically, an article picked up from the Associated Political Network—"Dole: Pressing Clinton on Health Records," states the title. One paragraph of the article tells us that "Clinton has not agreed to an interview about his health, as has Dole, who is 73 *and partly disabled from his World War II wounds*" (my emphasis).[7]

Politically, then, we can have our politician either way—disabled or not. It depends on the circumstances (and those hidden handlers). And yes, too, on the "fortunate" coincidence that Dole's "disability" can be cashed in as a patriotic chip—as a badge of honor, a war wound—and not as some congenital defect or the misfortune of (preventable, curable) disease or accident. What was once hidden (perhaps considered disadvantageous?), now becomes clearly a wedge worth working, a catapult to advantage in the campaign polls. This, then, is but one illustration of how disability is both constructed and constructive.

Deafness is perhaps no less constructed or constructive, and it offers, in and of itself, a core example of the politics of disablement. Certainly, as I will argue in chapter 2, it is no less *instructed*. Deafness as disability? as pathology? as culture? The case is anything but clear, the verdict still out—way out. As the Americans with Disabilities Act (ADA, 1990) goes into full swing (people who are deaf receive "services" and "access" guaranteed under this act), as the nearly two generations of completely mainstreamed "hearing-impaired" students (the bumper crop that came out of the 1975 "Education for All Handicapped Children Act") go to college at Gallaudet

University and elsewhere, as cochlear implants, assistive listening devices, and technologically sophisticated new hearing aids flood the audiological market, the debates over "deafness" have never been louder or longer. And these are debates the deaf hear quite well.

The debates occur, I think, in three principal arenas: within Deaf communities and strongholds of Deaf culture, at locations like Gallaudet University; within education; and within science—primarily within medical science. I contend—and I am not alone in this contention, of course—that the institutions of science (particularly biomedicine) and education (particularly in literacy instruction) have played key roles in these rhetorical constructions of selves and societies.[8] This book ultimately serves as an illustration of these contentions; it uses the case of deafness, particularly as it is rhetorically constructed by science and literacy education as either a culture (Deafness) or as a disability/pathology (deafness).[9] So, to come back to my point—science and literacy education have, by and large, rhetorically constructed deafness (primarily in the lowercase sense of "disability" and "pathology" and sometimes, although rarely, in the uppercase sense of "culture"). What is odd is that science and literacy education have interpreted and constructed without much attention to, communication with, or regard for d/Deaf persons themselves; they have tended not to listen, not to lend their ears, to those they are speaking for and about. To borrow again Thomas Farrell's terms, they have largely left the motives of the competing parties unintelligible, rendered the audience unavailable, relinquished reciprocity, and created "norms" that are not translatable. The silences, however, have been (increasingly) noticeable.

It is those silences that I try to take note of here, even as I try not to turn the proverbial deaf ear to those who have already and continually spoken long, loud, and quite rhetorically. Perhaps because the space I am studying (d/Deafness as disability, pathology, or culture) and the space I study it from (as one who was born with sensorineural deafness but who has been raised and educated, for the most part, as "hearing") are chimerical, my method for noting—and interpreting—these silences is itself a categorical chimera. Chimerically, too, I am calling my method primarily rhetorical analysis.

So, what do I rhetorically analyze? Scientific, biomedical, technological, educational, literary, and popular media constructions of d/Deafness *in addition to, alongside of,* and *in complication with* the "voices" of d/Deaf persons themselves as they too construct and interrogate the ways they have been constructed. Although the debate over marking d/Deafness as either a disability, a pathology, or a culture has been central to studies of deafness for some time now, only recently has this debate been heard outside the research communities. Recent public and media attention to deafness, not surprisingly, has followed significant events affecting the lives of both d/Deaf and hearing people: the mainstreaming movement set in motion in 1975 by PL 94-142, the Education for All Handicapped Children Act; the graduation of America's first crop of mainstreamed deaf children; the ADA, which greatly complicates deaf persons' labeling themselves as "disabled" or not; the linguistic mapping of American Sign Language as a natural language; the educational debates over whole language instruction and the place of ESL, "remedial," and/or "at-risk" students in U.S. colleges; the explosively controversial technology of cochlear implants and the rapidly changing technology for hearing aids; the widely publicized 1988 "Deaf President Now" (DPN) protest at Gallaudet University; and even the crowning of America's first deaf Miss America, Heather Whitestone, in 1995.

I have gathered my data for this analysis by conducting literature reviews and textual analyses of holdings from the specialized collections of places such as Gallaudet University and the Volta Bureau (the premier "oralist" organization) as well as from general collections. But my data and analysis also center on and are guided by conversations I have had with people involved in all these rhetorical constructions of deafness. In some forty interviews and untaped, informal conversations too numerous to recount over the course of five years, I have listened to deaf and hard-of-hearing students from both residential institutions and "mainstreaming" programs in public schools, from both Gallaudet and "hearing" colleges. I have also listened to audiologists; to Deaf artists, poets, performers, and scholars; to sign language interpreters; to lawyers working in "disability" law; to those who educate deaf persons and those who conduct research on or about deaf persons; to my own conscience and experiences; and finally, to the conscience and experiences of people such as my husband, my sisters, my children, my parents and grandparents, my friends—those who, as David Wright claims, realize the "converse aspects of deafness," who make up the other half of the dialogue" as those "people involuntarily but intensely involved" with deafness and its various constructions.[10]

Of course, there are those I did not listen to, those who would not or could not, for various reasons, have conversations with me. And I must admit that some of these voices—their silences, their absences—continue to haunt me. There were those who felt threatened (from outside), angry (from inside), or apathetic (from no side—or perhaps all sides) in the face of the questions I wanted to ask. There were those whose personal or professional realities and obligations made silence necessary. There were those who just didn't have the time to talk, those who didn't show up for an interview, those who never responded to my requests for conversations. I mention them now for two reasons: first, to record respect for their silence, and second, to confess that my account here remains partial, in both senses of the word. My certainty is anything but absolute as I myself have created various constructions of deafness.

Myself in the Middle; or, Notes on Rhetorical Form

Uncertainty loves a hyphen. Rhetoric does too. Elsewhere I have written of my inability to maintain a "still-life," either personally or professionally, as I have spent my doubly hyphenated "hard-of-hearing" life doing what anthropologist Michelle Fine calls "working the hyphens."[11] I'm still there in this book—in between rocks and hard places, "still" and "life," "participant" and "observer," and "hard" and "hearing." As one whose life has been spent always feeling one step behind in a conversation, usually caught in the exchange between two speakers and never quite "there" at the moment any one person is speaking as I scrabble to process what I *have* heard, to fill in the many missing high frequency consonants that I *haven't* heard, to attend to ways that minimize background and interfering sounds, to construct a more accurate picture from the context surrounding the conversation (reading lips, attending to body language, noting facial expressions, trusting tone)—as such a one, I do anything but stand *still*. As such a one, too, I am anything but silent (still).

I shift stances and voices often. And this business of stances and voices—of shifting and sifting them, exploring all their available means—conducts the business of rhetoric at large. Even Donna Haraway, primate anthropologist turned feminist and social-scientific critic, takes up rhetoric, theoretically and practically, admonishing that "abundance matters. In fact, abundance is essential to the full discovery and historical possibility of human nature."[12] While I am sure that I do not discover *all* the available means of persuasion here, I do aim wide, cast long: I write from an academically distanced stance in places, quoting authorities, analyzing critically and carefully, matching warrants for claims; I write too with a personal voice, shouting my subjectivity, telling tales, crafting sentences and deliberately stylizing as I go. Generically, I wander: story, memoir, essay, article, poetry.

Perhaps, like Jamaican Michelle Cliff, this wandering maps my "journey into speech." Cliff writes of her own journey:

> The first piece of writing I produced, beyond a dissertation on intellectual game-playing in the Italian Renaissance, was entitled "Notes on Speechlessness," published in *Sinister Wisdom,* no. 5. In it I talked about my identification with Victor, the wild boy of Aveyron, who, after his rescue from the forest and wildness by a well-meaning doctor of Enlightenment Europe, become "civilized," but never came to speech.[13] I felt, with Victor, that my wildness had been tamed—that which I had been taught was my wildness.
>
> My dissertation was produced at the Warburg Institute, University of London, and was responsible for giving me an intellectual belief in myself that I had not had before, while at the same time distancing me from who I am, almost rendering me speechless about who I am. At least I believed in the young woman who wrote the dissertation—still, I wondered who she was and where she had come from.
>
> I could speak fluently, but I could not reveal.[14]

Like Cliff, for me it took a dissertation—an act of intellectual game-playing about nothing less than the writing of deaf students at Gallaudet University—to gain both the belief and doubt in myself that would lead to the writing of a book like this one. And I have quoted Cliff at length here because my journey, like hers, has led me sometimes to "write this in fire."[15]

I have also written this in another kind of fire and spirit as well: I have tried to fashion my text in the spirit of ancient sophistry, a spirit Susan Jarratt has sought to revive in *Rereading the Sophists: Classical Rhetoric Refigured,* particularly for feminists, and even more particularly for feminist writing. My words lie somewhere between mythos and logos (see Jarratt's second chapter). I realize the culturally constructed "truth" and spirit of Jarratt's claim that "the devaluation of both the sophists and women operates as their reduction to a 'style' devoid of substance."[16] And I sometimes write in fire here, seeking to burn that truth.

As a sophist (there, I've said it), I replace Plato's "truth" with sophistic "situation," Aristotle's *logos* with Isocrates' *kairos*. The question of what argument surrounding deafness is *most reasonable* (the truth?) does not concern me so much as uncovering what the various and *situated* reasons for any one argument might have been, might still be. To get at these situations, to employ sophistic theory, I practice sophistic style—as practiced, according to Jarratt, by someone like philosopher Hélène Cixous, and likewise condemned by Aristotle and Plato for its "uses of antithesis and fondness for contradictory arguments, along with [a] propensity for poetry's loosely connected narrative syntax in prose . . . generic diversity, loose organization, a reliance on narrative, physical pleasure in language production and reception, a holistic psychology of communication, and an emphasis on the aural relation between speaker and listener."[17]

Finally, but with hardly any finality to it, I have written this book as a cyborg. As a "bionically enhanced" being—half-human organism, half-machine—I am, as Donna Haraway defines me in her "Manifesto for Cyborgs," "resolutely committed to partiality, irony, intimacy, and perversity."[18] Hyphenated, I write from a "fractured identity," trying to make the most of my "oppositional consciousness," a model offered by Chela Sandoval (and advocated by Haraway) that is "born of the skills for reading webs of power by those refused stable membership in the social categories of race, sex, or class."[19] To those categories I add, of course, "disability"—in a move I have come to call squaring the triangle of "otherness." Stuck between "hard" and "hearing," I have come not to pay much attention to categories . . . even as I have also come, as a rhetorician, to seek them out, conscious not only of their *constructedness* but of their ability to further *construct*. I pay attention to the rules. But then again, I don't.

Cyborgs, Haraway tells (warns?) us, are like that: "Cyborgs are not reverent; they do not re-member the cosmos. They are wary of holism, but needy for connection—they seem to have a natural feel for united front politics, but without the vanguard party. The main trouble with cyborgs, of course, is that they are the illegitimate offspring of militarism and patriarchal capitalism, not to mention state socialism. But illegitimate offspring are often exceedingly unfaithful to their origins. Their fathers, after all, are inessential."[20]

With Aristotle and Plato as my academic fathers, with hearing histories of deafness that usually do not even include me, with years of speech therapists, audiologists, and rhetoricians alike willing me to speech, I *write* here, wary of holism but needy for connection.

THE OTHER HALF OF THE DIALOGUE; OR, NOTES ON RHETORICAL CONTENT

My need for connection dwells, for example, between rhetoric and deafness. Perhaps even more than this is a book about rhetoric, it is a book about deafness; but for me, as I claimed at the outset, it is not easy to separate deafness from rhetoric. Nor is it easy to separate the rhetorical tradition, the theory and practice of rhetoric for some 2,500 years now, from the "problems" that deafness poses for a cultural imperative to speak and speak well. The legacy and residue of what James Fredal calls rhetoric's powerful "will to speech" in our culture are nowhere more evident than in the constructions and cases of deafness. Although there are instances of its imperative before then, particularly in Enlightenment Europe, this will to speech led philosophers and rhetoricians as diverse as the Spaniard Juan Luis Vives, the Englishman John Locke, the Frenchman Abbé Condillac, and the nineteenth-century elocutionists—including James Rush, Joshua Steele, and Thomas Sheridan—to posit the human voice, the ability to speak words, as both the vessel and content of Reason. And in this age, Reason was, of course the essence of being human. The syllogism created—rhetorical, faulty, and enthymematic as it is—sounds like this: *Language is human; speech is language; therefore, deaf people are inhuman, and deafness is a problem.*

I believe that it is no small coincidence that deaf education (as the first version of "special education") and the "speech sciences" begin in this era as well.[21] This will to speech is both oppressor and creator of deafness in its various forms—as disability, as pathology, and even as culture. That tradition of rhetoric—grounded in the will to speech—is the central point I wish to have ringing in my readers' ears as they continue; it is the point of departure and return for each of my three sections, for each of my nine pieces. For most of the book, to be sure, deafness will stand in the spotlight. But rhetoric is in charge of the curtains.

The curtain call comes with two questions: "How is d/Deafness variously constructed as a disability, pathology, or culture through the institutions of (literacy) education and science/technology?" and "How do these constructions fit with those of deaf persons themselves?" In part 1, "Deafness as Disability," terminology undergirds this interpretation of deafness. Terms created primarily by legal and educational institutions, in consort, are the principal markers of deafness as disability. In chapter 2, "Deafness, Literacy, Rhetoric: Legacies of Language and Communication," the territory of deafness as it is mapped into, on, and as an issue of literacy is discovered—with rhetoric as my compass. Proceeding from lists of terms surrounding deafness when it enters the educational arena, and by looking at the terms of deaf education's history, in chapter 2 I explore the lineages of seeing literacy as either *language* or *communication,* a lineage carried forward through the history of rhetoric, beginning with the Roman educator Quintilian (C.E. 92).

This lineage is carried forth in a controversy—the debate over "manual" versus "oral" communication methods in deaf education—that has again multiplied both quantitatively and qualitatively in current times since the passing of two key federal laws, the Education for All Handicapped Children Act in 1975 and the ADA in 1990. The controversy currently plays out over the issues of "mainstreaming" deaf children into public schools and of providing them with a "bilingual-bicultural" education. Here I turn to terms that are readily read on the lips of lawyers, judges, teachers, educational administrators, and school psychologists as they construct what they determine is the "least restrictive environment" for deaf students: terms such as *oral, manual, inclusion, mainstreaming, equal access, bilingual-bicultural, whole language, remedial, at-risk,* and *second-language learners* crop up in the literature surrounding literacy and deafness. A vision of deafness as disability creates this vocabulary and has striking rhetorical consequences in the daily lives of deaf individuals.

I elaborate on these consequences through conversations and case studies, through teaching, tutoring, and talking with deaf and hard-of-hearing students at both Gallaudet University and Ohio State University. Stories of the violence—and triumph—of English literacy in deaf students' lives grow from each of my terminological interrogations here.[22]

Thus, in Quintilian's tradition, this chapter ends with good people—both men and women—speaking *and signing* well as they tell tales of their educational experiences, as they map their lives as deaf and hard-of-hearing students in the late twentieth century, an age greatly influenced by major mandates such as PL 94-142 and the ADA, and an age rich with promising—and threatening—technologies that fundamentally affect their abilities to participate in educational and civic spaces.

In such participation, labels stick, categories matter, and "passing" is essential. This is a point Aristotle makes quite clear throughout his treatise on rhetoric. It is the point that runs throughout chapter 3, "'It's So Hard to Believe That You Pass': A Hearing-Impaired Student Writing on the Borders of Language." Here I listen harder and longer to just one such student, Anna, as she charts the border territory of one who stands—sometimes firmly, sometimes precariously—between "deaf" and "hearing," between English and American Sign Language literacy. Titled by a quotation from Anna herself, this chapter offers a case study of her attempts to pass through her Basic English course at Gallaudet University. In Anna's passage I illustrate how disability and deafness have danced, in and out of step, to the tune of what Susan Foster has called "same but different":[23] in some ways Anna's "deafness" is like (and of) disability, yet in other ways it is not.

The pathological view of deafness aligns itself with the medical model of disability and the "pity industry" (see, for example, Harlan Hahn, Anne Finger) and characterizes another construction that is explored in part 2, "Deafness as Pathology."[24] While disability and pathology certainly supplement each other—and I explore their various supplementary angles here, too—I have distinguished them in parts 1 and 2 primarily by the institutions behind them: literacy education finds itself most intertwined with attitudes and assessments of disability, while science—particularly biomedicine and its technologies—paves a way to pathology.

Exploring scientific constructions of deafness as a pathology, chapter 4 presents a rhetorical analysis of "the audiological moment." In "Diagnosing Deafness: The Audiologist's Authority," I come back to the will to speech and the way it plays out "logically" in an audiological examination, in the ethos of the audiologist herself, and in the pathos surrounding a diagnosis of deafness. I begin with the first step that rhetoricians call *invention*—exploring the history of audiology, excavating its various sites of invention, tracing its lineage with other sciences. With a tradition under way and a paradigm invented, audiology now begins (as do most sciences) to *arrange* and *stylize* what it has invented. Textbooks, as Thomas Kuhn, historian of science, tells us, play a major role in these arranging and stylizing acts. And so I turn to a rhetorical analysis of contemporary audiology textbooks, looking principally for the way in which they carry out audiology (and rhetoric's) will to speech.

But carrying out a paradigm (such as the will to speech) is not enough. To really matter, to make a mark in history, to rhetorically reverberate, such paradigm-driven discourse must memorialize. Memory must be created around the ideas of that paradigm. Following a model offered by Alan Gross in *The Rhetoric of Science,* I analyze the scientifically saturated moments of precise observation and prediction and of classification; the role of audience and authority (in the relationship between audiologist and her client, the person who is usually only "hearing-impaired"); and the promise—the *presence,* as rhetorician Chaim Perelman would have it—of a "cure" that hinges on basic amplification for the patient alone, thus locating the problem only in the body of the hearing-impaired audience and not in a shared responsibility between speakers and audiences, clinicians and patients. These are the scientific acts that memorialize audiology.

The stakes and strategies for logos, pathos, and ethos only get higher and more complicated, the will to speech only stronger yet, when I turn at the end of this chapter to the *delivery* of audiology's promise. A bold new line of "assistive listening devices," spurred on both by acts like the ADA and by technological advancement at large, and the highly controversial surgical act of a cochlear implant bring out perhaps the best and the worst of arguments surrounding deafness. Here technology delivers: it is variously seen as a godsend (as an ear from heaven, the road to "normalcy," and a journey back out of isolation, chronic misunderstanding, and self-deprecation) and as the devil itself (in posing a severe threat to "Deaf culture," in eradicating difference through not-fully-understood intervention, in testifying that deaf lives aren't worth living, and in creating a further self-deprecating cycle of technological [inter]dependence). I emphasize, yet again, the crucial role of rhetoric in pathologizing deafness and in ensuring that deafness is, remarkably and disturbingly, passed over in the current academic proliferation of work on "the body" and "the cyborg state."[25]

While d/Deafness continues to be passed over in academic discussions in which it would seem likely to consistently interrupt the conversation, if not control it, it has been speaking for itself of late as a culture with a unique linguistic heritage and worldview.[26] In section 3, "Deafness as Culture," I explore two instances of deafness's "coming out." Chapter 5, "The Coming Out of Deaf Culture: Repeating, Reversing, Revising Rhetorics," looks at the rise in cultural awareness of deafness, both by those who are deaf and by those who are hearing. Here I examine rhetoric principally as it is rooted in key events such as the linguistic verification of American Sign Language (ASL) as a "real" language (now the fourth most common language in the United States) and the "Deaf President Now" protest that galvanized Gallaudet University and captured the imagination of deaf and hearing persons as it also marked what many have called a major moment in the entire movement of civil rights for the disabled.[27]

In chapter 5, I analyze the DPN protest as a rhetorical situation, paying attention not only to its resonance within the rhetoric of social movements and the rhetoric of public address, but also to the way DPN creates rhetoric in a new key altogether.[28] With these two dominant models for rhetorically analyzing political discourse as my guides, however loose, and with an ear tuned at least partially to dominant discourse (especially as it is characterized by these two models), I examine how DPN triply encounters and employs rhetoric: *repeating* dominant political discourse models, *reversing* dominant political discourse, and finally, most provocatively, *refiguring* dominant political discourse in a revisionary rhetoric on entirely new ground, as it "hears" arguments differently.

Quite connected to a key coming out event like DPN, I argue, is the formal recognition of sign language literature, particularly poetry. In chapter 6, "Words Another Way: Of Presence, Vision, Silence, and Politics in Sign Language Poetry," I try out rhetorical analysis on poetry that is performance art, quintessentially postmodern in its presentation and provocative in adding the dimension of space to language: it can never be "disembodied." While I work to expand the possibilities for contemporary poetry at large in this chapter—by drawing sign language poetry within its circle—I also work to foreground sign language poetry as a rhetorical act in and of itself, as a unique literature just beginning to grow out of a culture and language that has, too, just come out. The interanimation of "voice" and "vision," the signification of silence, the power of (embodied) "presence,"[29] and the politics of performance all play out in sign language poetry. Thus, while it incorporates some of the traditional features we often expect in poetry, sign language poetry charts new territory in postmodernism, poststructuralism, political literature, and performance art. It stands to break ground, too, in the study of visual rhetoric, visual literacy, and visual culture.[30]

Also breaking ground in a culture desperately trying to define itself are those who sit on the borders, for various reasons, between "Deaf" and "Hearing," between "deaf" and "hearing." As Homi K. Bhabha tells us in *The Location of Culture,* "the borderline work of culture demands an encounter with 'newness' that is not part of the continuum of past and present. It creates a sense of the new as an insurgent act of cultural translation."[31] The occupation of those borders in the "state" of "deafness" constitutes what one sign language interpreter I have interviewed, Cynthia, calls a "precarious placement"—a place characterized, even, by what Bhabha calls its "insurgent act[s] of cultural translation." Who is "d/Deaf" and who is "h/Hearing" is a question often very much up for grabs, one whose answer cannot necessarily be easily placed. And in the grabbing and placing, rhetoric once again guides the grasp.

Along the way, I too grasp at my relationships to my locations within and outside of "Deaf culture," "disability," and "pathology." I do so with a series of interludes following each of my three sections; these interludes are essays and poems that touch on my own experiences as a disabled, pathologized, cultural entity. "On (Almost) Passing," the two "interpellation" poems, and "Are You Deaf or Hearing?" are yet another part of the arguments about deafness, yet another interpretation, yet another insurgent act of cultural translation. In line with Foucault's notion of genealogy, they "oppose . . . the search for 'origins,'" and "refuse the certainty of absolutes."[32] And yes, they are rhetorical, too.

CODA

Throughout this book, then, I speculate on deafness *as* rhetoric, on what Lennard Davis has called "deafness and insight," and on the way we might reconceive rhetoric by listening to deafness.[33] I aim for conceiving a "will to listen" that is born, ironically enough, from listening to deafness. Here I speak (or rather, write—they are not, after all, the same) of concepts quite familiar to Western rhetoric—of "speaking subjects," the "good man [*sic*] speaking well," and the Aristotelian tradition of audience analysis. I question a tradition that places all the burden for understanding on listeners, but all the authority on speakers. In rhetoric, we have, for instance, absolutely no tradition for "listening," no "art of listening well" to accompany 2,500 years of theory and practice in "speaking well." And finally, coming from the constructions of deafness I have examined, I suggest space for a rhetoric of silence, as well as time for a rhetoric of responsive and responsible listening that matches our rhetorical responsibilities for speaking—time for a rhetoric that lends its ear.

NOTES

1. Rhetoric as the art of "see[ing] all the available means of persuasion in each case" is Aristotle's oft-cited definition (*On Rhetoric* 1.1.14).

2. Oliver, *Politics of Disablement.*

3. L. Davis, *Enforcing Normalcy,* p. 2.

4. Indeed, I should not be surprised about this erasure of disability when I reflect on the "splendid deception" and magnificent manipulation of Franklin Delano Roosevelt's own presidency: he was a president we never saw in his wheelchair, who feigned walking with the aid of his sons and agents, and who never allowed himself to be photographed or publicly seen in either his wheelchair or, say, struggling to get out of a car; see Gallagher's book-length account, *FDR's Splendid Deception,* and L. Davis, *Enforcing Normalcy,* pp. 92–99. Likewise, even more recently, during his own presidency Ronald Reagan's "hearing loss" (hard-of-hearing? deaf?) and his struggles with both Alzheimer's and cancer were quite carefully "managed." So too has Bill Clinton's recent acquisition of hearing aids been played as an accessory—something akin to a hat: "he'll wear them when he needs them," announced the press.

5. See "Italian Town Hails Dole," *New York Times,* 17 August 1996, 1:8. The reasons for this change of view, for now emphasizing what was once deliberately hidden, are not clear and are surely complicated. However, one interesting event that intersects well with Dole's "coming out" as disabled in the post-convention months is the stirring speech delivered at the Democratic National Convention (which followed the Republican convention) by the movie star Christopher Reeve (Superman!), injured while riding a horse and now paralyzed from the neck down, who delivered a remarkable speech, respirator and all.

6. I don't doubt that there are other direct mentions of his disability or even photos taken in his political career—but as a native of Kansas, Dole's home state, and as someone who has followed the '96 campaigns in my local newspaper, I have not seen any this direct.

7. "Dole: Pressing Clinton on Health Records," *Columbus Dispatch*, 22 August 1996, A3.

8. A small sampling of recent work that posits the role of science (especially bio-medicine) as a large one in current configurations of "self" and "culture" might include Gould's *Mismeasure of Man*, Gross's *Rhetoric of Science*, Haraway's *Simians, Cyborgs, and Women*, Harding's collection *The "Racial" Economy of Science*, and Schiebinger's *Nature's Body*. Likewise, a sampling of work illustrating the interplay between literacy education and interpretations of self and society might include writings by Linda Brodkey, Henry Giroux, and Mike Rose (including pieces by Glynda Hull and Rose); Delpit's *Other People's Children*, Hirsch's classic *Cultural Literacy*, and Stuckey's *Violence of Literacy*; and collections such as Kintgen, Kroll, and Rose's *Perspectives on Literacy* and Lunsford, Moglen, and Slevin's *Right to Literacy*.

9. Here I follow the convention within the Deaf community, apparently begun by James Woodward in a 1972 course he taught, of distinguishing between functional hearing loss, an audiological deficit (deaf), and identification with a cultural community (Deaf).

10. All names used in reference to interviews throughout this book are pseudonyms. Wright, *Deafness*, p. 1.

11. Michelle Fine's piece "Working the Hyphens" was my inspiration for "Still-Life." In that essay on my precarious methodological positions, on occupying the hyphen between the anthropologically sanctioned role of "participant-observer" while I conducted ethnographically oriented research at Gallaudet University, I elaborate on the absence of a "still-life" position in such work and how it was that I "worked the hyphens" even as they worked me.

12. Haraway, *Simians, Cyborgs, and Women*, p. 68.

13. Victor and his "well-meaning doctor," Itard, will figure significantly in my own chapter on audiology later in this book.

14. Cliff, "Journey into Speech," p. 56.

15. The essay that follows Cliff's brief "Journey into Speech" is her potent and more sustained "If I Could Write This in Fire, I Would Write This in Fire." This essay is often assigned, and always controversial, in college classrooms today. The writing in "Fire" is, as she presages in "Journey into Speech," "jagged, nonlinear, almost shorthand." She occupies various positions—most of "hatred and bitterness"—railing against the colonizing British (the parts most students pay attention to as, aghast at Cliff's burning vehemence, they often begin building their own counterfires), but against her "white supremacist" colonizing tendencies as well: "we were colorists and we aspired to oppressor status" (p. 78). She tries, she says, "to write this as clearly as possible," but realizes "that what I say may sound fabulous, or even mythic" (p. 78)—hardly

academic, reasoned, objective. Her fragmented essay is rich with stories, tensions, interweavings, complications, emotions. It is also very well-written.

16. Jarratt, *Rereading the Sophists,* p. 65.

17. Ibid., p. 72. I practiced this style, though, long before I knew it had a name like "sophistry." As early as my journals and poetry, both at the age of ten, these features are evident. My classroom writing as far back as third grade—term papers, book reports, and the like—also evince a tendency to narrate, loosely organize, generically diversify, stylize even as they also exhibit carefully documented, thesis-controlled, logic-driven prose.

18. Haraway, *Simians, Cyborgs, and Women,* p. 151.

19. Ibid., p. 155. Haraway credits Sandoval, "Dis-Illusionment and the Poetry of the Future."

20. Ibid., p. 151.

21. See Winzer, *History of Special Education,* for a discussion of deaf education as the first "special education."

22. Reference to "the violence of literacy" borrows on the argument behind—and title of—a 1991 book by J. Elspeth Stuckey.

23. Foster, "Examining the Fit," 1996.

24. See, for example, Lane, "Constructions of Deafness" and *Mask of Benevolence,* and Woodward, *How You Gonna Get to Heaven?,* for discussions of the "pathological view of deafness"; see Hahn, "Politics of Physical Difference" and "Toward a Politics of Disability," and Finger, "And the Greatest of These," for two considerations of the "pity industry."

25. See, for example, Aronowitz, Martinsons, and Menser, *Technoscience and Cyberculture;* Gray, *Cyborg Handbook;* Terry and Urla, *Deviant Bodies.*

26. Notable exceptions to the silence surrounding literary and critical scholarship at large regarding deafness comes from the work of scholars such as Lennard Davis and H. Dirksen Bauman.

27. See Shapiro, *No Pity.*

28. See Jankowski, *Deaf Empowerment,* for example.

29. The rhetorical concept of "presence" is key in Chaim Perelman's work on rhetoric, particularly in *The New Rhetoric.*

30. "Visual rhetoric" is featured in some of Sonja Foss's scholarship, such as "The Construction of Appeal in Visual Images" and "Judy Chicago's *The Dinner Party,*" while "visual literacy" concerns Chris Jenks, among others.

31. Bhabha, *Location of Culture,* p. 7.

32. Foucault, "Nietzsche, Genealogy, History," pp. 77, 87.

33. See L. Davis, *Enforcing Normalcy.* Davis is himself a "CODA"—the acronym adopted for hearing children of deaf parents (Children of Deaf Adults). By some accounts, the term "CODA" befits these children well since they are, like their musical counterpart, "a passage of more or less independent character introduced after the completion of essential parts of a movement, so as to form a more definite and satisfactory conclusion" (*Oxford English Dictionary*, s.v.). Much of the folklore by and about CODAs records how they became, even as very young children, the "ears" for their parents—taking on adultlike responsibilities in their speaking *and* listening roles (see, for example, Preston's *Mother Father Deaf* and Sidransky's *In Silence*).

PART 1

Deafness as Disability

CHAPTER 2

*D*eafness, Literacy, Rhetoric: Legacies of Language and Communication

Almost since its inception the education of deaf people has been marred by divisive controversy concerning the most appropriate modes of communication.

—MARGRET WINZER, *The History of Special Education*

. . . an inability or unwillingness to deal with deaf children in terms of their own needs and capabilities. In 1880 this was understandable, as education for deaf children was in its infancy. But in the 1970s?

—RICHARD WINEFIELD, *Never the Twain Shall Meet*

I think the boundary [between deaf and hearing] is made up by society, the educational system. What caused the separation? I think education, the system.

—ELLEN, *Gallaudet graduate and American Sign Language teacher*

"Deafness is a big country," writes Owen Wrigley in one of his chapter titles in *The Politics of Deafness,* as he seeks to ethnographically document the "land," the "absent anchor," of the people who belong to the culture he writes about—the culture of the Deaf.[1] For all its nonexistence in chartable, tangible terms, the territory of "deafness" looms large. It is, as I now look out, simply huge; its terrain is vastly diverse and the possibilities for negotiating and navigating in it—or around it—abound. Maps are many. And both their multitude and their various and often conflicting representations guarantee that the going might in fact be made harder by using them.

23

The resources and richness of the land, too, are not diminished by physical absence: there is precious ore to be mined here. The size of its population alone guarantees that. Depending on different accounts, on which map is consulted and what criteria for establishing "deafness" are used, the count varies: from 15 million worldwide—"on par with a modest size nation" when commitment to cultural Deafness is the marker in one rendering; to 13.3 million in the United States (or 6.5 million or even 1.7 million, depending on which specific terms and classifications are used to define deafness); to 21 million in the United States by yet another definition. These are just *some* of the available sets of figures.[2]

Despite the diversity and preciousness of its resources, there are also dangerous subterranean mines in this country—mines long abandoned and not carefully marked, mines boarded shut, with warnings of "Danger! Keep out!" There are land mines as well, in a potentially explosively field. The promise and perils of educating deaf students have been (and continue to be) laid out in such possibly active minefields. Education matters, literacy matters—sometimes violently.[3] Furthermore, education and matters of literacy explode (like the "stop," the "plosive," the most articulate of our speech sounds) on the figurative tongue of deafness, when we look at (lipread?) the rhetorical constructions of deafness.

The ways I might look at the rhetorical constructions of deafness in education are many—frames, maps, primers, and the like prove plentiful. I might, for example, abbreviate most of the longer histories I have encountered, creating my own rhetoric and literacy-minded chronology:

A (Partial) History of Deaf Education

ca. 355 B.C.E.	Aristotle (*Politics*) advocates infanticide for "deformed" children; Cicero follows suit in 55 B.C.E.
380–420 C.E.	St. Augustine of Hippo claims "Faith comes by hearing" and excludes deaf persons from Christian faith
533	The Code of Justinian classifies deaf persons (both separately and among all other disabled persons)
1578	Pedro Ponce de León undertakes educating deaf Spanish nobility
1662	The Royal Society of London inspires inquiry into the nature of language and the teaching of deaf and blind persons
1720	Daniel Defoe writes *The History of the Life and Surprising Adventures of Mr. Duncan Campbell*—the first popular book about the lives of deaf persons
1745	Jacob Rodrigues Pereire begins working with deaf students

1751	Diderot publishes his study on deaf people
1760	Abbé Charles Michel de l'Epée founds the Institute for the Deaf in Paris
1779	Pierre Desloges, a deaf man, defends deaf education based on sign language in a widely circulated pamphlet
1789	Abbé Sicard takes over the Institute for the Deaf in Paris
1799	Jean-Marc Itard, trying out the language philosophies of Condillac, begins working with "Victor," a feral boy who cannot speak and is kept at the Institute for the Deaf in Paris
1817	The Reverend Thomas Hopkins Gallaudet opens the Connecticut Asylum for the Education and Instruction of Deaf and Dumb Persons (first American school for the deaf); educates Alice Cogswell, a deaf girl; and introduces manual methods for deaf education
1850s	Printing becomes popular trade for deaf persons (primarily through training in trade schools)
1851	Thomas Gallaudet founds first American church for the deaf
1857	Columbia Institution for the Deaf and Dumb and the Blind is incorporated on two acres of land in Washington, D.C.
1864	National Deaf Mute College (also known as Columbia Institution for the Deaf and Dumb) founded in Washington, D.C. (later Gallaudet College, then Gallaudet University)
1864	Alexander Melville Bell designs "Visible Speech"
1867	Clarke Institution founded (premier oralist school) and full-fledged campaign for oral methods begins
1871	First successful aural surgery
1871	Alexander Graham Bell begins teaching his father's method, "Visible Speech," to deaf students
1880	Milan Conference, an international meeting of educators of the deaf, outlaws use of sign language (manual methods) to teach deaf students
1883	A. G. Bell delivers and a year later publishes *Memoirs upon the Formation of a Deaf Variety of the Human Race,* a eugenicist tract decrying the marriage of (and potential child-rearing by) deaf couples
1886	A. G. Bell tests hearing of Washington, D.C., students (first audiograms)
1890s	A. G. Bell and Edward Miner Gallaudet lead "communications debate" between oralism and manualism, respectively
1893	National Deaf Mute College renamed Gallaudet College at the request of the alumni association

1895	A. G. Bell and E. M. Gallaudet square off at Convention of American Instructors of the Deaf
1909	First compulsory school attendance laws for deaf (and blind) children enacted
1954	By an act of Congress, the corporate name of the Columbia Institution becomes Gallaudet College
1958	Public Law 85-926 provides grants for training special education personnel
1963	The Division of Handicapped Children and Youth is established within the U.S. Department of Health, Education, and Welfare
1969	Model Secondary School for the Deaf (MSSD) established on Gallaudet's campus
1970	Kendall Demonstration Elementary School (KDES) established on Gallaudet's campus; "Deaf Studies" chair established at Gallaudet
1975	Public Law 94-142, the Education for All Handicapped Children Act, is passed by Congress
1980s	Like most U.S. colleges, Gallaudet has significant enrollment increase; cochlear implants offered
1986	Gallaudet College becomes Gallaudet University; the Education of the Deaf Act (PL 99-371) signed
1988	"Deaf President Now" protest—students close Gallaudet University campus; Irving King Jordan becomes first deaf president of Gallaudet University; Philip Bravin becomes first deaf chairman of the Board of Trustees
1989	International "Deaf Way Conference and Festival" held at Gallaudet
1990	Harvey Corson appointed as Gallaudet's first deaf provost
1990	The Americans with Disabilities Act (ADA) signed into law
1990	PL 94-142 revised and renamed the Individuals with Disabilities Education Act (IDEA)
1993–present	Gallaudet University enrollment begins to decline—federal funding declines and programs, services, personnel, departments are cut
1998	Gallaudet students actively campaign to replace a recently reelected English Department chair, purportedly because of her politics and pedagogy in literacy instruction

Sources: Gannon, *Deaf Heritage;* "Gallaudet"; Gallaudet, *History of the College;* Winzer, *History of Special Education: From Isolation to Integration;* and my own memory. I repeat that this list is partial, in all senses of the word: it selects for events that line up with my own senses of rhetoric and of literacy education.

Histories are surely useful, but they can also carry a rhetoric all their own in their partiality, in their "official" disguise, in their tendencies to cast change as "progress" moving toward things always bigger and better, and, finally, in their penchant for not being a history *of* the people even as they are *about* that group of people. And since my own proclivities and training have centered far more on qualitative research and a cultural studies approach to rhetoric than on historical research, I have not followed a historical map. Yet my vision has been imprinted by more than enough variant renderings of "deaf history" and "the history of deaf education."

I might, too, have undertaken a study of the rhetoric of deaf education by surveying relevant terms and categories, by examining the production and utility of all the labels and landmarks in the vast land of "deafness." The topographical variety is certainly not lacking here: deaf; hard-of-hearing; hearing-impaired; the silents; deaf and dumb; dumb; mute; limited hearing; auditorially impaired; acoustically handicapped; disabled; handicapped; prelingually, postlingually, or prevocationally deaf; mild, moderate, severe, or profound hearing loss; binaural, sensorineural, conductive, mixed, or central hearing loss; the least restrictive environment; appropriate placement; special needs; full or partial integration; self-contained classrooms; inclusion; audiological, psychological, occupational, physical, communicative, and social "assessment teams"; parent education; aural/oral rehabilitation; speech therapy; lipreading; speechreading; cued speech; fingerspelling; simultaneous communication (SimCom); total communication (TC); Pidgin Sign English (PSE); Signed English; Signing Exact English (SEE); American Sign Language (ASL); bilingual-bicultural (Bi-Bi); support services—note takers, interpreters (oral or sign language), tutors, FM loop systems, closed and open captioning, telecommunications devices (TTYs/TDDs), telephone relay services, real-time transcriptions, light alarm systems, bed shakers; resource rooms; hearing aids—in-ear, behind-the-ear, digitally programmable; cochlear implants; mainstreaming; residential institute; day institute; technical and trade institutes.[4]

Enough. To be certain, rhetoric is fond of terms, categories, division, classifications. We have Aristotle, first and foremost, to thank for that. But while I will be more than a little concerned with the production, reception, and utility of terms, I do not want to make them the focus of my discussion. Rather than turn to the text, as Aristotle might prefer, and analyze the terms on its page, I favor a more process-centered and person-dominated over a product-centered and strictly linguistic approach.

Michael Oliver and others in disability studies might call this a "sociological approach," and Kenneth Bruffee and others in composition and rhetoric studies might call it "social constructionist"; [5] I choose to call it a rhetorical-cultural approach. I want to consider where (and who) the terms come from, the social and rhetorical milieu surrounding their inception and usage, how they are used, and, certainly, who they are used on as well as how those persons react to them.

I could have proceeded by conducting a critical rhetorical study of those who "serve" in the "deaf education system" (what Harlan Lane has called, disapprovingly, "the audist establishment").[6] That is, I could have looked at the acts, words, and values of any of the following who work with and depend for income on deaf persons: audiologists, hearing aid salespersons, ear-nose-throat specialists and surgeons, speech pathologists, speech therapists, aural (and/or oral) rehabilitation specialists, school psychologists and counselors, social workers, interpreters, parents with deaf children, special education teachers, deaf education teachers, English as a Second Language (ESL) teachers, "regular" classroom teachers who encounter deaf students in mainstreamed situations, genetic counselors, school principals and superintendents (of both deaf residential and mainstreamed programs), English and American Sign Language teachers in particular, academic counselors, coaches, tutors, job counselors, literacy workers, civil rights and disability lawyers. Again, we have a long list that is both incomplete and daunting. This list—these persons and their work and lives in relation to those of deaf persons—is promising, too, for rhetorical analysis.

But still, I'm headed elsewhere in this chapter—headed to some "place" where the terms and people interact. And in heading there, I would surely have to pass by or through—perhaps even stay in—the lives of deaf students. My map codes them as the indigenous population of the country of deafness, long since taken over by terms, traders, teachers, missionaries, lawyers, medical practitioners, scientists, politicians—colonists all, if you will. By and large their colonial enterprise has been situated around issues of (il)literacy—literacy *of* and *for* the deaf, the illiteracy that is often equated with deafness.[7] This colonial form of literacy is one of "other people's children," as Lisa Delpit characterizes it, a literacy usually advocated and carried through "with the best of intentions by middle-class [and usually white, and usually hearing] liberal educators."[8]

So it is that—as a white, middle-class, liberal, but not very hearing educator—I turn my discussion of the rhetorical construction of deafness (as a disability) in our educational system to "literacy." In using literacy as my frame, my lens, and indeed my photo I hope to superimpose, quadruply expose—and simultaneously lay side by side—all four of the possible maps I've just considered: the history of deaf education, the terms of and in the deaf educational system, the people "giving" to the deaf educational system (who are, of course, doing plenty of taking, too), and, finally, the people "taking" from the system (the deaf students who irrefutably give as well).

In constructing this rhetorical-cultural map within the grids of literacy, I cannot avoid the significant "problem of speaking for others"; I realize that "the neutrality of the theorizer can no longer, can never again, be sustained, even for a moment."[9] I would not pretend otherwise. But still, I must write (which I also submit is different than speaking), and I must theorize and go about "naming silenced lives."[10] I try to do it with sensitivity to those silences, with respect for the ruptures that even I have surely created within the system and within the lives of those who work in the mines of deaf education and of those, too, who try to navigate through its minefields. In some ways I am each of them; in some ways, I am not any of them.

My combinatorial method is thus somewhat Ciceronian—the Cicero who opens the second book of *De Inventione* (2.1). Here he relates the story of the "citizens of Croton" who sought out a famous painter (Zeuxis of Heraclea) to paint for them "a picture of Helen so that the portrait though silent and lifeless might embody the surpassing beauty of womanhood."[11] Zeuxis proceeded by gathering all the city's most beautiful women, then selecting the five most beautiful from among them "because he did not think all the qualities which he sought to combine in a portrayal of beauty could be found in one person." Thus, his finished portrait was a beautiful composite representing a beauty, Helen. Cicero follows this example in writing about rhetoric: "In a similar fashion when the inclination arose in my mind to write a text-book of rhetoric, I did not set before myself some one model which I thought necessary to reproduce in all details, of whatever sort they might be, but after collecting all the works on the subject, I excerpted what seemed the most suitable precepts from each, and so culled the flower of many minds."[12]

In similar fashion, when the inclination arose in my mind to write a book about the rhetorical constructions of deafness it seemed that the most gifted of speakers and writers in the classical period, Cicero, might serve well enough as my model. My portrayal here is surely neither the most true nor most false (nor the most beautiful): it is a composite of excerpts—relying on personal interviews and published materials, collected works, and suitable (and perhaps unsuitable) precepts. In that composite sketch, the three sections that follow redraw, rhetorically, the territory of deafness as a disability in the nexus of literacy. First, I consider the "problem" of deafness in education from a rhetorical framework, taking Quintilian's concept of the *vir bonus dicendi peritus* (the "good man [*sic*] speaking well") as my cue. Second, at the heart of my own argument about deafness, literacy, and rhetoric, I explore a highly problematic conflation: what I call the "literacy legacy" of viewing literate acts (reading, writing, speaking, listening, gesturing) as either *language* or *communication*. Theories and practices of literacy—as either product or process, as oral or literate, as cross-cultural or community-based, or as academic or "critical"— come into consideration here, particularly as they intersect constructions of "deafness" in deaf education. Third, in an act of opening more than of closure, I turn to the subjects, turn to lend my ear to those who have been (or are being) educated in the deaf educational systems; I turn to see what signification they make, what maps they draw, of their own literate lives.

When Education Falls on Deaf Ears

As he begins book 12, which closes his voluminous *Institutio Oratoria,* the Roman educator and orator Quintilian turns back to the goal of the lifelong rhetorical education he has just set forth in these synoptic books— he turns again to consideration of the *vir bonus.* Can this "good man speaking well," wonders Quintilian, can this Perfect Orator be indeed a good *person* as well as a good *speaker?*

The answer to this question, claims Richard Lanham, "has underwritten, and plagued, Western humanism from first to last"—both in our considerations of *how* citizens/students ought to be taught (indeed, even in educating "students" to become "citizens") and in considering *what* they should be taught. Furthermore, in attempting to answer the question "in the West from the Greeks onward," Lanham posits that we have tended to offer two defenses. The first, "the Weak Defense," simply begs the question, "argu[ing] that there are two kinds of rhetoric, good and bad. The good kind is used in good causes; the bad kind is bad. Our kind is the good kind; the bad kind is used by our opponents." The second, and far more interesting and relevant for my own argument here, is the "Strong Defense," which "assumes that truth is determined by social dramas, some more formal than others but all man-made. Rhetoric in such a world is not ornamental but determinative, essentially creative. Truth once created in this way becomes referential, as in legal precedent."[13]

It is just such a "strong defense" for the goal of Western education at large—particularly, I believe, since the eighteenth century, with the rise of mass literacy—that has stood at the center of deaf education. It is no mere coincidence that deaf education and its concomitant social drama "came of age," and have remained of age contentiously, at the point in Western history when literacy became more commonplace and education (a rhetorical education, at that) was made available beyond the aristocracy and clergy. Nor is it coincidence either that a tradition of educating "the good man speaking well" would come to see deafness as a puzzle at best, an ugly hole to fill at worst.

For how might deaf people come to be taught what was *good* if they could not hear the wisdom of the ages? This is a concern carried forward from St. Augustine, who interpreted the Pauline dictum "Faith comes by hearing" quite literally to mean that "those who are born deaf are incapable of ever exercising the Christian faith, for they cannot hear the Word, and they cannot read the Word."[14] If we carry this exclusion from the word of God over to exclusion from the "voice of reason" and then to exclusion from the word(s) of law and order that govern a land and its people, we see, as Lennard Davis has argued, that deaf citizens become, in their ignorance, "a threat to the ideas of nation, wholeness, moral rectitude and good citizenship."[15]

Deaf persons were doubly damned, unable to gain access not only to the moral content of proper rhetorical education but also to the right "style" of speaking. "Eloquence," offered Augustine, was really a matter of imitation, and thus achieved principally by "reading and hearing the eloquent," by "reading and listening to the orations of orators, and, in as far as it is possible, by imitating them."[16] More particularly, a deaf student entering upon a rhetorical education, pursuing the path of the *vir bonus,* could barely be expected to master the nuances of correct pronunciation, to produce the right tones and the "exactest expressions, nicely proportioned to the degrees of his inward emotions," that Thomas Sheridan, the "champion of the elocution movement in the eighteenth century," claimed was a "necessity of [the] social state to man both for the unfolding, and exerting of his nobler faculties."[17] Thus the plight of deaf students hoping to receive a rhetorical education appears even more dire— how might they become good *speakers* when they have never heard words, let alone tones and pronunciations, themselves?

If we turn to Quintilian's own definition of rhetoric, we see the potential of deafness to disrupt the ear and the order of rhetoric itself: rhetoric, he writes, "will be best divided, in my opinion, in such a manner that we may <u>speak</u> first of the *art,* next of the *artist,* and then of the *work.* The *art* will be that which ought to be attained by study, and is the *knowledge how to <u>speak</u> well.* The *artificer* is he who has thoroughly acquired the art, that is, the orator, whose business is to <u>*speak well.*</u> The *work* is what is achieved by the artificer, that is *good <u>speaking</u>.*"[18] *Speaking:* Quintilian's definition of rhetoric, intertwined as it is with a definition of education as well, quadruply repeats (stutters?) the central precept of speech.

By the Enlightenment, when literacy and education became more widespread, this precept sometimes fell on deaf ears. Literally. As Davis tell us, "before the late seventeenth and early eighteenth centuries, the deaf were not constructed as a group"; furthermore, when the attention of philosophers and educators during the Enlightenment did turn to deafness, "one might conclude that deafness itself was not so much the central phenomenon as was education."[19] Thus, it was through and in education that deafness began to be known as a group trait, as a sociocultural category rather than as an individual difference—as it seems to have been referenced in writing about deafness before this point, in the Old and New Testaments and in works by Aristotle, Descartes, and others.

Looking back at my partial history of deaf education, we can see that the birth of deaf schools—or rather the separation of deaf persons from any educational "mainstream" by placing them primarily in deaf "institutions" or "asylums," as they were often called—began both in Europe and then a little later, here in North America, during the Enlightenment. The management of deaf lives—particularly through their education and their language—has been tied up in the legacy of Quintilian's "good man speaking well" who lies at the heart of our humanistic tradition. He [*sic*] who does not speak well must be trained, maintained, contained, restrained. In training the deaf person (who was long designated as "deaf-mute"), deaf education is part of the entire aggressive humanistic tradition of (rhetorical) education that Lanham asserts we have carried forth from that initial "'Q' Question": "humanism, construed in this rhetorical way, is above all an education in politics and management."[20]

For the most part, those political and educational moments of "management," both at large and more specifically as they pertain to how best to educate a deaf student, are hammered on the mettle of literacy, mined from sources where literacy is seen as either language or communication. It is from the realm of literacy that deafness, following the multiple possibilities of my metaphor, might be mined as precious ore or explosive danger.

LITERACY FOR COMMUNICATION; LITERACY FOR LANGUAGE

Richard Lanham claims that the "'Q' Question"—the matter of educating the "good man speaking well"—all comes down to the motives for education and to the curriculums we must always design in response to them. I couldn't agree more. I only beg to differ in naming what those essential controlling motives are: for Lanham they are "play, game, and purpose";[21] for myself and my argument here they are *literacy seen as a matter either of communication or language.* When I look to the recent explosion—both beautiful and dangerous—of research on literacy, I see its products and processes categorized and shelved all too simply; as often as not they are divided into literacy for and as communication (as a product) and literacy for and as language (as a process).[22]

I might go back again to Quintilian. Even in the consummate product of a lifelong process of rhetorical education—even in the *vir bonus*—I think the division potentially appears: being a "good man" as one goal and "speaking well" as the other. The rhetorically educated good man uses literacy for and as language; he desires, attains, and uses literacy to convey thoughts, morals, ethics—both his own and those of the community, nation, or culture at large. Here literacy is a process, a means of exchange and change, a way of belonging to a place and people: a language.

At the same time, the rhetorically educated man speaking well stands in for literacy as communication—here he masters the "products" of literacy, attaining and retaining skills of style, delivery, memory, pronunciation, tone, gestures, diction, and so on. Later, in the age of print, he masters further skills such as punctuation, paragraphing, spelling, penmanship. His goal is the correctness of his language, the appearance of the product itself, his ability to convey information "accurately."

Both being the good man and speaking well, to be sure, are worthy goals; and both, to be just as sure, were goals in tandem for Quintilian. It is equally interesting and indeed perplexing to see how these two have been separated out in literacy education at large and—even more sharply (and yes, painfully)—in deaf education. Let me labor a moment then at mapping them in literacy education at large so that I might turn, in my final section, to show some of the ways they play out—violently and sometimes with casualties, sometimes with goods gained—in the lives of deaf students.

Communicating a Product

As a means of learning to communicate, literacy is a skill to be obtained and retained. Such a perspective tends to hold literacy in stasis, setting it up as an end in and of itself. Moreover, such a perspective makes literacy an *individual* attribute rather than a *social* achievement and also foregrounds what Deborah Brandt calls the "strong-text account of literacy," in which becoming literate is becoming textlike—"logical, literal, detached and message-focused."[23] Literacy as a communicative product turns the individual into either a *have* or a *have-not*. Finally, considering literacy as a product focuses on the consequences of being either a have or have-not—as do some fairly familiar accounts by literacy scholars and public-intellectuals, including among others Jonathan Kozol, E. D. Hirsch, Jr., Jack Goody and Ian Watt, Walter J. Ong, and David R. Olson.[24]

And what the literates have are textlike qualities themselves. To be literate in the strong-text descriptions that have characterized literacy education in the United States, Brandt argues, is to "force attention away from the world and onto the text" and to "transcend dependency on social context"; she criticized product-centered theories for "making meaning out of the fixed, semantic resources of language-on-its-own."[25] On this account, becoming literate is anything but a dynamic, interactional, involved process (i.e., it is anything but *language*); instead, it requires divorce from context and lack of involvement with the world and others, while wedding oneself to the text and the text alone. And the text one weds is, of course, itself a product, fixed and unchangeable—a text that "communicates," that imparts information—a text like the one in the middle of the old sender-message-receiver conduit of communications theory. Literacy, then, becomes a matter simply of getting it right, of passing the message the sender intended through a conduit and making it completely understood by the receiver on the other end. This is literacy for communication only.

In her often-cited three metaphors for literacy, Sylvia Scribner also relies on the dominant product-centered theories. Scribner posits that the attainment of literacy leads to three possible metaphorical ends: literacy as adaptation, literacy as a state of grace, and literacy as power. "Literacy as adaptation" is primarily an individual achievement, which she dates to the specification of basic literacy skills needed to be a modern soldier during World War I; it currently goes under the guise of "functional literacy" and is defined, multifariously, as a level of reading and writing proficiency necessary for "effective performance" in any particular setting.[26] It is the "standard" measured on most types of standardized tests of English language skills and, as such, it is the type of literacy that deaf students are most familiar with.

Also individually achieved but usually socially sanctioned by some dominant force or culture is "literacy as a state of grace." Here the literate individual knows and can speak what Henry Giroux calls "the dominant social grammar" and is thereby considered "cultured" and endowed with special, significant virtues. An individual can effectively communicate with and through the dominant social grammar although he or she may not still be a member of that dominant group. Those who succeed have learned the code and passed—but it is also likely that in such passing they have put at risk, if not lost, any prior identification with the nondominant group. In their popular literacy autobiographies, Mike Rose, Richard Rodriguez, and Michelle Cliff all write of the dangerous, seductive, paradoxical gift of the dominant culture's "English."[27] This too is the "gift" of "hearing" literacy that some deaf students wish for and, often as not, never receive; it is a gift typically of one-way communication, of skills.

More balanced, although still significantly lopsided, is Scribner's third metaphor, "literacy as power," which "emphasizes a relationship between literacy and group or community advancement."[28] This metaphor is more socially oriented than the other two: it offers power to nondominant

classes and culture in exchange for their having learned the dominant social grammar—though note how the dynamics of exchange reflect the un-
equal powers of the groups. Because literacy is typically and historically a
tool for maintaining hegemonic power in almost every Western
society[29]—just as the Plato of the *Phaedrus* feared was the case with the
tool of rhetoric—its attainment affords nondominant classes and cultures
the opportunity to share in that power, to increase their social and political participation in the hegemonic society that oppresses them. Thus "literacy as power," literacy that establishes more than one-way communication (or that, at the least, turns that one way into the other direction for
once), is currently quite desirable in Deaf culture and among many deaf
individuals.

In all these metaphors there reside, of course, possibilities for process,
for individual and social change. But because functional literacy—literacy
principally to "communicate more clearly," as one of my student-subjects,
Anna, put it—is the metaphor controlling most of American education
and our culture at large, literacy is usually seen as a product to be bought
and used, according to the package instructions, by illiterate consumers
(those who *have not*), "sold" to them by its literate owners (those who *have*).

Processing a Language

When literacy is viewed as a process, students—both deaf and hearing—
have a chance to become involved in language, to interact with the process
of language, to change and fashion it, and to place themselves somewhere
in the activity. This kind of process is what I claim happened at Gallaudet
University in 1988 when deaf students, buoyed by recent linguistic legit-
imization of American Sign Language and by their own growing pride in
their culture and its unique language, and angered by the selection of yet
another hearing president, closed the university for several days until their
demands were met (see chapter 5).

When literacy for and as language stands at the center of educational
and social institutions, then literacy becomes about social identity, about
power, about self-transformation, about speaking and listening to others,
and, perhaps most important for my argument here, about changing
schooling and other social institutions from the inside out and the bottom
up—about changing them by engaging students and citizens in "critical

literacy."[30] To teach critical literacy, as Giroux describes it, requires teaching more than just communication: it requires a focus on language. When literacy is about language and its roles and shapes in society, then students engaged in such literacy learning are gaining "critical skills that not only help them understand why they resist, but also allow them to recognize what this society has made of them and how it must, in part, be analyzed and reconstituted so that it can generate the conditions for critical reflection and action rather than passivity and indignation."[31]

In fact, what Giroux would have these students analyze and reconstitute are the very "mechanical approaches" to reading and writing that he characterizes as the "instrumental ideology" of literacy education. Within an "instrumental ideology of literacy," writing is "strip[ped] of its normative and critical dimensions and reduce[d] to the learning of skills."[32] The instrument here is communication: when literate acts are seen as being only about or for the *purpose* of communication, when literacy is only about or for the correct use of skills to convey a message clearly—a message that goes one way—then the beauty, of what *language* can do, as well as its power, is lost. And with the loss of language comes the loss of culture, of communities, of ethics, of morals.

Indeed, this singular potential for language and rhetoric sheerly as a skilled "craft" was what so alarmed Plato in the *Phaedrus.* If the explosive and beautiful possibilities were taken away from language; if the complexity, complications, and contradictions of social and individual nuances that make up language were entirely given up in favor of "only information" and "clear communication"; if its cultural, moral, critical, and ethical content was removed; then the "good man" also potentially disappeared. Stripped of these things, there might still be communication, there might still be someone "speaking well," speaking pretty and pleasing words, clear and even classically sublime words—but the words might be false, or empty, or even immoral. There would be no language.

"I'M ALMOST THERE"
"I'm Ready to Roll Up and Pass It"

Let me now try to illustrate how the separation of literacy into communication and language affects the lives of deaf students. In these brief and loosely stitched stories we see the range of possibilities—literacy as primarily communication, literacy as principally language, and even literacy as some of both—in the tradition of Quintilian's *vir bonus* (whom, I think it is important to remember, Quintilian claimed it took an entire lifetime to educate and create).[33]

If I had to think of one central concept that might possibly hold a composite of deaf students that I have known, talked with, worked with, and taught, it would be that of *passing*. In virtually every interview I conducted and in informal conversations too numerous to remember, let alone mention, we turned always, at some point, to passing. Even in an interview with a hearing person who was the "assistive listening device (ALD) consultant" for deaf persons at a local speech and hearing clinic, the issue was not passed by: "I noticed you had a lot of questions about passing. Is that going to be a focus of your work?" she asked me toward the end of our conversation.[34] Her question came, too, after she had told me at least half a dozen stories of "people who walk in the door" and their various degrees and successes with passing in the hearing world.

Most memorable for me were stories of the students at the state university in town who refused to use the "services" offered to them by the university's Office of Disability Services—primarily because those services, either an interpreter or, more often, the use of an FM audio loop system, prevented them from "passing" in one way (culturally) even as it jeopardized their passing (academically) in another. The ALD consultant, Sue, explained the "typical" situation with using the "FM system"—the "sender" (the instructor) wearing the system microphone and speaking directly into it, and the "receiver" (the deaf/hard-of-hearing student) wearing the "unit," the box around his or her neck with earphones (somewhat like hearing aids): "If you have a student who is eighteen years old, and just starting out in college, they don't want to wear it. It's not a bulky unit, but it's extremely obvious and they don't want to wear it. They would rather get Cs in class because they can't hear the professor very well, than get As or Bs because they're wearing this unit."[35] Indeed, two of the students I interviewed told me of their experiences trying to pass in hearing colleges and also tell me of their refusal to wear FM systems: Paul spoke of his discomfort with the FM system because of his effort to "be like them," and Lynne also confessed, "I don't know why, I just feel that I was embarrassed or something [to wear the FM system], because I was with hearing people . . . you know?"[36]

What I do know is the painful paradox in that by passing as hearing when they don't use an "aid" such as the FM system in a "regular" classroom, these students put at risk passing in the other necessary ways—in the academic and in the communicative arenas. They risk ever "speaking well"—or learning to speak well; they risk active participation and communication in the classroom; they risk knowledge; they risk understanding. Two women I interviewed, who were part of "mainstreaming" efforts in their early days (the late 1970s and early 1980s), told me stories about the price of passing, socially or academically, when communication is the key in the literacy learning classroom. One, now very successful social worker, remembers some of her struggles this way:

> Among my deaf classmates [during her elementary and junior high years in public schools], I was the brightest; among my hearing classmates, I was not. I didn't understand that my deafness had a lot to do with that. When you're young, you don't see it that way, and you compare yourself without knowing that there's a difference between you and other hearing peers, so my self-esteem was not really very high. . . . And I can remember feeling much more inferior to my classmates in reading and English, because I always had to struggle with it. I had a lot more corrections on my papers than my hearing classmates.[37]

Because of those painful never-quite-passing experiences, Kathy now heads a community-wide program to help fill social voids and provide (deaf) role models for those students currently in educational mainstreaming experiences. The program organizes a monthly social gathering for deaf/hard-of-hearing students in area schools, and Kathy describes its inception and philosophy:

> And so we called thirty different youth programs in _____ County, to find out if any provided programs for deaf youth in this area and if they'd had any involved in their programs. Out of the thirty of them, only two said they had deaf kids involved in their programs. The other thing is that a lot of times, for deaf kids to feel equal to their peers, it would be very difficult to do that because you would have to place a third person in that situation, an interpreter. And if there's not an interpreter, they wouldn't understand everything that's going on, they would feel left out. So we started the program with the concept of wanting to provide a social need to fill that void that many of them had in the mainstreaming programs.

We also wanted to give them something that other [youth] programs for kids had been doing for years, and that is, giving them self-esteem, and confidence.[38]

The self-esteem inherent in passing, in being able to fit in the dominant culture and in being able to communicate effectively in what Giroux calls that culture's "social grammar," is no small goal for many deaf students. The other woman I interviewed who spent most of her life, like Kathy, struggling in the mainstream, once wrote me a paper explaining the premium she placed on passing: "When I went to a high school, I wanted to be in a regular english class with other hearing students. The reason why I wanted to be in it because I would like to take this class for a challenge. I was trying to be like them but my english teachers think it would be too hard for me. They decided to put me in a special education class. I really didn't learn much english in high school [*sic*]."[39] Later, Anna amplified that story verbally: "I opened the book [in the 'regular' English classroom] and thought, 'Whoa . . . this is hard.' But I don't care if I get an F and fail, I want a challenge. But right away when they found out I got an F on my first test, they took me out and put me in a special education class again. I'm not going to learn anything about English. I was not happy."[40]

Anna is also the interviewee who best exemplifies for me the key role played by literacy understood as communication, and as communication only, in the road to passing that many deaf and hard-of-hearing students take. Indeed, it is Anna who becomes the focus of my next chapter and who years ago gave me its resonant title: "because it's so hard to believe that you pass," she told me tearfully on the day she discovered that she had—on her third try—passed the "basic English" course at Gallaudet University. That phrase has stuck with me, has reverberated through all the thinking and writing and teaching I have since done about and with literacy, whether with deaf or hearing students, native English or non-native English speakers.

What has stuck, too, are Anna's words, both written and spoken, about what "English" literacy *is* and what it is *for*. When I once asked her for a short paper that defined or explained "writing," she wrote: "Writing is part of english to have good communication. Writing have grammers in it. It can help some people what the paper is telling when you write something on it."[41] While the grammatical and communicative ironies abound here, this short statement has also come to represent for me the mode of literacy that as often as not engages (and disengages) deaf students.

When literacy is about communication, and thus is about grammar, about usage, about vocabulary (another overwhelming concern of most deaf students that I have worked and conversed with)—it is about passing. Just passing. Barely passing. Getting through. Getting by. Adapting, functioning, getting graced (with that grade). I think again of one young Gallaudet student who told me of her past two—failed—efforts at passing the basic English course. "This time," Bev said, with the same kind of hope Anna once had for those brief moments in that "regular" high school English class, "this time, I think I'm ready to roll up and pass it."[42] In failing once again to "speak well" and carry the English idiom through, Bev rolls up not just her colloquial sleeves but her entire self.

How fitting a metaphor I have found in Bev's skewed idiom: the carpet of literacy, extended when literacy is taught as a mode and means of communication only, can and will get rolled up at any moment, often without advance warning. And as often as not, the student, having missed the moment of communication, will get rolled up in it. What's more, the carpet creates a mirage—the moment of perfect communication is always out there somewhere, always just a little beyond where the student is right now, always there with the *next* level achieved, the *next* test passed, the *next* grade gained. "I'm almost there," says one of the students at Gallaudet that I have known for five years as he tells me—on the eve of his college graduation, a week before he is to turn forty-five—of his literacy levels being quite near what he has "heard" is Gallaudet's goal of "eighth-grade literacy skills." "I struggle and struggle," Charlie tells me at the conclusion of his interview, "but I haven't quite reached that level."[43]

"Because English Can Express It Beautiful"

Where I think Charlie would really like to get is past the mirage of literacy sheerly for communication and on to holding literacy as language. He is, in fact, moving close these days, grasping, "almost there." He and several of the other older and residentially educated Gallaudet students I have known and interviewed have made it clear that while communication is good, right, and a worthy goal for literacy, communication is, in the end, not enough. I have seen them sign of *language* as the goal of literacy—insisting that the person who "speaks well" must also be a "good person," a person who uses language for more than just dress or perfection or the "getting-the-message-across" informational conduit.

To be sure, Charlie has spent more than enough of his educational time trapped in that one-way conduit; when I asked him to bring me up to speed on what has happened to him at Gallaudet since I had last interviewed (and tutored) him five years previously—when he was struggling through Gallaudet's infamous basic English literacy course for the third time—he told me an alarming and lengthy story about the violence of literacy in his recent life:

> Last time we talked, in English 50 after you were with me, I passed English 50, and then I took 102 [the next English course required for anyone intending to take a degree at Gallaudet]. I didn't know who the teacher was when I signed up. I went into the classroom and didn't like the teacher; it was a strange teacher. He'd be writing and writing at the blackboard, and then when he finished he'd sign Exact English [a non-ASL pidgin form] what he just wrote. Why did he repeat what he just wrote? The exact same thing. I read it, I understood it. And his structure of expressing the meaning [in ASL] wasn't accurate; conceptually, it wasn't appropriate. And so I failed 102. So I repeated 102 with a better teacher and I improved a great deal. I still had some problems, but I passed and took 103 [the second in the four-course required sequence at Gallaudet] and failed that two times. The third time I took 103 I passed, and the teacher thought that there was something wrong with me, that I might be learning disabled and asked me if I was. I said I never knew. Who, me? Possibly, I don't know. So I thought I might need to get myself checked out. So I took 203 [the third required English course], and again, I failed. And I thought well, maybe I have a learning disability. I took it [English 203] again and again. Finally, after I became a junior, I passed and I had to select a major and I chose ASL. And then I took 204 [the last required English course] and got another lousy teacher, slow signs and difficult to understand, wasn't clear, so I withdrew from that and took it the second semester and finally passed and got a C, a 72, so that was, OK, I was frustrated but satisfied. So then I applied to be an ASL major, and the person said, well, you've got this C in English; I have a friend who is an English teacher, why don't you come down and get tested and see if you have a disability. Go ahead and try. So I took the evaluation, and found out that I have a reading disability, I reverse letters and words. Dyslexia, yeah,

[signing directly to me] remember I showed you my evaluation paper before? So they waived the C and I became an ASL major. But now I learned that I had a disability and they give me accommodations.[44]

I have let this story unfold in its full telling because it is full of telling.

There are several remarkable things going on here. First are the facts of Charlie's identity beyond that of "student": he is a nontraditional student, in his mid-forties, who had a successful career as a drafting engineer, who has experience (and accolades) as a deaf actor, and who happens to be one of the most skilled, beautiful users of his native language, American Sign Language, that I have personally known. He may not necessarily "*speak* well," but Charlie surely uses language well. The second remarkable point is his incredible perseverance in the face of what could be only called an absolutely appalling experience with English literacy. When I add up all the multiple attempts he made at passing from English 50 through the four required English courses at Gallaudet, I count twelve classes in all.[45] Third is Charlie's late-discovered learning disability, his documented dyslexia. Try to imagine: he sat in twelve introductory-level English classes before someone—notably, not an English but an ASL teacher—made sure he got tested for learning disabilities. Were they all so convinced that Charlie's inability to learn English, his inability to pass at basic English literacy, was just a function of his deafness that no one could see past their own limited expectations? What was going on here?

I don't know. But I do know that in the face of the limitations of literacy being taught as communication only, Charlie's passion for literacy as language was not squelched. And that, I think, is beyond remarkable. "Listen" to how Charlie summarizes "the English problem" at Gallaudet:

> One problem I feel is that for deaf students here it is difficult for us to learn English because of the teacher's signing skills. I think that is a direct relationship. The teachers, I feel, should learn two languages—learn both languages [English and ASL]. Because they work with the deaf they should learn our language. It would make teachers look good. And it would help students improve their skills. It's destiny—students would be destined for success then. If they've grown up with ASL, then the translation [from ASL to English] is a lot easier. *And writing [in English] is a beautiful language. It can be beautiful in English*—if the teacher knows how to teach from an ASL standpoint. If they want to improve our English and they are concerned with that then they need to learn our language.[46]

Here is someone who cares not just about *his* language, ASL, but who respects the beauty and capabilities of any language, all languages. Here is someone who has experienced literacy learning for the sake of language—seemingly *in spite of* the educational system that focused mostly only on literacy learning for communication. Here then, in Charlie, is what I think Quintilian would have been proud of—a good man speaking [*sic*] well.

Another Gallaudet graduate (and perhaps not surprisingly, another gifted user and indeed noted teacher of ASL), Ellen, might illustrate the same point. Despite the enormous troubles she has had, and continues to have, with English, Ellen professes a "love" for it. She has a history with "lousy grammar"—a picture of herself as a somewhat "screwed up" user of English that she's come to internalize after all these years: "I always had a problem with writing because [just as] with lipreading, I could catch certain things, but then I would miss so much. I put things together, but it was usually screwed up."[47] Like Charlie, she has spent more than enough educational time trying to learn to just *communicate* in English—time that she indicates was equally fruitful and fruitless: "And I was giving up my recess at the deaf school so that I could have private speech lessons one on one. I benefited, yeah, because I can communicate with my family better and with some people. And sometimes I feel like I can talk and that is really nice. But really skilled sentences, no. Little phrases I can say, short and sweet."

Maybe Ellen is not exactly what Quintilian had in mind, then—but I would not be too sure. She is, by her own account and that of others (who kept mentioning her name when I told them of my project and who kept recommending that I interview her), a skilled user of language *and* a "good person" who uses language thoughtfully, to make meaning in herself, her community, her world: she is a known comedian, storyteller, and poet in the Deaf community; she teaches American Sign Language and Deaf literature to both deaf and hearing students; and she teaches future ASL teachers.

She stays connected, too, to English. She is currently enrolled in a Ph.D. program in a state university, and it is through that program, she tells me, that she continues to use and attempt improving her "English reading and writing." And she does so for far more than purely functional, instrumental, communicational reasons: "I love English because it really broadens my horizon so much. I feel like I want to express things and I can't through ASL always. And English helps me to express more, writing jokes and stories—like that. ASL is great for videotaping, but hearing people don't appreciate that. I want people to appreciate both [languages, ASL and English], so I use English for that and I find it a challenge to find a way to say things that will make people laugh in English too." Thus, Ellen sees literacy as more than just a matter of communicating, as more than just achieving the functional necessities that impart information but that still, I argue, keep the boundaries clear and contested between the haves and have-nots in any culture, in any language.

For Ellen, I think, literacy (and the educational process it is learned in) is not about building and maintaining "standards" and communicational borders, whether imaginary or real; instead, literacy is about "broadening" oneself and one's community—about expression, laughter, challenge, and appreciation shared across, through, within that language. As someone who is herself a product of "the system," who has taught deaf students in the public schools, and who now teaches at Gallaudet University, Ellen knows about the boundaries established by education, the lines drawn tight by literacy. When I ask her where all the current categories and classifications that characterize "deafness" so variously now might have come from, she responds quickly, definitively—drawing the map with bold strokes: "I think the boundary is made up by society, the educational system. 'The deaf can't function in the hearing world. They're stuck and they have to go to a deaf residential school.' [She is imitating hearing educators here.] I think that kind of thing has set up a boundary. . . . I wish that the deaf and hearing worlds were mixed from the beginning, that hearing people could talk and sign and deaf people could talk and sign. What caused the separation? I think education, the system."

And it is a system that, for deaf students, tends to separate out *language* from *communication,* emphasizing the latter over the former; in doing so, by its own "audist" terms, it leaves deaf students linguistically lacking, audiologically disabled, civically crippled, culturally deprived. These communicative portraits are most often drawn by what Harlan Lane disdainfully calls "the audist establishment"—a colonial mechanism that keeps the deaf dumb, unable to communicate, never speaking (let alone writing) well enough, while hearing people remain in power, victorious always through a violence of literacy that sets communication and language against each other, severing Quintilian's twin goals of being the "good man" who *also* "speaks well."

NOTES

1. See the opening chapter of Wrigley's *Politics of Deafness,* esp. p. 13.

2. These three sets of figures appear, respectively, in Wrigley, *Politics of Deafness,* p. 13; Schein and Delk, *Deaf Population of the United States,* p. 16; and National Information Center on Deafness (NICD), "Deafness."

3. See Stuckey, *Violence of Literacy.*

4. My four primary sources for this list of associated terms are Brill, MacNeil, and Newman, "Framework for Appropriate Programs"; Moores, *Educating the Deaf;* NCID, "Deafness"; and, as always, my own thirty-eight years of experience in the "deaf education" system.

5. See Oliver, *Politics of Disablement and Understanding Disability;* Bruffee, "Social Construction."

6. See Lane, *Mask of Benevolence.*

7. Paulo Freire, Henry Giroux, and numerous other scholars in literacy studies remind us that most colonial enterprises are, in fact, predicated on the sustained illiteracy of the colonized.

8. Delpit, *Other People's Children,* p. 28.

9. Roof and Wiegman, *Who Can Speak?,* pp. 97, 102.

10. *Naming Silenced Lives* is the title of a 1995 book by McLaughlin and Tierney.

11. It is no coincidence that my example involves a painter commissioned to portray "silent and lifeless" beauty—an all-too-common portrayal in the history of attitudes about deafness.

12. Cicero, *De Inventione,* pp. 167, 169.

13. Lanham, "The 'Q' Question," p. 654.

14. Winzer, *History of Special Education,* p. 22. This damnable dilemma—a dilemma of inevitable damnation—is played out and played on in an often-cited book on Deaf culture by sociolinguist James Woodward, *How You Gonna Get to Heaven If You Can't Talk to Jesus?*

15. L. Davis, *Enforcing Normalcy,* p. 82.

16. Augustine, *On Christian Doctrine,* 4.4–5; translated in Bizzell and Herzberg, *The Rhetorical Tradition,* p. 387.

17. Bizzell and Herzberg, *The Rhetorical Tradition,* p. 649; Sheridan, *On Elocution,* Lecture VI, p. 730.

18. Quintilian, *Institutio Oratoria* 2.14; italics mark the translator's emphases (in Bizzell and Herzberg, *The Rhetorical Tradition,* p. 318) and underscores mark mine.

19. L. Davis, *Enforcing Normalcy,* pp. 51, 52. Davis's own double-edged argument about the construction of deafness and the "moment of deafness" that began in the Enlightenment is fascinating—and one I will take up again in this book. He describes how deafness became recognized and studied, and how deaf people became grouped together—both results of the theories of language and education at the time. But also, all the more interestingly, he makes a case for how eighteenth-century Europe became itself "deafened" as literacy rates rose and people engaged more in the "deaf" acts of reading and writing more and less in the "hearing" acts of speaking and listening. This swing from speaking/listening to writing/reading is, I might add, a major one in the history of rhetoric.

20. Lanham, "The 'Q' Question," p. 692.

21. Ibid., p. 691.

22. I am wary and weary of the all-too-traditional and reductive move—a classically rhetorical one, a classical rhetoric one—of dividing, categorizing, classifying. I might attempt to exculpate myself by noting that I am only "discovering" the truth that was already there, that was created before me. But sadly, I know that not to be the case; I know instead that the "discoverer" of categories continues the splitting and ensures the existence of categories, carries out their creation, by using what she claims to have "found." For now, I plead guilty as charged. Later, as my argument advances and I come to some "conclusion," I hope also to work my way out of this thought knot.

23. See Brandt, *Literacy as Involvement,* pp. 7-8. Scribner distinguishes between literacy as an individual or social attribute in "Literacy in Three Metaphors."

24. Kozol, *Illiterate America;* Hirsch, *Cultural Literacy;* Goody and Watt, "Consequences of Literacy"; Ong, "Some Psychodynamics" and *Orality and Literacy;* and D. Olson, "From Utterance to Text."

25. Brandt, *Literacy as Involvement,* pp. 7, 8.

26. Scribner ("Literacy in Three Metaphors") locates its point of origin in World War I; I might note further that literacy standards were of significant concern at Harvard University in the 1890s when the faculty established what was, essentially, the first "basic writing" (remedial composition) program because they felt too many of their students were poorly prepared to meet the demands of college writing.

27. Rose, *Lives on the Boundary;* Rodriguez, *Hunger of Memory;* and Cliff, "If I Could Write This in Fire."

28. Scribner, "Literacy in Three Metaphors," p. 75.

29. See Freire, *Pedagogy of the Oppressed;* Giroux, *Schooling and the Struggle for Public Life;* and Goody, *Literacy in Traditional Societies, Logic of Writing,* and *Interface between the Written and the Oral.*

30. For work on literacy as social identity, see Gumperz, *Language and Social Identity,* and Kannapell, *Language Choice Reflects Identity Choice;* for literacy as power, see Fairclough, *Language and Power,* and Foucault, *The Order of Things;* for literacy as self-transformation, see Stromberg, *Language and Self-Transformation;* for literacy as speaking and listening to others, see Miller and Mc-Caskill, *Multicultural Literature and Literacies;* Geissler and Jessup, *Situated Stories;* Weis and Fine, *Beyond Silenced Voices;* and Street, *Cross-Cultural Approaches to Literacy;* and finally, for critical literacy, see de Castell, Luke, and Egan, *Literacy, Society, and Schooling,* and Giroux, "Literacy, Ideology" and *Schooling and the Struggle for Public Life.*

31. Giroux, "Literacy, Ideology," p. 231.

32. Ibid., p. 212.

33. As I begin to discuss interviews and conversations I have had with deaf or hard-of-hearing students, I enter into a significant interpretive dilemma. In some cases, even though I have moderate skill in American Sign Language, I used an interpreter (usually when the person I was interviewing was a native signer and/or he or she requested an interpreter); in some cases, no interpreter was used (as with Anna, the "subject" of the following chapter) and the interview tended to proceed with any of the various forms of English-ASL "contact" languages—SimCom and Pidgin Sign English most notable among them. With or without an interpreter, I was left with the interpreter's dilemma when faced with transcribing the interviews and again when choosing to use quotations from them in my text. Because I am well aware of the way "broken English" tends to get translated in our culture as "broken intelligence" (indeed, that is part of the point of this chapter), I have chosen to interpret, transliterate, and then quote what was "said" into its approximate English equivalent, as well as I could. However, all quotations from a student's *written* text reproduce the original text exactly.

34. Sue, 11 April 1996.

35. Ibid.

36. Paul, 21 May 1996; Lynne, 30 October 1991.

37. Kathy, 20 June 1996.

38. Ibid.

39. Anna, 8 October 1991.

40. Anna, 30 October 1991.

41. Anna, 12 November 1991.

42. Bev, 5 September 1991.

43. Charlie, 9 May 1996.

44. Ibid.

45. English 50, the basic English course that Charlie took three times before he passed it, is not a required course, nor does it count toward requirements for graduation at Gallaudet. It is only seen as a "voluntary" preparatory course for those entering Gallaudet students whose "language skills" are not quite up to par in English, as determined by a four-part test that comprises reading comprehension, vocabulary, structure (an alias for grammar), and a 150-word writing sample. The part that most students have the most difficulty with, long after they might have achieved "passing scores" on the other three parts, is the writing sample, which asks them to use English as *language*—to think originally and compose a thoughtful argument, description, or narration in response to a question/prompt. The other three parts of the test are aimed at testing literacy for *communication,* literacy as "functional adaptation" (see Scribner, "Literacy in Three Metaphors") that can be tested for standardization, literacy as "instrumental" (see Giroux, "Literacy and Pedagogy"). It is also worth noting that the pressure on "at-risk" students to take this voluntary course is enormous. Until they pass the English Language Placement (ELP) test, with or without English 50, they cannot be admitted to Gallaudet as "regular" college students. They have four chances (four semesters) to take the ELP; failure brings disenrollment from the university. When I was at Gallaudet in the fall of 1991, 51 percent of students did *not* pass the ELP on the first try (and were, therefore, likely to be enrolling in English 50). What is more, the attrition rate is quite high: many of those enrolling in English 50, having not initially passed the ELP, *never* pass the test—either because they fail all four times or, more often, because they just drop out before making that final attempt.

46. Charlie, 5 December 1991; my emphasis.

47. Ellen, 3 June 1996. All subsequent quotations from Ellen are from this interview.

CHAPTER 3

"*I*t's So Hard to Believe That You Pass": A Hearing-Impaired Student Writing on the Borders of Language

This case study of Anna addresses the *processes,* the language, of literacy.[1] I examine literacy as both contextualized and cognitive processes, as both a social restriction and an individual accomplishment; I also examine how the concept and label of "remediation" is primarily a social construct.[2] Through Anna's case, I look at the weave and patterns constructed between an individual's cognitive processes, her social and cultural contexts, and the larger literacy standards of written English. And in so looking, I see the precarious spaces she occupies—as one who is variously disabled or not—on linguistic, cognitive, and literate borders.

OCCUPYING THE TERRITORY

To begin, the cultural and social context of Gallaudet University presents a unique literacy situation: it is the only liberal arts university for the deaf in the world. Deaf, hard-of-hearing, and hearing-impaired students from all over the world come here to study,[3] and regardless of their skills in *any* signed or spoken language, they are generally expected to become skilled users of Gallaudet's two dominant languages—American Sign Language (ASL) and Standard Written English (SWE). While ASL, a visuospatial language, is the dominant language used in daily interactions by most students and faculty, students are not only expected but *required* to demonstrate proficiency in reading and writing the English language. Thus, within the same institution, two very strong—but opposing—literacy messages are being given. The opposition is particularly stark because ASL and English differ radically—syntactically, conceptually, modally—in al-

50

most every way.[4] Most significantly, perhaps, ASL has no written component. Thus, for native ASL users the task of learning a "written" language is a twice-over, conceptually tangled act of translation.

Furthermore, I have labeled the two languages (ASL and SWE) as "opposing" because of my sense that both the faculty and students at Gallaudet tended to see them that way—as if becoming too fluent in one language would somehow automatically jeopardize if not eradicate one's skill in the other, thereby also threatening one's position in a culture.[5] To further compound these linguistic and cultural problems, some students and even some faculty come to Gallaudet having almost no skills in any sign language, having been educated primarily by oral methods; just as many arrive having almost no skills in any oral or written language, having lived and been educated primarily in a sign language. And as if the language oppositions weren't enough, Gallaudet is also, as one student's hearing mother put it, "occupied territory" in terms of cultural conflict: relations between hearing and Deaf culture are always tense, often volatile.[6] While on Gallaudet's campus, I keenly felt the tensions of such past and present cultural conflicts. The 1988 "Deaf President Now" rally, during which the students made national news by barricading and closing down campus for one week until their demands for a new deaf president were achieved, still resonated as a key event in the lives of most of the deaf students I met there in 1991.[7] The campus also remained tense over the death earlier that year of a disgruntled student, Carl Dupree, at the hands of five Gallaudet security personnel who did not understand him as they "restrained" him outside the student center following his angry protest of his failing English 50 grade. Born profoundly and prelingually deaf, Dupree did not speak English intelligibly; the guards did not know ASL.[8] A year later, my own English 50 students took up the death of Dupree in a computer network discussion I was leading one day: they had been revealing their own fears about the upcoming English Placement Test (EPT) at the end of the semester when one student warned the others, "Beware the English 50 Monster. . . . English 50 monster love staff not students. . . . English 50 monster kill Carl Dupree."

Suffice it to say that English 50—or any English class, for that matter—was not highly regarded by most students. I strongly sensed that even within the overall university structure, the English department was often under fire and little esteemed by the university's other departments. Contributing to this controversy, the process of electing a new English department chair had split the department itself between linguistic and cultural affiliations: the debate over the two candidates centered primarily on their opinions of language use in the classroom (did the candidate advocate ASL or [oral] English?) and their own cultural affinities (was the candidate d/Deaf or h/Hearing?).[9]

The politics and position of the English department within the entire Gallaudet University structure, disregarded if not outright disdained by many students there, were made clear by 1997 Student Body Government (SBG) President David J. Kurs in the student newspaper, the *Buff and Blue*. In a piece titled "Da Faculty: Discourse, Interaction, and O'Connor," Kurs comes down hard on "the paternalistic attitude set forth by the English department," which he feels "does much harm to Gallaudet's morale, and it serves as an anti-recruiting tool." Although Kurs finds this attitude particularly oppressive at the moment because the former English department chair, Dr. Diane O'Connor, has just been reelected—"As long as O'Connor reigns as chair, she will continue to keep the English Department down under as the worst department on campus"—he also emphasizes that the trouble with the English department is not just a current event, not just centered on a particular election. "I told the Board of Trustees last February," he adds, "Gallaudet will become a truly better place if two issues are confronted and resolved: Communication and the English department."[10]

The English department "issue" rose with nearly volcanic force in the spring of 1998, as the English department was yet again holding elections for a new chair. The issues surrounding that election, and the Gallaudet students' volatile reactions to the eventual reelection of Dr. Diane O'Connor, were and continue to be "complex"—the term used by both a Gallaudet English department faculty member and student to characterize "the DOC situation." ("DOC" stands for Diane O'Connor, whose name sign is also represented by these initials.) In assessing the DOC situation—or the "Complexities of the English Issue," as one *Buff and Blue* headline put it—opinions were far more varied than Kurs's article might suggest: it was evidently the hottest issue all year on Gallaudet's campus. It was perhaps made even hotter by the difficulty in obtaining truths and insider information. *Buff and Blue* Opinions Editor Louise Stern writes, two pages after Kurs's curt assessment of O'Connor's "reign": "It is always difficult for us here at *The Buff and Blue* or for other organizations to get documentation about this issue, because there are so many sticky, political complications. The people who really know what is going on work for the Department, understandably, are unwilling to put their jobs at risk by going on the record."[11]

As neither a member of the *Buff and Blue* staff nor any other organization, occupying instead what one Gallaudet English department colleague called "both insider and outsider" status there as researcher and teacher, with continuing contacts through the 1990s, I too had great difficulties obtaining information beyond the published *Buff and Blue* articles. Friends and colleagues in the English department who had long been willing to discuss with me literacy at large and at Gallaudet in particular understandably backed away from this topic. They felt they had not only careers but personal lives to protect. Some apparently key students in the events surrounding this situation also e-mailed me with polite regrets: "I'm just too sick and tired of all this for now," one stated. And others, both faculty and students, simply never responded to my inquiries at all. This account of the chair question and the English Language Program (ELP) remains partial.[12]

Still, some talked. Some wrote. Some sent me on paths toward other sources, other articles, other contacts. Some sent me whole stacks of past *Buff and Blue* articles on the DOC situation. From these I pieced together a picture that made it look very much like "the English 50 Monster" was still lurking in the halls of Gallaudet's English department. Only now, Gallaudet students were stalking him back. Things apparently got rowdy, just as they had done with the Deaf President Now protest a decade earlier, shortly before spring break on Gallaudet's campus. At that point the *Buff and Blue* editorialized on "English Department Hijinks," citing a list of complaints against the department—beginning with O'Connor's being "inaccessible and unwilling to accommodate [us]" and concluding with metaphors and analogies (or rhetoric: see chapter 5) that could hardly be ignored: "Is this the end of the list of issues that students are grumbling about regarding the English department and the captain of their capsizing ship, O'Connor? No. We've just barely begun to cause ripples in the water. It's been 10 years since Deaf President Now. Maybe it's time to mount a movement for Concerned English Chair Now."[13]

The movement mounted against the English issue, the DOC situation, revolves yet again around literacy—standards for literacy, achievements at literacy, testing for literacy, failing at literacy. That focus becomes evident in student resistance to what one faculty member called "the big

one [area of student concern] of the barrier testing system."[14] The system
came up at an SBG meeting on 9 February 1998, when a town hall meeting was called expressly to "give any concerned students an opportunity
to speak about the English Department." A panel of four English department faculty, including the chair, Diane O'Connor, attempted to address
student concerns and answer angry questions. The questions and comments reported by the *Buff and Blue* all seemed to center on literacy issues:
"The first question asked O'Connor why the EPT (English Placement
Test) had a high failure rate"; "Another question asked them the reasons
for the high failure rate of students enrolled in conditional English 60 and
70 courses, and if it was because of the rigidity of the course itself and its
restraints on the teachers"; and, finally, a student complained "that many
teachers couldn't sign or understand ASL enough to be able to TEACH."[15]

Adopting the rhetoric of "oppression" and "barrier" that occupies
much of the student discourse about the ELP at Gallaudet (as I report here
and elsewhere), a student closed that SBG meeting with yet another
powerful metaphor, giving "a soliloquy in which he painted a picture of a
fort with its gates open, representing the English department, with horse-
back warriors wielding spears and riding towards the fort, which represented the students, but just as they reached the fort, the fort slammed
shut, catalyzing a war, where there is already one casualty. [Note: Darnall
was referring to the 1990 death of Carl Dupree, a former student who died
after being restrained by the DOSS after he claimed that he had been
treated unfairly by his English teacher.]" (brackets in original).[16] Even one
faculty member who is heavily involved in both the English department
and the Deaf studies program at Gallaudet draws the scene in such strokes,
in language of "oppression" and "battle," although widening the picture
far beyond just DOC—the chair against whom eventually some 600 students signed a petition, requesting that the administration force her resignation. After telling me that "the chair situation was so very complex,"
this faculty member goes on to express a position that looks much like the
one I take not only here but also in my 1992 dissertation, written after my
five-month experience in Gallaudet's English department. "The situation," he currently writes,

> is wider than that; the battle over DOC in many ways is a symptom of a
> larger ideological battle over bilingualism, over definitions of literacy, and
> the politics of pedagogy. DOC is of the school that chooses to ignore the

politics of literacy issues and focus only on basic mastery of memorized vocabulary, rote grammar lessons and prescriptive writing. Language is disconnected from personal identity, socialization and enculturalization. Language in a vacuum. The assessment mechanism that bears her fingerprints does not test literacy as it is used in students' lives, but it tests a student's ability to memorize. Memorization is not literacy. Whether the students could articulate this or not, they feel a stream of oppression in the education they receive here. The students recognized it; some faculty recognize it; and clearly the program review team recognizes it.[17]

In this exploration of the politics of literacy, plenty of manipulation also gets uncovered. Students not only express persistent and mounting frustrations over failing literacy as it is taught and tested in Gallaudet's ELP, but they also recognize what several have publicly professed to be an unchallenging, ultimately insulting system.[18] In "Confessions of an English Major," the *Buff and Blue*'s editor in chief, Terry Giansanti, asserts, "I am not proud to be an English major." He goes on—reversing the rhetoric of "bad attitude" and "lack of motivation" that is commonly used to explain why Gallaudet students so often fail in the ELP—to blame the uninterested, uncommitted attitudes of most of his English professors: "Some English teachers complain that their students appear unmotivated, so why should they put forth the effort? Well, it takes good teachers to motivate students."[19]

Similarly, one *Buff and Blue* staff member parodies the English education received at Gallaudet in a spoof based, unfortunately, on "factual examples" from Gallaudet students' writing: "My English are much good. I come Gallaudet of University for want study grammar and grow my vocabulary. I want expand education for get degree B.A. job good money future support family children. My favorite part Gallaudet are VAX [the e-mail system] and much poster on wall in hall dorm HMB Ely Center and room of bath. Why? Is because I read lot learn new word for grow vocabulary how through VAX and poster."[20] Ironically, this article—"I Are Learn English from Gallaudet!"—sits right next to Stern's piece addressing the "Complexities of the English Issue." In her column, the opinion editor seeks to encourage all to make informed judgments about the issue. While Stern wants everyone to realize that some manipulation of information might be occurring—"Diane O'Connor is *not* the Devil incarnate," "Some teachers who complain about the way they have been treated by the Department actually are not telling us the whole story," and "We students are much more at fault than one would imagine from what has been said lately"—the neighboring spoof offers a very different view of the manipulation of literacy issues.

Indeed, the manipulation magnifies on various literacy screens here. One faculty member told me, "When we did have the new election [that would either remove or reinstate Diane O'Connor], a fairly large block of the department boycotted the meeting, trying to prevent us from having enough members present to have the election."[21] And one student who was apparently quite involved in and vocal about the whole issue expressed distress over the possible doctoring of the numbers and percentages of students who pass the ELP; another student believed that "DOC was punished for sticking to her beliefs" and that other "professors then manipulated students into starting an uprise against DOC."[22] Finally, even Diane O'Connor, "speaking" in a *Buff and Blue* article on 13 March 1998 through the voice/pen of Stacy Novak, claims that she herself was manipulated, since members of the English department "don't set the English requirements. The University faculty does"; further, the students "don't want to face reality [i.e., their poor English skills], so they beat up O'Connor for telling them the truth."[23] In all this manipulation, blaming, metaphor making, frustration, and outright anger, it is hard to know, with certainty, what *the truth,* let alone *a truth,* might be. But one thing does seem clear: the politics of literacy, the premium on passing, occupies all at Gallaudet; it draws territorial boundaries, especially in and around the English department, daily.

Finally, as one last example of the unique literacy oppositions and cultural border tensions that characterized Gallaudet, I myself often felt split between these affiliations of language and culture. Any time I was introduced to someone new, either faculty or student, he or she usually first wanted to know whether I was "Deaf" or "hearing." In short, my new acquaintance wanted to be able to draw quick linguistic and cultural borders around me, to name me as one of either *them* or *us*—a move to which I return in this book's final interlude.

My central question for this chapter grew out of all these linguistic and cultural tensions: How and how well, I wondered, can a deaf student write publicly "in English" at the same time she is using and emphasizing personal ties to a very different culture (Deaf culture) and language (ASL)? In what ways is Anna "disabled" within either culture or either language? In what ways is she not? And as these arguments about Anna's abilities and positions are made, as Anna is constructed, how is she a rhetorical subject?

SUBJECTING ANNA

Like me, Anna was an ambiguous subject—someone not clearly named as "Deaf" or "hearing," and therefore someone sometimes "disabled," sometimes not. Now thirty-one years old, Anna was educated as a mainstreamed student in a small midwestern town. She is the daughter of two hearing parents. She has some residual hearing and wears hearing aids, refers to herself as "hearing-impaired" (rather than "deaf" or even "hard-of-hearing"), and did not learn ASL until she was nineteen. At that time, she was attending Johnson County Community Junior College, a junior college in Kansas City, Missouri, that has a significant deaf student population and a good reputation for providing them with adequate services. She learned ASL from other deaf students there. She reads lips with a good deal of success, and although her own voice tends to be loud and lacking in tonal modulations and careful enunciation, she can be understood. She prides herself in having "gotten along in the Hearing world."

Anna is a returning student; she has credits and experiences from two junior colleges, but she stopped going to school in order to work full-time. Before enrolling at Gallaudet in fall 1990, she had been working in a machine shop for eight years, "reading blueprint." Now she finds herself wanting to fulfill her dream of being a "leader and role model" for younger deaf students as teacher and administrator in deaf and disability education. And so it is that she has found herself back in school at Gallaudet University.

Anna spent her first year at the Northwest Campus (NWC), Gallaudet's preparatory school (since closed), before coming to the main Kendall Green campus near Capitol Hill in the fall 1991 semester. She was still, however, a student in the English Language Program and was enrolled in one of the English 50 (basic) classes for which I served as a teaching assistant. She had already passed three of the four required sections of the English Placement Test—reading, structure/grammar, and vocabulary. What remained was the fourth part, the most difficult one for *all*

Gallaudet students: the "English Language Sample" in which "students are required to write approximately 100–150 words expressing an opinion on some topic that has a tangible referent and with which they can be expected to have personal everyday familiarity."[24]

Both her regular classroom teacher and I thought that Anna had a good chance of passing the English language sample and exiting the preparatory ELP. She was certainly motivated enough to do so, and her general written English language skills were strong enough that with conscious, persistent effort—something she would exert plentifully throughout this semester—we had confidence in her chances of success. She did, in fact, pass the writing sample and exit the ELP; all of her scores on the four sections significantly improved by the end of the semester. What follows is an investigation into the context and cognitive processes of Anna's writing during this successful semester in English 50.

The Borders of Language

What is meaningful and ironic in this account is that while the literature on mainstreaming tends to point to "academic challenge" as its major benefit, Anna's own tale of her educational background as a mainstreamed student tells a very different story.[25] She herself admitted often in the interviews that she was never really challenged in her English classes, that she was kept out of the "mainstream" and placed instead in special education classes, and furthermore that she never really understood what it meant "to write *in English*" (her emphasis) during all those years. In many ways, then, the ideally enabling environment of mainstreaming proved to be disabling for Anna. With double irony, she thought she first and finally learned something about English at Johnson County Community College—at the same time and place that she was among other deaf students and was learning sign language for the first time in her life. It seemed to me that aside from her hearing mother, who gave Anna endless hours of tutoring while she was being mainstreamed in public schools, Anna had no teachers who were capable of teaching English to a young, bright, but "hearing-impaired" student in all those years—no teachers capable of bridging linguistic and cognitive gaps for her. She had to wait for junior college at age nineteen, and for Gallaudet's preparatory college at age thirty, to provide that service. And that is a long time to wait to learn skills in a first language.

Language, of course, is more than just skills. It is culture, communication, community; it is what creates and is created by social and individual lives. And what Anna may have lacked during most of her experience in mainstreamed public schools was not just *skills* in a first language but all those other things that come with language. I want to argue that Anna occupies a unique (and largely unenviable) border position both in the "hearing" and "Deaf" cultures and in using either of their languages, English or ASL.

For example, Anna strongly believes that ASL and English should be kept separate when she is learning English.[26] She told me early in the initial interview that *talking* to herself while she writes is what helps her writing the most; furthermore, *signing* and writing simultaneously did not help at all. When she makes a mistake she tries to understand why she missed that word "*in English.*" "ASL," she concluded, "makes your writing messed up."[27] And because ASL "messes up" her writing, Anna is adamant about keeping ASL out of the English classroom. In an interview, Anna complained to me about her English 50 teacher's frequent request in class that the students sign (in ASL) an English sentence so they could discuss the differences (and similarities) between the two sentences. "Why?" she asked me. "This is not sign language class. That's confusing. I don't want to know how to write an ASL paper." I tried for a moment to explain that perhaps such a comparison helps some students know more clearly the differences between the two languages—so that the students do *not* confuse them. But she did not buy my argument. "That's the problem," she concluded emphatically, "ASL and English *don't* combine. It's confusing."

Because of her belief that the two languages only conflict with and confuse each other, Anna became quite upset at the end of the semester when the English 50 teacher suggested, as a strategy for taking the English Placement Test, that she "try [to] sign ASL in English" as she writes. "I told him," she said, "I don't know any ASL deep—it's *sign language* [as she tells me the story she emphasizes those two words]. All I know is talking English [long pause]. That's the only way I pick up my English—writing and reading. If I do that I'm not going to use sign language much."

Anna makes a point here: ASL is *not* her native language—English is, regardless of how literate she is, or isn't, in it. This is why she claimed, "I don't know any ASL deep." (And perhaps it is because she is also aware how weak her literate skills in English actually are that she said, "All I know is *talking* English.") While I could also argue that she doesn't know English "deep," Anna herself seems aware that (oral) English is, whatever her degree of fluency, her first and native language.

Anna, it seems, is caught on the borders, in the no-man's-land of the ASL and English/oralism issue. And while she consciously rejected the interference of sign language with her written English, much of her rejection was only lip-service. That is, while Anna may have railed against using signs to "translate" her English or vice versa, and while she may have advocated instead (English) "talk-write" strategies for writing and revising, her actual process of composing showed something very different going on. Both in her daily classroom writing and in the writings I videotaped during our interviews, Anna used both talking and signing to get herself through a written paper.

Anna did most of her classroom writing, responding to one of the prompts given each day in class, with her chair pushed back in an isolated corner. From this corner, she often "mumbled" to herself—doing the talk-write method she claimed works best for her, reading sentences over to "see how they sound" and to see if she had the grammar right. This is the strategy she readily told me about when I asked her how she helps herself with her writing and what her process is.

What she did not tell me about is the signing she also does while she writes. Though her signing and fingerspelling as she rehearses just-written text is not as frequent or as noticeable as the oral mumbling that always accompanies her writing, it is there nevertheless. For some reason, during the second writing she did on videotape for me, her reliance on signing was especially strong. On this occasion, she stopped to work through passages five times: three of these involved her use of "oral" skills, but the other two—each lasting a significant time—involved her signing to herself as she reread her own text.

Thus, Anna's theories about crossover between sign language and English don't match her practice. Out of her mouth comes the opinion that ASL only "messes up" her English writing, and therefore she avoids using it when she writes, but her hands tell a different story: she sometimes signs and fingerspells her way through portions of her written text—as she is writing. Again, it seems that Anna is caught between the arguments and the languages. And even if she is right in claiming that ASL confuses her

English (and I think she is), she still somehow cannot avoid using ASL when she writes in English.

What Anna seems painfully aware of is her own questionable communication skills—she can neither talk clearly or well enough in English to make herself always understood by hearing people, nor can she sign clearly or well enough to make herself always understood by deaf people. At the close of the last interview with her, I suggested that people probably have difficulty understanding her voice. She agreed and then stressed that because of this communication problem, writing well has become all the more important for her: "Yeah, that happens a lot. That's why I'm trying to find a way to communicate with other people. So maybe if they can't understand you talk, they'll be able to understand you write. Gotta be able to write good grammar . . . make more clear so that person understand. Because it's a part of a career to communicate." For Anna, then, the "language issue" is not really about whether one uses or chooses sign or voice, English or ASL, but about whether one is *communicating* or not. Anna sees writing as an essential part of communication in her life—as "part of a career" and even as a way to be understood when neither her voice nor her signing will do.

As I watched the videotapes of my interviews with Anna six months later, I was struck—much more than I had been when I was engaged in the process and context of communicating with her—by how garbled and ungrammatical her speech actually is; but I was struck just as forcefully by how garbled and ungrammatical her signing is, especially in viewing the two tapes on which there is a great deal of microphone distortion, when I needed to rely primarily on her signing to transcribe the conversation. She seems without solid skills in either language, and I can't help but wonder if she is perhaps "disabled" in both cultures.

Yet between the two, Anna has managed to find a way to communicate and has managed to enhance her own abilities. To give up either language—as deaf people are often forced to do in choosing between living in Deaf or in hearing culture—would surely leave her at a great loss, would surely leave her "disabled." The risk of such a loss entangles a student like Anna more tightly in the issues of language. Perhaps that is why she works so hard to become at least minimally competent and comfortable in a third communicative option—*writing* in English. The more options Anna has, the better chance she has of being understood in whichever world—hearing or deaf—she might find herself. The more options, the more abilities; the more options, the less likely the label of disabled. As yet another option that may stave off her being labeled as disabled, writing, as much as speaking or signing, takes on great importance for Anna.

And in Anna's context, it looms particularly large—though paradoxically, in a way that threatens to cripple—in the immediate future: writing, and writing well, is necessary to pass the English Placement Test and exit from the English Language Program at Gallaudet. This exit is the entrance to a "real" education at Gallaudet; for only when a student passes the EPT can she truly begin a degree program.[28] So significant is this event in the lives of Gallaudet students that most of them taking it only *hope* they will pass; they are never truly sure that they actually will. And so, at the end of the semester, when the results of the EPTs are announced to Gallaudet students, the halls echo with whoops, guttural yells, and weeping. Like Anna, most students cry if they find out they have passed because, as she said simply in her final interview, "it's so hard to believe that you pass." For Anna and others like her, the borders of literacy (especially the achievement of SWE) are rigorously patrolled; passing seems to take more luck than skill.

Bound by a Writing Process

Here I focus on some of the most interesting and important features of Anna's writing process during this semester, using models and results from composition research on hearing student writers as a foundation and comparison. I examine the ties that bind—or variously elude—Anna in her writing process.

Anna's Attitudes about Writing

Attitudes and affect, motivation and emotion, argues Alice Brand, are the "why" of cognition in the composing process.[29] Like other student writers—indeed, like *all* writers—Anna is governed in part by her attitudes toward writing. Some of those attitudes, as she expresses them in her eight interviews, are unique, I believe, while others are fairly typical. Writing is obviously a great challenge for Anna, but a challenge she is eager to meet; writing is a functional necessity—something she needs to do in order to make it through college and have a better job; writing is something she does not particularly like to do, but wants to do well because it is so necessary for school and job success; and finally, writing is something she wants more closely connected to reading in all of her classes, but particularly in English 50, since she believes that the connection between these two skills is the key to her success in school and life.

Anna also has strong attitudes about the topics she chooses or is asked to write about; the *why* of her cognition while composing (her feelings and motivation) seems to affect the *what* of her composition (the topic). While Anna told me of some remarkable purposes she has in writing—sharing information, communicating "pictures" and "emotions," getting a better job, and passing the EPT—what is perhaps even more remarkable about this list is all the purposes she has left out. Many she omits are those we teach and theorize about in composition studies: writing to communicate ideas, thoughts, opinions, arguments, and experiences (i.e., writing as a rhetorical act), not just to relay raw information.[30]

I believe that these are not casual omissions on Anna's part. She clearly does not like to express her ideas or opinions or to argue and take sides. Topics that require such responses usually seemed to her "negative." According to Anna, "bad" or "negative" topics ask her to express a personal opinion or idea, to take a stance on an issue, to make an argument for or against something (e.g., "How should the government spend its money?"; "Should teens be required to have parents' consent for birth control measures?"; "Should Judge Thomas be confirmed?"; "Should [older] 'children' who work and live with their families still be required to sign contracts and pay rent?"). At the same time, topics she designates as "good" or "positive" are usually the ones that ask her to tell a story, narrate an event, explain a positive personal experience (e.g., "Memories of being __ years old"; "This weekend was __"; "What I did for Homecoming '91"). Arguing one's opinions is what schools often advocate as the primary purpose of communication—whether written or spoken. In Deaf culture, however, as in most nonacademic arenas, telling stories and sharing experiences make up a good deal of what communication (and language as well) is all about. Perhaps in this regard, Deaf culture has influenced Anna more than she is aware of. For Anna, as in Deaf culture, stories are to be shared, but opinions are "your own."

Another attitude Anna embraces about writing and all communication that may have been influenced from her position within Deaf culture is her emphasis on *control*. Like most deaf people, Anna is aware that in any conversation with a hearing person she is more than likely to have to bear the responsibility, to take all control, for the success of communication; it will be her task to make sure that she both understands and is understood. As Deaf author Shanny Mow writes, the burdens of communication and control are often crushing for deaf people, particularly among their hearing families:

> You were left out of the dinner table conversation. It is called mental isolation. While everyone is talking or laughing, you are as far away as a lone Arab on a desert that stretches along every horizon. . . . You thirst for connection. You suffocate inside but you cannot tell anyone of this horrible feeling. You do not know how to. You are expected to spend 15 years in the strait-jacket of speech training and lipreading. You learn not how to communicate, only how to parrot words, never to speak your own. Meantime your parents never bother to put in an hour a day to learn the sign language or some part of it. One hour out of twenty-four that can change a lifetime for you. . . . It has never occurred to them that communication is more than method or talk. That it is a sense of belonging, an exchange of understanding, a mutual respect for the other's humanity.[31]

Like Mow, trying to gain and exchange respect and understanding, Anna finds it important to gain and maintain control in communication, which includes her writing. Regardless of how paradoxical or even impossible it may be for any person, deaf or hearing, to be completely in control of her or his writing processes and products, Anna still strives toward that end.[32]

Anna is especially cautious about, and strives particularly hard at, maintaining control over her vocabulary when she writes. For the most part, she seeks such control because she is aware that letting go of the reins when choosing words will court grammatical disaster: "I try to understand—to be sure I know what the vocabulary means before I use it. If I don't know, I refuse to use it. Because I know it will cause me problems with grammar writing. Because I feel I'm not ready for it. I not feel safe with new vocabulary. If you're using vocabulary, you're not going to understand grammar. So I prefer to throw out vocabulary and concentrate on grammar. Do things step by step. I have to." Anna shows great sophistication in realizing that she can cognitively handle only so many elements of the writing process at once. She seems to recognize that there is not enough space in her "working memory" to handle new vocabulary and correct grammar at the same time.[33] And because Anna's writing process focuses intensely on grammar—a point to which I will return shortly—she chooses to "leave the dictionary alone" and thus control both elements.

In addition, she demands more control of both her own written product and process. When Anna, who was almost always smiling and cheerful, arrived one day late in the semester, scowled, sat down, crossed her arms across her chest, and said bluntly, "I don't feel like writing today. I am not happy in English class," my plans to do another writing session changed. Instead, I listened to Anna's emotional outburst.

She instantly began listing grievances about her English 50 class. Her most emphatic complaint was about being "lost" in the way the teacher "graded" their papers. She conveyed in dramatic signs how she would write a paper in class, hand it in, and then "he [the teacher] slashes through it—wrong, wrong, wrong." Even worse, she added, he sometimes crossed a word of hers out and put in his own. "That's not the point," she exclaimed, "that's not what I was talking about." And because he gave "not enough information" about why she was making mistakes, she could respond only with sheer frustration: "Why? What's the point? I don't learn that way. No way. I don't want to change it immediately without explaining. We're just writing but we don't know what's going on. How do I know? I'm lost." In fact, here Anna sounds much like the basic writers Mina Shaughnessy describes in her introduction to *Errors and Expectations:* "Confusion, rather than conflict, seems to paralyze the writer at this level. Language learners at any level appear to seek out, either consciously or unconsciously, the underlying patterns that govern the language they are learning. . . . This is less a choice they make than an urge they have to move across the territory of language as if they had a map and not as if they were being forced to make their way across a mine field."[34] What I "hear" Anna asking for here is some of the "error analysis" and evaluative techniques long since advocated by composition teachers and scholars such as Mina Shaughnessy, David Bartholomae, Bruce Horvath, Barry Kroll, John Schafer, and Nancy Sommers.

Anna's Self- and Audience-Awareness in Her Writing Process

Perhaps because she feels she has no control in the process of her writing, Anna is not very aware of her own composing process. She cannot see any self-improvement over the semester in English 50; as she told me in the last interview, "I didn't realize how I was improving in writing. I can't see it for myself." In addition, she sometimes does not detect errors in her own product (a point I will come back to when discussing her focus on grammar). When she wrote for me as she was videotaped, she was not aware that she sometimes signed while she wrote and reread her text; neither was she aware of how often she stopped while writing to reread or reconsider (she marked very few places with the *x* designated for pausing, although she paused numerous times). And finally, when I focused on some element of her process, asking how indicative or characteristic it was of what she normally did, she almost always backed away from such questions with an ambiguous "sometimes" or "it depends" answer.

While her awareness of her own process is weak, her awareness of an audience is even weaker. From the beginning of the semester, Anna rejected any suggestion by me that she share her papers with fellow classmates (although she was always eager to have me or the teacher read them); an audience beyond those who do the grading did not seem to matter much to her. Also telling is her insistence on communicating "information" as the primary purpose for writing. One of Anna's favorite phrases was "sharing information." At various points in the interviews she told me that communication was for "sharing information"; reading was for "sharing information"; writing was for "sharing information": all of education, in short, was for "sharing information." In fact, the first piece of advice she said she gave to other deaf students was that they "must learn to return back and control the information in a conversation in order to communicate." As Barry Kroll has outlined it, the "informational perspective" of writing, in which "writing for an audience can be viewed as a process of conveying information, a process in which the writer's goal is to transmit, as effectively as possible, a message to the reader," is "too mechanistic and reductionistic[,] . . . failing to consider reading as an act of personal interpretation, evaluation, and affective response."[35]

Given that Anna is usually asked to write in rhetorical and social vacuums (at least in English 50, where only once during the entire semester were the students asked to share their writing with each other), it is not surprising that she takes such a purely informational stance toward writing, nor that she can see little reason to be concerned about audience. The writing she does in English 50 is like the writing done in the kind of courses that Mike Rose critiqued in "Remedial Writing Courses": it tends to focus on "simple, personal topics" so that errors can be more easily isolated instead of on challenging topics that emphasize connections with other academic reading and writing.

Focus on Grammar and "Rigid Rules"

What Anna lacks in audience awareness, she makes up for in grammar and rule awareness. Her near obsession with error is characterized by Shaughnessy as another feature of basic writers: "So absolute is the importance in the minds of many writers that 'good writing' to them means 'correct writing.'"[36] Reading functions primarily to give Anna "ideas for new or good grammar [to try] out in your writing," and she insists that what English 50 most needs is a book with "grammar work" in it. Her definition of writing, though short (and, ironically, grammatically incorrect), is sure to include grammar: "Writing have grammers in it," she once wrote. And when I asked her what she thinks about as she gets started writing on a paper, she mentioned the "order" of her paper first, but quickly added, with a laugh, "and you're also thinking, 'watch out for grammar.'" Which Anna always does.

There are rules for all of this grammar, and like almost every deaf student I encountered in any English class at Gallaudet, Anna is obsessed with the rules. But like the basic writers Shaughnessy describes, Anna looks for a map of these rules and comes up with a minefield instead. Nowhere is her struggle with the rules of grammar more evident than in her account of how she struggled particularly hard with the structure/grammar portion of the EPT:

> But one area I get stuck is that structure. Because there's so many sentences sound right and trying to figure out which sentence is proper. . . . Because I had to figure it out on scrap paper trying to figure out rule, which one is right or not rule. Because I have to write on scrap paper in order to know if that means the same thing or what? They look so close, have the same meaning, but a little bit different grammar. You're thinking and reading it over and over to make sure it have the right one or wrong one. I keep tell myself, "Try the best I can. Try, try. Think for awhile." That's when I need close my eyes and yeah, I'll pick that one. It depends on [long pause] which grammar to use.

It is no wonder that Anna had tears in her eyes throughout most of this final interview—tears for having made it through the stress and strain of such an experience: "It took a lot of patience, a lot of work," she summarized, "but . . . whew . . . I'm through with it."

But is she? Though Anna has certainly mastered the multiple-choice grammar test students are given for the EPT, and though she has proved (after two unsuccessful attempts) that she can produce an "acceptable" 150-word "language sample" to a formulaic topic structure with which she had a year's experience of almost daily writing—the question remains as to whether she can actually write any "better." If "better" is limited to the formula she has been using for a year, if "better" is limited to literacy in the purely functional sense, then the answer is probably "yes." But if the question is asked of her ability to produce text outside the formula, to produce text that is rhetorically sensitive, social, fluent, and audience-engaging, the answer is probably "not really."

Other evidence of how strongly rules function in her writing process comes from her stiff, formulaic use of transitions. Halfway through the semester, the English 50 students in my two classes were introduced to transitions, given a list of them, and ordered to write, for several days, papers that use "at least three" transitions in them. Like Anna, the students all become rather good at inserting transitions at the beginnings of paragraphs (and sometimes, for the brave few, at using them to begin various sentences within paragraphs). But these insertions are generally stiff and meaningless—a transitional word serving as a bridge where no foundations have been built in the first place.

Such rigid rules affect even the physical details of Anna's writing process. She was obviously upset in the two videotaped writing sessions when I asked her not to use a pencil (so I could see the errors that she would otherwise erase), although I assured her that I did not care if it looked messy and that, in fact, her errors were part of what I was curious about. She was not assured. Her first comments at the end of both sessions were about how messy her papers looked.

In class it was often Anna who was the most insistent on and persistent in getting the sentences exactly right on the weekly "what's wrong with this sentence?" exercise. When she came up with a slight variation from the "correct" sentence, she usually made sure that her version was also recognized as "OK." And Anna had to have the perfect place and situation to write in or else she was likely to complain—as she did after one practice

EPT test that she failed (with a 60)—that it was too hot in the room, there was too much noise and distraction, it was too late in the day, and so on.

To be sure, what Mike Rose called the "rigid rules and inflexible plans" of many unsuccessful student writers tend to govern Anna's composing process.[37] Yet they do not seem to help her write any better. The transitions, in fact, got her all tangled up in both videotaped sessions: twice she tried to use "finally" for a concluding paragraph; twice she tried to use "in short" in the same position, and then had to spend a while thinking her way out of the repeated transitions. When she added a new thought or bit of information, she used a transition such as "also" or "addition" (incorrectly for "in addition"), and then broke off for a new paragraph that presented no separate thought. Yet Anna herself insisted that these transitions are helpful for both her and her reader: "It's really helpful to clearly understand and also I understand myself when reading that." Finally, despite the rules she follows and the care she takes with grammar, it is grammar that particularly begins to crumble when Anna leaves the safety of the "what is good/bad about __" formula given to her daily in English 50. This is evident in some of the extra papers I had her write for me throughout the semester, as part of both her tutoring and the interviews I conducted; I have quoted from many of these papers already.

Revision and Recursion

Strategies already discussed—getting the grammar right, using transitions, and making sure the information is both "clear" and "enough"—principally guide Anna's writing and final revising. She told me in one interview that "sometimes" she changes the order of her paper. But in all the papers she wrote for me and her classroom file, I never saw such an organizational change, beyond the shifting of a transitional word from one paragraph lead to another.

Anna's strategies and attitudes about revision are yet another instance of her relative inflexibility, and they parallel many of the characteristics of the "student writers" in Nancy Sommers's groundbreaking case study research presented in "Revision Strategies of Student and Experienced Adult Writers." Like Sommers's student writers, Anna never fully engages with the concept of "revision." Instead she focuses on "scratching it out and doing it over again," or "adding" a word or phrase (and in some instances, an entire sentence) when she wants to make something "clearer." Thus, as

Sommers explained, for inexperienced writers revising is based primarily on lexical rather than semantic changes. So it is that Anna worries, as do Sommers's student writers, about repetition (for Anna the repetition of transitions is particularly troubling).

And given how her English 50 teacher corrected her writing in class, it is not surprising that Anna revises her own text outside of that class in just such a mechanical way. Papers she turned in to the teacher each day were quickly checked for their lexical and grammatical correctness and then handed back for her to rewrite again with the correct grammar, diction, and missing information. I cannot remember a true semantic or organizational change ever being requested of a student writer in these classes; such changes were simply not discussed unless they were directly related to a lexical change. Thus Anna and Sommers's inexperienced student writers approach their task similarly:

> These revision strategies are teacher-based, directed towards a teacher-reader who expects compliance with rules—with pre-existing "conceptions"—and who will only examine parts of the composition (writing comments about those parts in the margins of their essays) and will cite any violations of rules in those parts. At best the students see their writing altogether passively through the eyes of former teachers or their surrogates, the textbooks, and are bound to the rules which they have been taught.[38]

Yet in spite of her "teacher-based," lexically focused revision strategies, Anna does employ some recursion in her composing process. When I asked her in the writing sessions why she stopped and began "rereading" (or rehearsing in sign language, as was sometimes the case), she told me she was checking for "sense" and "fit": "to see what I was talking about and see if I made sense." The videotapes make it obvious that she employed this recursive strategy—checking herself in the middle of composing for sense and fit before she went on to the next bit of text—at several different levels: she sometimes stopped to reread only a sentence or a phrase, sometimes a paragraph or whole page. Her endings, especially, rely on a recursive fit with what has gone before. When I asked her how she knew when and where to end a paper, she explained, "When I'm satisfied—stop right there. You just feel it inside," echoing the essence of Sondra Perl's famous observation. These kind of feelings, Perl maintains, are part of "the felt sense," a necessary component that is extremely difficult to document in the recursive process since it refers "not to any words on the page nor to the topic but to feelings or non-verbalized perceptions that surround the words, or to what the words already present evoke in the writer."[39] Although Anna seems to possess a felt sense for what she does wrong, she seems to lack any awareness of what she does right. And at least in her recognition of something specifically wrong in her text, she appears far more sophisticated than are the majority of inexperienced student writers either I or other researchers in composing have worked with over the years.

"Pseudo-Hearing" Writer

In the early 1990s Lorna Mittelman and Larry Quinsland designed a "cognitive fluency assessment model" for teaching written English to deaf students, and in many ways their model summarizes some of the cognitive and contextual features I have been discussing so far. Their model places deaf student writers in ten possible groups; members of the first group are most skilled at English and are part of the hearing world, and those in the last are "seriously fragmented" in their knowledge of both languages and cultures. At the middle level is the "true bicognitive" deaf student writer who has fluent skills and knowledge in both cultures. In this model I see Anna falling best into the fourth category, just short of the middle ground, as a "pseudo-hearing" student writer. Pseudo-hearing writers, like Anna,

> have generally grown up in English language environments, have hearing families, and have attended mainstreamed programs. They may have learned some form of Pidgin Sign English, but they usually have not been exposed to ASL before attending college. Their thinking has developed primarily within an English framework, and students in this group usually identify themselves as hearing-impaired. . . . Although these students appear to be quite fluent in English, due to excellent speech skill and mastery of many colloquialisms, an analysis of their spoken and written English reveals these students have not developed the cognitive activity that forms the basis of meaningful communication. There is a similarity between this student and the hearing student who has grown up in a language-deprived environment.[40]

On almost every count, this description of student and learning environment fits Anna. As she would admit herself, she has speech skills that are good enough to allow her to pass (though sometimes with difficulty) in the hearing world, and her English vocabulary is good. But she still struggles to weave that vocabulary into "meaningful communication" (I would substitute "language" here). As Anna repeats often and then reminds me once more in the final interview, such meaningful communication is the force and focus of her motivation to become fully literate, to improve her writing skills. Nowhere is this struggle between simply knowing and using words and actually having them produce meaningful communication more painfully evident and ironic than in the short definition of writing Anna offered me: "Writing is part of english to have good communication. Writing have grammers in it. It can help some people what the paper is telling when you write something on it."

At every turn, this short piece perplexes. The words are all there, and even the ideas behind them are good. But somewhere, in the actual process of writing it down, is it possible that Anna loses some kind of cognitive control, and thus short-circuits "meaningful communication"? All three sentences are ungrammatical, even though the definition emphasizes grammar. Two of the sentences also stress writing as "good communication," but again neither of them communicates the idea very well. The context and cognition of Anna's writing are such that, at this point, she can pass and produce writing that fits certain formulas in certain controlled circumstances. She can *communicate* in writing now, just as she can communicate in speech and sign (especially when contexts are controlled). But whether she can consistently produce meaningful, flexible *language* is still an open question.

Framed/Disabled?

The question of Anna's ability to use language hinges on perspectives of disability.

That the deaf and hearing-impaired students (like Anna) in Gallaudet's English Language Program by and large have little understanding of the process of their own writing or literacy acquisition was one of the most disturbing and significant conclusions of my work with Anna. That she was clearly framed as a disabled subject seemed painfully clear to me; even though the frame did not fit well, it was the window that Anna was all too often seen through. From the outset, the language of federal law

(PL 94-142 and its revision in 1990, the Individuals with Disabilities Education Act) marked her as "disabled" and set out to build for her, by the designs of educators who were predominantly hearing, a "least restrictive environment."

The picture that balloons up from these terms is not pretty: the environment, even at its "least," is certainly "restrictive." The frame remains. Anna's abilities, as she herself points out, are hampered when she is literally forbidden to meet "challenges" in her early educational days, placed—against her own will but supposedly for her own good—in "special education" classes where she learns nothing about English. Then, as an older, nontraditional college student at Gallaudet University, the system again places her in basic English classes where she sits, usually off in a corner, diligently trying to compose 150 words of "good English" about topics that are inane, if not insulting: "What is good about fall? What is good about having a roommate?" And what could one write anything with real substance in a mere 150 words on such cookie-cutter topics?

So Anna is framed again. The wings of ability clipped, the door to challenge slammed shut—she is disabled not by her own capacities but by what disability studies scholars metaphorically call "the built environment." The design that writes Anna out of the picture, the barrier that forbids her access isn't, of course, a flight of literal stairs, or an actual doorway too small; it is a doorway to nowhere that envisions her as a subject of communication, not as a user of language.

I would like to envision something on the other side of that door, to rebuild the steps and even the landing at the top of them. We might want to try imagining, for example, the degree to which, and manner in which, most deaf student writers, like Anna, view writing as a purely "functional necessity," devoid of all the rhetorical purposes we in composition studies attach to it. And we might want to imagine this not by arguing, in an audist frame and tone of voice, about what Anna *can't* do, but by exploring where she is in her literacy learning and focusing on what she *can* do. Instead of wondering what is wrong, and why, we might ask: What are the major uses and purposes for writing among deaf students? Do these purposes vary with educational or family background, degree of hearing loss, relative ASL and English skills, future life and career plans? In these questions, we would follow the lead established by Shirley Brice Heath in her classic study *Ways with Words,* as she examined the uses and purposes for literacy within two Carolina Piedmont communities.

In a later study, "Protean Shapes in Literacy Events," Heath offers another valuable lead for exploring the purposes and effects of literacy, particularly among deaf students at Gallaudet, by assessing the effects on them of the English Placement Test, Gallaudet's premier "literacy event." What are the attitudes and issues surrounding this key language event—as expressed and perceived by both faculty and students at Gallaudet? How do these attitudes affect university policies and decisions, faculty and student interactions and perceptions of each other, and even the Deaf community outside of Gallaudet?

One possible literacy event has already received some attention, but it produces more questions than answers: What are the direct and indirect effects of a unique visuospatial, conceptual language such as ASL on the writing process of deaf students who use ASL as their native language? How might ASL interfere with or aid these students when they write "in English"?[41] Are the interferences primarily translation problems of the same sort encountered by most ESL students? Or does the use of a unique real-time, oral, nonwritten, and visuospatial language create unique kinds of problems in translation and the composing process? Aside from possibly providing deaf educators with more strategies and knowledge about teaching writing to deaf students, attention to these questions could also benefit the larger community of composition scholars and teachers. In some striking ways, many of the students we now teach in college composition courses are like these deaf students who use ASL. They, too, live in a primarily oral and real-time world, with little exposure to print.[42]

Longitudinal and in-depth case studies of deaf students acquiring literacy—particularly writing skills—in English also need to be conducted (as do longitudinal, in-depth studies of hearing writers, an argument Stephen North convincingly makes in *The Making of Knowledge in Composition*). This second-level inquiry would continue the first-level inquiry I have begun here. As North notes in arguing for the value of case studies, "clinical knowledge accumulates by accretion[;] . . . it approaches the world it studies by examining phenomena again and again, looking at them from different angles, probing them in differing ways, aiming to render a composite."[43] In seeking to create such a composite, these extended case studies could tell us much about the differences and similarities—qualitative and quantitative, positive and negative, cognitive and contextual—between deaf student writers and their hearing counterparts. These kinds of case studies might then inform us of what is "foundational" to the composing process, regardless of which language we "speak" or use. Furthermore, longitudinal case studies might also illustrate the cognitive uniqueness and complexity of composing not only in a second language, but in a language occurring in a different receptive and expressive modality from the writer's native language.

Finally, I believe that by addressing literacy acquisition among deaf students more as a process and act of involvement, and less as a static product, we might gain some significant steps, moving us more smoothly through (and beyond) binary arguments about deafness and literacy—in which language is lost at communication's expense or communication is circumvented for the sake of language. Literacy needs to be offered to deaf students as a process within which they have some power, input, and effect.[44] And then their response needs to be carefully considered, studied systematically and sensitively. What happens when deaf students are given a chance to explore and analyze their writing and reading processes, to learn to analyze their errors, to take part in designing the standards of literacy by which they will be evaluated? Here, of course, I am thinking particularly of such a study being done within the English Language Program at Gallaudet. From my perspective, this is the most pressing and provocative area for revision and rebuilding—precisely because it involves a rhetoric of "lending an ear" rather than one of merely "speaking at" an audience.

If literacy for deaf students were indeed approached as a rhetorical process of language in which they might fully participate, it is my belief that deaf, hard-of-hearing, and hearing-impaired students (i.e., both those like and those unlike Anna) might come to have some power over and in their own literate lives. They would no longer be "disabled," in theory or practice—unless, of course, they chose to label *themselves* as such. They might simply be "different." As it stands now, the majority of deaf students I met in Gallaudet's English Language Program were much like Anna in that they felt they had no such power: literacy and rhetoric—and thus their lives as successful, educated, self-sufficient human beings—belonged not to themselves but to the "hearing world," who dictated the products and standards of literacy without ever offering them a chance to be a part of that process. It is time that these deaf students—as well as other "remedial" students with cultural and linguistic backgrounds outside the "mainstream" and on the borders—be given a chance to explore, understand, and even change, if they wish, their own contextual and cognitive processes for composing. It is time to refit the frame of deafness as disability, to realign the borders that disable students like Anna. Although the loss of hearing certainly poses particular educational problems, deafness need not equal disability if the borders surrounding the "problems" of deafness remain fluid, negotiable, and part of a *shared* process of gaining literacy.

NOTES

1. All interviews with Anna took place during her second year as a Gallaudet student, from September to December 1991. There were eight weekly interviews and forty-two in-class observations of her as a student in English 50 at Gallaudet University.

2. This view of literacy aligns somewhat (though not entirely) with Stuckey's claim in *The Violence of Literacy* that "Literacy is a social restriction and an individual accomplishment. Individuals read or write, or don't, and individuals do with their literacy what they can. The subjectivities of minds and the ways in which people make their lives and thoughts, and the ways in which people are coerced, entrapped, colonized, or freed, must be addressed as processes" (p. 64). See also Hull et al., "Remediation as a Social Construct."

3. Despite a current trend to use the term "hard-of-hearing" (one I have always preferred to use in labeling myself) instead of "hearing-impaired," I have chosen the latter term here because it was how Anna described herself.

4. For discussions, sometimes competing, of the unique features of ASL that make it so different from English, as well as different from any other "spoken" and "linear" language, see Baker and Battison, *Sign Language and the Deaf Community;* Bellugi, "How Signs Express Complex Meaning" and "Link between Hand and Brain"; Hall, "Train-Gone-Sorry"; Kannapell, "Inside the Deaf Community," "Personal Awareness and Advocacy," and *Language Choice Reflects Identity Choice;* Kretschmer and Kretschmer, *Language Development and Intervention;* Lucas, *Sign Language Research;* Markowicz, *American Sign Language;* Mindel and Vernon, *They Grow in Silence;* Neisser, *The Other Side of Silence;* Quigley and Paul, *Language and Deafness;* Reagan, "American Sign Language," "Cultural Considerations," "The Deaf as Linguistic Minority," "Multiculturalism and the Deaf," and "The Oral-Manual Debate"; Sacks, *Seeing Voices;* Stokoe, *Sign and Culture* and *Sign Language Structure;* Stokoe, Casterline, and Croneberg, *Dictionary of American Sign Language;* Strong, *Language Learning;* Van Cleve and Crouch, *Place of Their Own;* Webster, *Deafness, Development, and Literacy;* and Woodward, *How You Gonna Get to Heaven?* and "Sociolinguistic Research."

5. This loss of one language (and concomitant loss of one culture) at the expense of and violence to another is an issue Richard Rodriguez has written about passionately in *Hunger of Memory.*

6. See Treesberg, "Death of a 'Strong Deaf.'"

7. Gannon's book and photo essay, *The Week the World Heard Gallaudet,* chronicles this significant event—as does Christiansen and Barnartt's *Deaf President Now.* I take up the rhetorical situation of DPN at greater length in chapter 5.

8. For a powerful account, see Treesberg, "Death of a 'Strong Deaf.'"

9. At the time I came to research and teach on Gallaudet's campus in 1991, the English department chair was deaf (although I sometimes saw the students and even her colleagues use the "think hearing" sign to describe her); in 1992, another deaf person was elected chair for a three-year term. Following his term (1992–95) a hearing woman, long involved in the English Language Program, was elected. She served from 1995 to 1998, and it was her reelection in 1998 that again occasioned so much controversy over literacy standards and politics.

10. David J. Kurs, "Da Faculty: Discourse, Interaction, and O'Connor," *Buff and Blue,* 17 April 1998, p. 5.

11. Louise Stern, "Complexities of the English Issue," *Buff and Blue,* 17 April 1998, p. 7.

12. Here again, as in chapter 1, I adopt the term *partial* in both its senses: my account is marked by admitted incompleteness and by partiality. As one who believes and writes as I do in this book about the situation of literacy instruction at Gallaudet, as well as at other sites of deaf education, I cannot pretend otherwise.

13. "English Department Hijinks," *Buff and Blue,* 6 March 1998, p. 4.

14. Dr. Y, 20 July 1998. Interestingly enough, one long-standing member of the English department replied to my inquiry for information about this "incident" with puzzlement: "why would you be planning to discuss this in a book about English literacy?" (Dr. X, 5 August 1998).

15. Jason Lamberton, "English Department Speak Out," *Buff and Blue,* 27 February 1998, p. 12. English 60 and 70 are two courses that have been added to the ELP since I taught at Gallaudet in 1991; they augment English 50.

16. Ibid.

17. Dr. Z, 28 July 1998. See also Brueggemann, "Context and Cognition."

18. One student expressed her discontent with the manipulation of persons and numbers in the ELP system at Gallaudet in an e-mail to me:

> The thing is that so many students keep on failing these courses and have to take them again as long as until they pass the elp exams, which are given out at the end of each semester—there must be some type of a problem! O'Connor FLATLY denied any problem and said there is an increase in percentage of students passing in the past ten years (not

exactly sure how long through) and said "MY research is correct." That's what she says ALL THE TIME, yet there are students lining up at the student body government office complaining EVERY semester. Indeed, there is a problem." (Ella, 10 September 1998)

19. Terry Giansanti, "The Chief Speaks: 'Confessions of an English Major,'" *Buff and Blue,* 6 March 1998, p. 6.

20. Sara Stallard, "I Are Learn English from Gallaudet!" *Buff and Blue,* 17 April 1998, p. 7.

21. Dr. Y, 20 July 1998.

22. Ella, 10 September 1998; Linda, 8 September 1998.

23. Stacy Novak, "English Dept. Chair O'Connor Speaks," *Buff and Blue,* 13 March 1998, p. 5.

24. "General Description of the English Language Program," p. 4.

25. Since the passage in 1975 of Public Law 94-142, the Education for All Handicapped Children Act, the debates about advantages and disadvantages of mainstreaming deaf children have been heated and frequent. To date, research remains inconclusive as to any significant advantage of mainstreaming into public schools versus remaining in a deaf residential institution. There seems to be a general consensus that mainstreaming offers substantial intellectual advantages, whereas the residential institution setting offers mostly cultural and social ones. So, while the argument continues, the opponents begin their arguing from different grounds. A small but representative sampling of the contentious literature on this debate might include Beaman, "Holy Cross Integration Project": Foster, *Impact and Outcome of School Programs,* "Life in the Mainstream," "Mainstreaming Hearing-Impaired Students," and "Reflections of a Group of Deaf Adults"; Foster and Brown, *Academic and Social Mainstreaming;* Foster and Elliot, *Alternatives in Mainstreaming;* Foster and Modgett-DeCaro, "Mainstreaming Hearing-Impaired Students"; Garbe and Rodda, "Growing in Silence"; Harvey and Siantz, "Public Education and the Handicapped"; Hemwall, "Ethnography as Evaluation"; Hodgson, "How to Integrate the Hearing-Impaired"; Jacobs, *A Deaf Adult Speaks Out;* R. Johnson, Lidell, and Erting, "Unlocking the Curriculum"; Robert Jones, "Can Deaf Students Succeed?"; Kennedy et al., "Longitudinal Sociometric Data on Mainstreaming"; Ladd et al., "Social Integration of Deaf Adolescents"; Libbey and Pronovost, "Communication Patterns"; Lou, Strong, and DeMatteo, "Relationships of Educational Background to Development"; Mertens, "Social Experiences"; Moores, Cerney, and Garcia, "School Placement"; Moores and Sweet, "Factors Predictive of School Achievement"; Reagan, "Cultural Considerations," "Multiculturalism and the Deaf," and "The Deaf as Linguistic Minority"; Schildroth, "Recent Changes in Educational Placement"; Sedey-Roman et al., "Enjoying Each Other's Company." There are also several col-

lections published by the National Association of the Deaf, such as *Deafness: Life and Culture* (ed. Merv Garretson), that feature numerous short opinion pieces on variations in deaf education.

26. Just as the benefits of mainstreaming are often debated in both Deaf culture and education, so too are the issues of teaching and using either sign language or oral methods in classrooms with deaf students. For some examples of recent research and criticism of the ASL/English (oralism) issue, see Gee and Goodhart, "American Sign Language"; R. Johnson, Lidell, and Erting, "Unlocking the Curriculum"; Kannapell, *Language Choice Reflects Identity Choice;* Lane, "Constructions of Deafness," *Mask of Benevolence,* and *When the Mind Hears;* Mayberry and Wodlinger-Cohen, "After the Revolution"; Moores, *Educating the Deaf* and "Reactions"; Reagan, "The Oral-Manual Debate"; Sacks, *Seeing Voices;* Stewart, "American Sign Language"; Trybus, "Sign Language, Power, and Mental Health"; Winefield, *Never the Twain Shall Meet.*

27. An interesting characteristic of Anna's writing is her use of the second-person pronoun *you* when she is referring to herself.

28. As such a rite of passage strongly connected with gaining literacy, Gallaudet's EPT constitutes what Shirley Brice Heath calls a "literacy event"—"any action sequence, involving one or more persons, in which the production and/or comprehension of print plays a role." The EPT, like any literacy event, has "an appropriate structure . . . [and] certain interactional rules and demands particular interpretive competencies on the part of participants" ("Protean Shapes in Literacy Events," p. 350).

29. Brand, "The Why of Cognition."

30. To be sure, these are purposes that ensure *academic* success and may not be much practiced outside school. Nevertheless, they still are linked to success, even in the "real" world.

31. Mow, "How Do You Dance without Music?" p. 38.

32. For an excellent critique of the "control metaphor" in composition studies, see Robert Brooke's "Control in Writing: Flower, Derrida, and Images of the Writers," 1989.

33. Lennard Kelly has argued that one thing deaf writers lack in helping them make correct grammatical decisions is "the working memory" aided by an "auditory feedback loop" like that used by hearing writers; see "Relative Automaticity without Mastery." While I do not agree entirely with Kelly's rather simplistic summary of how sound (the lack thereof) echoes through the correct use of grammar in SWE, I do see that deaf student writers may be operating under a different cognitive frame—without sound to rehearse the written language orally. But my work in composition studies as well as a teacher of writing for seventeen years also tells me that the problems in writing that *any*

student encounters, deaf or hearing, have roots far more complex than just the absence of an "auditory feedback loop."

34. Shaughnessy, *Errors and Expectations*, p. 7.

35. See Kroll, "Writing for Readers," pp. 176, 178. Here Kroll borrows his argument from G. Dillon's *Constructing Texts.*

36. Shaughnessy, *Errors and Expectations*, p 8.

37. Rose, "Rigid Rules, Inflexible Plans."

38. Sommers, "Revision Strategies of Student Writers," p. 383.

39. Perl, "Understanding Composing," p. 45.

40. Mittelman and Quinsland, "Teaching Written Language to Deaf Students," pp. 155–56.

41. This question guides part of a sociolinguistic study being done by Kathy Wood, literacy instructor at Gallaudet and Ph.D. candidate at Georgetown University, as she investigates the literacy "resources" and "constraints" in the literacy life stories of Gallaudet students.

42. This is the world of mass communications technology that Walter Ong refers to as manifesting "secondary orality"; see *Orality and Literacy.*

43. S. North, *Making of Knowledge in Composition*, p. 205.

44. Here we would be following the leads established by composition and literacy education scholars such as Henry Giroux, Deborah Brandt, Glynda Hull, Mike Rose, J. Elspeth Stuckey, and Andrea Lunsford—and by deaf education scholars such as Carol Padden and Carol Ewoldt.

Interlude 1

On (Almost) Passing

3. Reasons you cannot be deaf

You don't sound funny.
You don't talk too loud.
You have such a nice voice.
You're so normal.
You can wear hearing aids.
You can turn up your hearing aids.
You can try harder.
You don't have any trouble hearing me.
You can do better if you try.
You can hear anything you want to hear.
You can try harder.
You can never really learn sign language.
You didn't grow up deaf.
You didn't go to a deaf school.
You tried to pass as hearing.
You try to pass as hearing.
You don't fit in.
You don't get the jokes.
You don't understand the language.
You don't understand the language.
You just don't understand
the language.

Reasons you can't be hearing:

You can't hear.

—ILENE C. CAROOM,
"Like Love, This Choice of a Language"

It is much easier to pass as hearing than it is to feign deafness. To be hearing, you can try hard and harder, sound a little funny, talk a little too loud (and often, and fast), wear hearing aids (and hide them)—and you will, for the most part, pass well enough. I should know; I've done it all my life. If I were to write it, my brief biography would read much like Ilene Caroom's, the author of my epigraph: "Although she has a progressive hearing loss, Ilene C. Caroom was raised hearing, with hearing aids, and taught to lipread. She has a B.A. in English from Hollins College and a J.D. from the University of Maryland Law School."[1] While some particulars part us, the sum of our experience looks much the same: to hide my deafness, to pass as hearing, I've tried hard and done quite well. The reasons, as Caroom herself outlines them and unreasonable as they may seem to the hearing world, abound for why I cannot be d/Deaf.

It was not until I had embarked on my "coming out" as a deaf person that I considered my rites of passage and dwelled on my acts, both deliberate and unconscious, both past and present, of passing. Because my coming out was a midlife event, I had much to reflect back on and much to illuminate ahead of me. This passing through an identity crisis, and the rites of passage involved in uncovering the paths of my lifelong passing as "hearing," took place in a hall of mirrors. Later I would come to know this place as the art and act of rhetoric.

I think I first saw myself mirrored in several students I met at Gallaudet University. I was thirty-two and finishing my Ph.D., writing a dissertation—that quintessential act of literate passing. What's more, I was finishing it by doing an ethnographic sort of study on deaf student writers at Gallaudet University; thus, I was using the guise of an academic grant and a Ph.D.—producing project as a professional foil to make a personal journey to the center of Deaf culture.

I was always good at finding a way to pass into places I shouldn't "normally" be.

So, there I was, doing time as a teacher and researcher at Gallaudet, collecting data for my study, taking a sign language class, living with a d/Deaf woman and faculty member at Gallaudet, going to Deaf gatherings, tutoring some of the students. Mostly,

I was just trying to pass in ways that were both familiar and unfamiliar to me: to pass (unfamiliarly) as d/Deaf—and doing a lousy job of it—and to pass (more familiarly) as h/Hearing and thereby pass through this last of major academic hoops.

In this passing, I spent a good deal of time watching—an act for which I had, as a hard-of-hearing person, lifelong experience and impeccable credentials—watching myself, watching the students I was doing case studies of, watching everything in the ethnographic scene of Gallaudet Deaf culture before me. I kept seeing myself in and through many of the students I worked with in the "basic English" classrooms. They were the mirror in my ears. These students often had volatile, if not violent, histories of passing—especially academically. Most of them, by virtue of finding themselves "stuck" (there is a powerful sign for that—two fingers jammed into the throat, a desperate look on the face) in English 050, were still floundering mightily, struggling violently, to pass at basic English literacy. Having negotiated that passage rather adeptly I now, oddly enough, found myself struggling to squeeze through another doorway as I was myself engaged in a mighty, violent struggle to pass in basic d/Deaf literacy.

I don't think I ever got it right. Almost, but not quite. I couldn't be deaf any more than I could be hearing. I was hard-of-hearing; and therein I was as confused and displaced, in either Deaf or Hearing culture, as this multiply-hyphenated term indicates.

The mirror in my ears threw back odd images—distorted, illuminating, disturbing, fantastic, funny—but all somehow reflecting parts of me. It put my passing in various perspectives: perspectives of tense and time (past, present, future); perspectives of repeated situations and relationships in my personal and academic life; and perspectives about the ways that stories are told, identities forged, arguments made. These are but some of the things I saw as I passed through, by, on.

For some twenty-five years of my life, from age five on, I went to the movies. And while I think I always more or less got the plot, I missed everything in the dialogue. For twenty-five years

I sat, passing time with a Three Musketeers candy bar, some popcorn, a Coke. I sat with my sisters as a grade school child on weeknights when my Mom had to work and my Dad was running the film from up in the little booth (both my parents had two jobs). To be sure, we often didn't sit so much as we crawled the aisles, playing hide-and-seek quietly in an always near-empty theater. Sometimes, more sensibly, I went to the lobby to do some homework. Through some films, though—the Disney classics and the cartoons that opened and closed each feature film—I did try to sit, to listen and watch. I don't think I had a conscious knowledge of it then, but now I know that I heard nothing, that I was a pro at passing even back then.

I got better, too, with age and the requisite social agility that becomes most junior high and high school girls. On weekends in my very small, very rural western Kansas town, the theater was the only place to go, the only thing to do. Past the Friday night football or basketball game, the movies beckoned; we'd often go to the same film both Saturday and Sunday night. Going to the movies was the only date possible in Tribune, Kansas.

I dated. They took me to countless movies, and I never heard a word. What's more, in the dark of the movie theater, with no hope of reading my date's lips as he struck up conversations with me, I nodded and feigned attention, agreement, acceptance all the more.

It now all seems so ludicrous, if not painful. For years I have listened to my friends—especially my academic friends—rave about movies, past and present. For years I have shifted back and forth on my feet at parties, smiling, nodding, looking genuinely interested in the discussion of this film or that. Not that I felt left out of their discussions. I just felt somehow disoriented, out of step—not quite passing. Like many deaf people, I not only saw films but enjoyed them. What I didn't know in all those years of adolescent pretense, but know so well now, is that I tend to enjoy films differently than hearing spectators do. I came to know that while they were concentrating on clues to solve the mystery, say, in the dialogue between characters, my eyes, a little more attuned to detail than theirs, would see in the background the weapon of death or notice the facial tension and odd mannerisms of the guilty party.

Take one example: in my early years of graduate school, one of the last years I still let dates take me to movies, I saw David Lynch's *Blue Velvet.* Just recently I had a conversation with my husband about that movie; it was a conversation based on memory, and on memory in different contexts since we had not seen the film together or even remotely in the same place. What I remembered, what I talked about, were vivid visual details of the movie: the ear lying in the grass that opens the movie, the color of Isabella Rossellini's lips and the way they pouted and quivered, the tenseness in her body, the vivid surreal scenes splashed like canvases in a museum of modern art. And while he himself pointed out how visual the movie was (as indeed most movies are), what my husband remembered most clearly were the conversations. He knew that the severed ear in the grass belonged to Rossellini's husband, that the husband had been kidnapped, and that her actions throughout the movie were done as ransom to keep her husband alive (plenty of reason for body tension and quivering lips). My husband knew this, of course, because they talk about it in the movie.

But I didn't know this. I thought the ear was a symbol of all the scenes of eavesdropping that appear in the film, nothing more, nothing less. I thought the severed ear and the blue velvet forged some artistic link to van Gogh and to Picasso's blue period. This was the sense I made with one sense missing.

So, when the pieces began to fit together and I began, late in my twenties, to understand that I understood precious little of movies beyond the roar of the dinosaurs in *Jurassic Park* or the catchy little tunes of the latest animated Disney "classic," I just stopped going. I had better things to do with my time than hog down a Three Musketeers and bad popcorn. There were other options for dates—especially since my dates now preferred to actually talk about the movie after it was over with, trying out their latest readings in critical theory on the poor, defenseless film over coffee, a drink, dessert. I couldn't hold up my end of the conversation, so I let it stop before it could begin.

~

I could not always stop conversations before they began, though. (If a genie were ever to grant me three wishes, this would definitely be one of them.) And more times than enough, I found myself pressured into passing and then greatly pressured by my passing. Some days, you see, I could pass; some days I could *almost* pass; some other days the rug almost got yanked out from under me.

My first high school sweetheart was, now that I look back, a real sweetheart; when he could have yanked, he didn't. He let me pass, and he let me do so with grace, saving my hidden deaf face, as it were.

What first attracted me to him was his gentle manner, his quiet, soft-spoken demeanor. It was that demeanor, of course, that doomed our relationship. He was a senior, I only a sophomore— and although I felt enormously comfortable around him (maybe because he didn't talk much, so I didn't have to listen much?), I wanted greatly to impress him. Apparently I did so, because a short month after dating several times, we were cruising main (the only option in Tribune besides "parking"—which only bad girls or longtime steadies did—or going to the movies) and Steve asked me to go steady with him, to wear his gigantic senior class ring. Actually, he asked three times. I didn't hear a one of them. But by the third time—even across the cavernous distance of his big Buick's front seat in the dark of a December night—I could *see* that he was saying something, trying *hard* to say something.

So I said the words that are surely the most common in my vocabulary: "What? Hmmmmm? Pardon me?" (I don't recall exactly which variation it was.)

Now Steve could have been mighty frustrated, out-and-out angry (and I would have not been surprised, since this response is all too common when we are asked to repeat something)—but instead he smiled in his gentle way, the way that had attracted me to him in the first place. He pulled the car over to the curb on main street right then and there, and he shut it off. He turned to face me directly and I could read his lips then. "I said," he still barely whispered, "would you wear my class ring?"

It was a bitter cold, blustery, snowy December night on the western Kansas plains. But I was hot, my face burning. Shamed. And shamed not so much at having not heard the question the first three times, but also in having myself, my deafness, so thoroughly unmasked. It felt as if someone were holding a mirror up to the sun with the reflected sunlight piercing through me. The mirror in my ears hurt. And it hurt even more because in that one fleeting instant in that big Buick at the age of fifteen, I realized, too, how DEAF I was. And I knew I would have to say "no" to soft-spoken Steve, his gentle ways, his giant class ring. I was not hearing enough; he was not deaf enough. And although I couldn't voice it at the time, I knew even then that this was more than just a sheet of glass between us, more than a barrier we could "talk" to each other through.

And I think—in fact, I'm sure—that he knew this, too. But still, instead of saying "never mind" or "oh, nothing" to my "What?" (the other most frequent responses) he let the moment play through, let me have the benefit of the words I had missed. He let me play at passing, let me play it as if it could really be, our going steady, our promise as a couple. He could have ridiculed me with taunts of "Gee, you just don't hear *anything*," or worse, in its "innocent" ignorance, "What's wrong, are you DEAF?" Those, too, are all-too-common responses to my requests that statements be repeated.

So, the moment passed. Steve and I didn't go steady. Nearly a decade later, when he and I were both married (to different persons, of course) we recounted this scene for our spouses; we laughed, they laughed. For a moment, Steve and I locked eyes— and I read it all there: he had known then, as he knew now, that I was indeed deaf. But neither he nor I, then nor at the present moment, would say the word. We let it pass. The conversation went on elsewhere.

When I began talking and working with deaf students at Gallaudet University as part of my dissertation research project, however, the conversation always went there directly: how I, how they, how we, coped with our deafness in personal relationships, especially with lovers and other significant others. We were trying out our mirrors on each other, trying to see if these multiple mirrors would help us negotiate the difficult passages we always encountered in relationships.

One student, David, an older nontraditional student, had mentioned several times in the course of his interview with me that his wife was far more deaf (in strict audiological terms) than he. It came up most strongly when I asked him directly about how much time he spent with hearing people and in "Hearing culture" as opposed to with deaf people and in "Deaf culture." His answer hinged on his relationship with his wife: "I have a little bit of a struggle with my wife over this issue. She isn't comfortable socializing with hearing people she doesn't know or with my hearing friends who don't sign. So I would end up having to interpret for her or stay right with her to keep her company. So I would either go alone, or go with her with a group of deaf people. I didn't have problems with either group [deaf or hearing], but she did have a problem with the hearing group." I mentioned, smiling, that were he asked, my husband might say some of the same things. We left the issue at that, and I went on to other questions. But at the end of the interview, when the videotape was off and the interpreter we used had left the room, David turned directly to me and in both spoken English and sign language, asked, "I'm curious. You said that you and your husband have similar communication problems in hearing situations since you are hard-of-hearing and he isn't. How," David paused, with genuine pain on his face, "do you work around this?" I could see that this was a sore spot, a blemish on both our mirrors. And unfortunately, I didn't have any particularly inspiring answers—no secret passageways to divulge and to help us both thereby solve this mystery more neatly, more quickly. We were (and are) both just stumbling and groping, looking for light switches in the often dark hallways of our deafness within relationships.

∼

In the past, too, I had looked to others, more deaf than I, to help illuminate my way through the relationship with my new husband. When I first came to Gallaudet in 1991, I became good friends with a woman some ten years older than I. She had become late-deafened; her gradual deafness was probably genetic and the result of auditory nerve degeneration; her intellect, acumen, wit, and passion amazed me; she liked simple food and good beer and wine; she was the heroic single mother of four teenagers; and she enjoyed the company of men thoroughly. In the fantasizing way, I think, of adopted children who often feel as if they never quite fit with their own parents, and in this time of substantial identity shifting for myself (I was, you see, trying to come out in my deafness), I fantasized her as potential role model, a mentor, a long-lost mother—or maybe sister—of sorts. I held up the mirror to myself and saw her in it; I held up the mirror to her and saw myself in it.

What I watched most carefully in that mirror was my own just-married relationship with a hearing man and the various reflections of my newfound friend, whom I'll call Lynn, in her relationships with men, both deaf and hearing, past and present. It was not always a pretty sight—on either side of the mirror. What I saw in watching Lynn and in sharing many conversations with her about the dilemmas of life with a hearing man or life with a deaf man was as inspiring as often as it was scary. Either way, the specter of dependence, never really tangible in that mirror, always lurked: to marry a deaf man meant she (we) would be the one(s) that might be most depended on (especially because as late-deafened and exquisitely literate persons we had skills and experience well worth depending on)—and this, then, would leave us little room for the sometimes necessary dependence of our own; but on the flip side (the magnified side of that mirror?), marrying a hearing man might well mean we would come to be too dependent and would, therefore, put at risk our ability to pass on our own, as our own.

When the woman is deaf, in a culture in which the woman is still seen as typically more "dependent" in a male-female relationship, her further dependence on a hearing partner can dangerously diminish her autonomy. Yet at the same time men typically depend on women in certain specialized areas; as Bonnie Tucker has written in *The Feel of Silence,* her controversial autobiography about her deafness, men expect their female partners to carry out an array of social functions that demand precisely the kind of communicative competence that is challenging for the deaf. Women generally mediate between the home and the

world in arranging the social obligations and daily domestic du-
ties of (heterosexual) coupled and family life. This calls for
speaking with many people, a high proportion of them
strangers, both in person and by telephone (in stores, offices,
schools . . .), in contexts in which the conversations can't be carefully anticipated or controlled. Discussing her own earlier marriage to a hearing man, Tucker sees the disruption of these
cultural norms in the social parameters of male-female relationships as largely responsible for the fact that successful relationships between hearing men and deaf women are few and far
between.

Within Deaf culture, there is more at stake than the bounds
of the intimate relationship: to marry either deaf or hearing
marks one, proffers one a pass, in the eyes of Deaf culture. Often
immediately after the initial identity-confronting question that
greets one—"Are you deaf or hearing?"—comes the next test: "Is
your spouse deaf or hearing?" In the strictest of cultural terms,
to marry deaf is to be Deaf; to marry hearing is to be Hearing. Of
course, these strict terms constitute far more an ideal than a reality. Many deaf—and even Deaf—persons I know have nondeaf
partners. Still, according to surveys conducted by Jerome Schein
and Marcus Delk, over 68 percent of deaf people marry endoga-
mously, with 86 percent expressing a desire to do so.[2]

To marry one or the other, then, is to pass as one or the other.
Yet another reason why I have *almost,* but not quite, passed:
when Deaf culture seeks to identify me, it holds up the mirror
and sees my husband, a hearing man. He is a gentle man, a generally soft-spoken man—like the Steve I didn't go steady with.
And yes, I must often depend on him in ways I'd much rather
not—asking him to make phone calls for me, asking him to interpret or relay bits of conversation I've missed in social settings,
asking him to repeat what one of my own children has said, asking him to help me bow out of uncomfortable social situations,
asking him to order for me at restaurants, asking him to pronounce with exaggeration words I'm not sure of, and often, most
difficult of all, asking him to just intuitively know when I want
to pass on my own and when I want to depend upon him.

It isn't easy. Sometimes I feel like shattering the mirror: it
shows me as "crippled," as "disabled" in my dependence.

~

It was a young woman, a new and very much struggling student, that I met at Gallaudet when I first went there and was so engrossed in my own coming out, so obsessed with my own identity, who first showed me and let me feel the shards of that mirror. She had been a student in the English 50 class I was a teaching assistant in; I had also tutored her individually and she had served as one of my in-depth case studies, meeting with me weekly for interviews and videotapes of her in the process of writing. We had come to know each other well. And although she looked, figuratively or literally, nothing like Lynn, the older deaf woman I now know I fetishized, I think the mirror drew us to each other—in the way most of us can hardly resist glimpsing ourselves, can hardly resist turning to stare at ourselves, when we pass by any reflective glass. This younger woman (whom, interestingly or conveniently enough, I had assigned the pseudonym "Lynne") turned to me as her model and mentor—me the mainstreamed, academically and somewhat socially successful woman, who had married a hearing man and got along, so it seemed, rather well in the Hearing world.

I hadn't realized how much she had turned to see me in her mirror (and I, in that way that we do when the mirror flatters us, not only had let her but had probably encouraged her)—I hadn't realized until toward the end of the semester I received several desperate long-distance phone calls from her mother in Nebraska. Lynne was not doing well at Gallaudet. It wasn't just her grades, although those were bad enough, to be sure. (Lynne was one of those lifelong products of mainstreaming—now found in abundance at Gallaudet—who arrived as a college freshman with little sign language skills and found herself immersed, even drowning, in Deaf culture and the precedence of sign language—yet another language now, in addition to English, that she didn't quite get.) Lynne was failing miserably in the Gallaudet social arena: she was lonely, depressed, even cast out. She just didn't fit. And her mother suffered for her, with her.

Back home, it turns out, Lynne had a hearing boyfriend. In righteous anger, her mother wanted her out of the "meanness" of Gallaudet, and so she had begun contacting me to seek my counsel on both the meanness and on getting Lynne out. Essentially, she wanted me to talk to Lynne and encourage her to abandon her long dream of studying at Gallaudet. Lynn's mother, understandably, wanted her back in the hearing world. It was mean there, too—but I think her mother had forgotten about that for the moment. What's more, she wanted Lynne married to a hearing man.

In a bit of conversation that jarred my very bones, her mother asked me if I was married. "Yes," I replied tentatively, not sure why this question had come up.

"Is he hearing?" she probed further. And then I knew just why the question had come up and where it was headed.

"Yes, he is," I confirmed.

"Are you happy—married to him?"

I sputtered a little, I remember, not quite comfortable with the suddenly personal tack that this conversation with a stranger some thousand miles away had taken. But I didn't know how to turn either back or away (mirrors are like this). "Yes," I answered simply.

"Well, good—then there's hope for Lynne, too. Would you tell her that? Could you tell her that she could be married—and happy—with a hearing man?"

I don't know what I said then. Stories and memories are selective, and, as Benedict Anderson has written, "all profound changes in consciousness, by their very nature, bring with them characteristic amnesias";[3] mirrors simply cannot say and show it all. But I do know that I felt deeply the pain of a shattered mirror—the pain of trying to be Lynne's inspiration, her role model, her fetish, her whatever. I could barely get it right for myself, could barely pass either as clearly and securely "d/Deaf" or as "h/Hearing"—how could I ever show someone like Lynne which, if any of those, to be?

I felt very much nailed to the threshold with several tons of doors, from both sides, closing on me.

$\sim$

When I get to feeling this way—trapped, nailed, stuck in between overwhelming options—I tend to get frantic, nervously energized, even mean. And my will to pass, to get through and beyond at all costs, kicks in ferociously. Some animals freeze in fear, shut down in fright; I run—harder, faster, longer. I run until I pass—until I pass on, or out.

And that running always seems to lead me to stories. I have always been a storyteller, a writer, a talker. These "talents" pass me off as "hearing" even as they connect me to "the Deaf way." "The Deaf way" revolves around narrative, around sharing stories—and the narration itself is, in Deaf culture, far more than incidental to the experience. Using sign language, Deaf culture prides itself on its "oral" and "narrative" nature. And for Deaf people, *who* tells the story and *how* they tell it is every bit as important as *what* the story is. The narrator, then, is in control of the experience instead of vice versa.

I tend to control conversations. This is not always a truth I am proud of, but it is the experience I present, the face I show in the mirror. I can talk a lot. I ramble, I chatter—especially on the phone and in one-on-one conversations. It is safer this way: if I don't shut up, if I keep talking, then voilà, I don't have to listen. And if I don't have to listen, I don't have to struggle, don't have to ask for repeats, don't have to assume any of the various appearances that I and other deaf/hard-of-hearing people often appear as—stupid, aloof, disapproving, suspicious. If I keep talking, I pass. I thrive and survive in perpetual animation.

But in situations in which animation affords me no control—in social settings with more than two in the conversation, for example, or as a student in the classroom—I resort quite rhetorically to another strategy: I disappear to what my mother and sisters called "Brenda's La-La Land." I just fade away, withdraw from the conversation. Here it is safer not to speak at all. For if I do, I am sure to be off-topic, three steps behind, completely out of sync with the others. Or even worse, if I speak, someone might ask me a question—a question I would struggle to hear, would have to ask to be repeated (probably more than once), would fail then to answer with wit, intelligence, clarity, quickness. Passing is treacherous going here, so I usually choose not to even venture out, not to cross over the mythical yellow line that marks the divide between d/Deaf and h/Hearing.

When I do venture out or across, I've been trapped more than once—have talked myself right back into the deaf corner. You see, when I talk, people sometimes wonder. "Where are you from? You have quite an accent," I have heard times too innumerable to count—and usually from near strangers. The question is, I suppose, innocent enough. But my answer apparently isn't. For many years I used to pass myself off as German; it was easy enough since my grandparents were quite German and I, as the child of an army family in the 1950s, was born in Germany. Of course, having grandparents who once spoke the language and having lived there, attached to the U.S. Army, for only the first four years of my life didn't really qualify me as a native speaker, complete with an accent. But my interlocutors didn't need to know any of that; when I said "German," they were satisfied. "Oh yes," they nodded, completely in understanding.

But some years ago, as another act of coming out, I stopped answering "German." First I tried out a simple, direct, "I'm deaf." But the result was too startling—it rendered my audience deaf and dumb. They sputtered, they stared at me speechlessly, they went away—fast. It quite unhinged them.

So I have softened the blow a bit and begun to respond, "I'm quite hard-of-hearing." To this I get a split response, which probably fits those multiple hyphens in my identity—they will both smile and nod an affirmative, "Oh yes, I understand now" (although I know that they really *don't* understand the connections between hearing loss and having an "accent"), and they will also back away rather quickly, still reluctant to continue a conversation under these circumstances.

I didn't like passing as German, but I'm never sure I like their response to my real answer any better. When I see the fright in their eyes, the "oh-my-god-what-should-I-say-now?" look that freezes their face into that patronizing smile, I feel cornered again. I feel scared, too, for the way it reflects back on the way I saw myself for many years. I wish I had just stayed mute.

For all that it frightens me, though, when I get cornered and I see my scared, caught-between-the-hyphens, hard-of-hearing face in the mirror, something comes of it. This happened to me first, and I think most significantly, at my first successful academic conference. I had just finished my first year of graduate school and had journeyed to give a paper at the Wyoming Conference on English. I had attended the conference the summer before as well, but I had been in my silently passing mode. This year, however, I was animated by everything from a very positive response to my own paper on the first day, to the glitter of the featured speakers, to a headful of theory-stuff mixed near explosively with my first year of teaching college freshman in a university principally composed of minority and Appalachian, first-generation college students. I was primed. I was talking a lot.

On the third day of the conference we were having a picnic lunch up in the mountains; at a table with one of the conference's biggest stars, I was feeling lit up, I guess by the glitter he was sprinkling on me by showing genuine interest in my own projects and things I had said in earlier sessions. I was telling stories about growing up in western Kansas. Everyone was listening, engaged, laughing.

Then a woman across the table, slightly to the left of me, wearing a tag from some small place in Louisiana, I remember, asked me, point-blank, "So, how long have you been DEAF?" (And that word, especially, went echoing off the mountain walls, I swear.) The question did not fall on deaf ears. The table, full of some sixteen people, went silent—awfully, awesomely silent. They waited.

"A-a-all my life." Silence again. Eons of silence. Echoes of silence.

"Wow," said the star, and he touched my arm—a genuine touch, a caring touch, a you-don't-have-to-feel-bad touch.

But I felt plenty bad. I excused myself under pretense of wanting some more potato salad. Instead I went behind a giant pine tree on the other side of the chow table and tried to breathe, tried to think of how I could make it past those people, to my car, out of here, out of here, out of here.

I know that in this telling the incident may all sound quite melodramatic. But in that moment, I learned, if nothing else and quite melodramatically, that I am the narrator of my experience. I learned that there was a price for passing, that the ticket cost more than just a pretty penny, that the fear of always, at any moment, being "found out" was far worse than just telling at the outset. (Like telling a lie and having to remember who you told it to, who you didn't.)

And what was I so afraid of in the first place?

That moment in Wyoming, at the dawn of my academic career, shortly before I entered my thirties, was the first time I think I asked myself that question. And when I began asking it, I also began taking care and charge of narrating my own experience and identity. I began coming out. At the age of thirty, I took my first sign language class. And I cried mightily on the first night at the sheer thrill of not having to sit in the chair at the front and center of the classroom so I could "hear" the instructor—cried for the simple freedom of choosing my own seat. I also dreamed up a dissertation project, rhetorician that I was, that would take me into "deafness"—my own and others—and to Gallaudet University, to the "heart" of Deaf culture.

If nothing else, I could always write about it, read about it. I had been doing literacy, and doing it well, all my life as yet another supremely successful act of passing. In all those classrooms I disappeared from as I drifted off, when my ability to attend carefully was used up and I wafted away to Brenda's La-La Land, I made up my absence by reading and writing on my own. If nothing else, I could always write about it, read about it.

At Grandma's family gatherings for the holidays, Brenda was always in the other room, away from the crowds, reading. Nine times out of ten, when Brenda's high school friends went out for lunch and to quickly cruise main, Brenda went to the high school library and read (or wrote one of her crummy poems). The summer before she was to start college, Brenda spent her lifeguard breaks at the noisy pool in the corner of the office, plowing through a used introduction to psychology textbook she'd gotten from another older friend who was already at college. As it turns out, this plowing was what saved her when that fall she found herself in the cavernous intro to psych lecture hall with some three hundred other students—thankful that her name alphabetically allowed her to sit near the front, but still yearning to be an A so she could optimize the lecture from the choicest chair.

And she read. She bought or checked out a dozen more texts on psychology, biology, the skills of writing an essay. She took copious notes from each of them, recorded and memorized key vocabulary from them, read over those notes and her own in-class lecture notes (which she didn't trust) carefully each week, adding notes on top of those notes.

She spent most of her freshman year in the all-girl dorm holed up in her room, writing, reading, taking notes, passing. She went swimming—a silent, individual sport—for a "social" life. After that first frightful year of college it got better. The initial panic of failing, of being found out, subsided. She even skipped class now and then, forgot to study scrupulously for each and every test. She still passed quite well. She took a job— a safe one—lifeguarding in a tall, antisocial chair at the university pool on nights and weekends. She kept writing and reading, but now found her interests were far beyond ingesting college textbooks and taking careful notes; outside of her homework, she started working her way through Russian literature (don't ask me why) and writing short stories.

She avoided bars and parties—sooner or later a young man would come slosh a beer on her, ask her something, and not having heard him, but not wanting to appear any of those dreaded things, she would just nod "yes." It was not always the answer she meant to give.

Books were far easier to control. When she didn't understand a text, it didn't seem to mind her asking for a repeat. She could stare hard, be aloof, acquiesce without embarrassing consequences, speak out of turn, and question a book again and again. It didn't seem to mind. She wasn't deaf when she was reading or writing. In fact, she came to realize that we are all quite deaf when we read or write—engaged in a signing system that is not oral/aural and is removed from the present.

How many times must she have written—to herself or to someone else—"it's easier for me to write this than it is to say it; I find the words easier on paper." On paper she didn't sound deaf, she could be someone other than herself—an artificer (thus fulfilling Plato's worst nightmare about the rhetorical potential in writing). On paper she passed.

~

Through the years, although I've become more confident in public speaking and far more willing to unmask myself, my deafness, before others have a chance to, I've always been better at writing and reading than I have at speaking. In graduate school, I was given a prestigious fellowship—principally for my writing skills—and thus my colleagues, both the faculty and other graduate students, expected me, I think, to be a class leader, to speak often and well. I didn't. In fact, I later came to know that many interpreted my silence in the classroom as negligence about the reading, or just arrogant indifference. Negligence about reading was never a crime I was guilty of, although I might own up to some indifference. How could it be otherwise, when only two of my graduate school professors spoke loudly and clearly enough for me to understand more than half of their mumbled, head-down, lifeless, eyes-stuck-on-the-page lectures?

Mostly I was still afraid of myself—still scared of what I saw when I stood in front of the mirror and spoke. As long as I had a written text—something I had worked on and rehearsed in order to smooth out my odd "accent," my tendency for fast talk and illogical progression, and my tonal infelicities—I could be comfortable speaking from and through it. But just to speak well extemporaneously—this was risking breaking the mirror, seven years' bad luck. Writing smoothed the blemishes, softened the sharp edges.

Even when I teach, I teach from and with writing, thereby maintaining control. I avoid, at all costs, leading large group discussions that involve the whole class, discussions in which students might speak from the back of the room—from the places where even my hearing aids on the highest setting won't go. I put them in small groups for discussion and then I walk around, lean over their shoulders, sit down with a small group for a short time. Then I bring one group to the front of the class to help me lead the whole class through discussion, branching out from what they were talking about in their smaller groups. In this way, the students take charge of receiving the questions and become interpreters for me and each other. I like to argue that in this process they gain a new kind of responsibility and learning that they might not have had before; but I know, truth be told, that it's mostly just a matter of getting *me* past some of the more difficult parts of teaching.

My premier pedagogy for passing is, of course, writing. My students, even in the more literature-based classes, write a lot. They always keep journals; they always write too many papers (or so it seems when I'm reading and responding to all of them). And my students, for sixteen years now, are always amazed at how much I write in responding to their journals and papers. For here is a place where I can have a conversation, unthreatened and unstressed by my listening limitations. They write, and I write back.

Writing is my passageway; writing is my pass; through writing, I pass.

NOTES

1. Ilene Caroom's poem and her brief biography appear in Garretson, *Deafness*, p. 8.

2. These figures, to be sure, are likely somewhat outdated; see Schein and Delk, *Deaf Population of the United States*, pp. 15–34.

3. Anderson, *Imagined Communities*, p. 204.

PART 2

Deafness as Pathology

CHAPTER 4

*D*iagnosing Deafness: The Audiologist's Authority

The deaf believe that they are our equals in all respects. We should be generous and not destroy that illusion. But whatever they believe, deafness is an infirmity and we should repair it whether the person who has it is disturbed by it or not.

— PROSPER MÉNIÈRE, 1855 (RESIDENT PHYSICIAN
AT THE PARIS SCHOOL FOR DEAF-MUTES)

What, after all, is orality about, if not a performance of a person's mouth addressing another person's ear and hearing with his own personal ear the spontaneous personal reply? Here surely is the essence of communication, a process of spontaneous exchange, varied, flexible, expressive, and momentary[;] . . . relationships between human beings are governed exclusively by acoustics (supplemented by visual perception of bodily behavior). The psychology of such relationships is also acoustic. The relation between an individual and his society is acoustic, between himself and his tradition, his law, his government. To be sure, primary communication begins visually with the smile, the frown, the gesture. But these do not get us very far. Recognition, response, thought itself occur when we hear linguistic sounds and

This chapter would not have been possible without the assistance of Vic Mortimer, a graduate research assistant who aided me with the interviews and in a related project on audiologists within the scope of "women, authority, and deafness"—a project funded by the Coca-Cola Foundation for Research on Women. So, too, it could have not been completed without the remarkable insights of my own audiologist, called here Gwen, who has given me her time, her students, and her ear in talking over various issues treated throughout this text.

melodies and ourselves respond to them, as we utter a variant set of
sounds to amend or amplify or negate what we have heard.

　　　　　　　—Eric Havelock, *The Muse Learns to Write*

Deafness

For my sister

It is when I hear Mozart,
some birds, the scraping
of wind through pine and
she is there; sounds crowd
round her silence like clay.

It is then I hear the note—
an inkling of the sound
of death; not the mere
being without, but the not
knowing, at all . . .

　　　　　　　—Richard Ryan,
　　　　　　　"Deafness"

Deafness has long been the subject of, and subjected to, rehabilitation. Rhetoric has long been aligned with—if not often the very voice of—rehabilitation: as a "formal act or declaration" meant to "restore" someone "(. . . degraded or attainted) to former privileges, rank, and possessions," and furthermore "to re-establish (one's good name or memory) by *authoritative pronouncement*," the refrain "to rehabilitate" (as defined by the *Oxford English Dictionary;* my emphasis) might well be sung to the tune of rhetoric. For rhetoric, as for rehabilitation, the establishment of one's good name or memory, the attainment of privilege, rank, and possession, and the art of authoritative pronouncement all echo loudly down the corridors of the tradition. And again, specifically in the case of rhetoric, the emphasis on acoustics is no coincidence—to not hear the note is to not know: and this "inkling of the sound of death," as Richard Ryan puts it, transfers fatally to speaking. To not *speak* the note is to not know.

From at least the time of the famed early classical orator Demosthenes—who is said to have practiced his speeches with pebbles in his mouth and against the background of the roaring ocean surf in order to correct his defects in speaking—rhetoric (as both theory and practice) has been preoccupied with rehabilitation, bent on restoring, and even perfecting, authoritative oral pronouncement. Theoretically and practically, rhetorical treatises have been designed to rehabilitate the otherwise ignorant, to train the voice and mind not only to speak, but to speak well—and thereby gain privilege, rank, possessions. This refrain reverberates loudly in Roman rhetoric—in Cicero's texts (both his theory and his own speeches) and in Quintilian's concept of the *vir bonus dicendi peritus,* the rehabilitated, educated man who becomes the sum of a lifelong education whose description spans the twelve volumes of the *Institutes of Oratory.* The necessity of rehabilitating speech that so compels rhetoric carries forward to the Renaissance and the Enlightenment, connected with philosophical notions of speech *as* reason; elocutionary interests in gestures; emphasis on voice qualities; the role of women in the speaking, privileged world; and the movement of rhetoric into the "popular" cultural sphere.[1] And with this popular movement, the echo of rhetoric's rehabilitative function sounds in the broad rhetorical education that characterized the nineteenth century: from the formal lectures and textbooks of George Campbell, Hugh Blair, Richard Whately, Alexander Bain, and John Quincy Adams—to name a few of the more eminent—to the more informal and apparently ubiquitous "parlor rhetorics" found in the homes and on the coffee tables of many. In the late twentieth century we still place significant premiums on the rehabilitated "voice"—the continued success of a textbook like Edward P. J. Corbett's *Classical Rhetoric for the Modern Student* and our required courses in freshman composition and often in speech communication in colleges across the country might illustrate how pertinent the premium is.

But what does this have to do with audiology? As this chapter will show, audiology exists for much the same rehabilitative, speech-restoring, orality-facilitating purposes as does rhetoric, echoing the syllogism *Language is human; speech is language; therefore, deaf people are inhuman, and deafness is a problem.* The three epigraphs I have chosen represent a predominant (although not exclusive) "audiological perspective" on deafness—emphasizing infirmity and the repair of that infirmity "for the good of the patient" whether the patient necessarily chooses rehabilitation or not, and imagining the human world only and always in terms of sound. Beyond sound are no human relationships, no government, no equality of existence, no inkling of knowledge. (And yes, according to our tradition, not much rhetoric either.) To be sure, these views are not original with audiologists. They come from culture, transmitted through rhetoric—both in practice and theory. Audiologists, as "scientists" in a field that they claim has existed only since World War II, did not make them up. It is my belief that the development of audiology as a full-blown field since the 1940s represents what rhetorician Alan Gross calls a "scientific-social drama"—something akin to the discovery of DNA, the recombinant DNA debates, and the Copernican revolution that Gross himself analyzes. Prosper Ménière, writing long before there was a field of audiology, and Eric Havelock—who is anything but an audiologist—writing 130 years later in 1986, both make clear that the audiological perspective is not just something on sale at the local Miracle-Ear franchise or the speech-language-hearing clinic in town. In this chapter, I will trace it from its originary moment through its self-presentation in audiology textbooks and the rhetoric of the "audiological moment"—the point at which a diagnosis of deafness is made—to, finally, cochlear implants, the cyborg creation delivered by the audiologist's authority.

INVENTING AUDIOLOGY

Half a dozen current audiology textbooks tell me that audiology is a "new science" and that its "lineage" comes from World War II, when soldiers suffered hearing losses en masse and found, on their return to civilian life, little "rehabilitation" offered for their difficulties in functioning in the postwar, hard-of-hearing world.[2] War is always good for medical and technological advances, and audiology, it seems, walked right out of just such an opportunistic moment. One popular audiology textbook (first published in 1958 and in its sixth edition in the 1990s) even figuratively casts audiology as "the offspring of two parents: speech pathology and otology," who were "wedded in World War II in the so-called aural rehabilitation centers established by the armed forces for the benefit of hearing-impaired service personnel."[3] Audiology as baby boomer.

Its recorded fathers are "Raymond Carhart, a speech pathologist recruited for Army aural rehabilitation work, and Norton Canfield, an otologist who was serving as consultant to the War Department."[4] Thus, the figure is a bit vague, the metaphor a bit mixed, as audiology's lineage really has no mother of record (though more than 80 percent of practitioners in this field are female). And yet, in several textbook accounts, speech pathology plays the mothering (and some would say, smothering) role while otology—as befits a medical, military father—is absent yet all-powerful and authoritative. The drama continues as audiology, the baby boomer, grows up a little and her (I take poetic license in assigning the pronoun here) parents separate, though never really divorce. She goes to live principally with her mother, speech pathology, and remains there, with much Sturm und Drang, a bit past her adolescence. The house is in her mother's name; it began as the American Speech Correction Association and only later was changed to include audiology (the American Speech, Language, and Hearing Association), although by some accounts it still does not really recognize the "adult" in audiology—reluctant, for example, "to embrace such issues as audiology licensure, hearing aid dispensing, and the Au.D. [Doctor of Audiology] as the entry level [degree] for our profession."[5]

In this and other ways explored below, audiology usually locates her identity in her mother: most audiologists begin their careers as undergraduates in speech-language pathology and only later, in graduate school, take up audiology specifically. She debates often—with her mother and herself—the efficacy of an autonomous existence outside her mother's name, house, identity.[6] Much as she seems to try, she cannot shake speech—particularly the pathologies of speech and her investment in rehabilitating it. She is, after all, her mother's daughter.[7] But this inability to move out or beyond her mother's primary identity leaves her stuck in adolescence, suffering an identity crisis. My own audiologist—also an academic who trains students for their master's degrees in audiology—explains "about audiology being in its adolescence" this way:

> I think what you said about college students, we're sort of in the same place as a profession. We've taken philosophies from lots—from medicine, from speech pathology, from deaf education—and we like a lot of those philosophies, and we're trying to evolve some of our own philosophies, and I think that training audiologists is where that happens most. I don't know if anyone has talked to you yet about the issue of the Au.D., the audiology doctorate. Right now there's a push to make audiology a

doctoral level profession [it is now almost exclusively a master's level profession, while a doctorate can be obtained in speech-language pathology] . . . but I think we haven't evolved into what's the best way to train an audiologist. No one can seem to agree on that. Makes my job hard.[8]

The difficulty of the audiologist's job is compounded from her father's side as well. The otologist—the medical and missing, although still powerfully "present," patriarch—commands her not only to serve her patients—through testing, evaluation, and rehabilitation—but to conduct research on them as well. And this research proceeds from the notion that all hearing loss is a pathology—a disease to be understood, held in check, and then, it is hoped, someday eliminated. In this scenario, though, she becomes "merely" a technician (much as rhetoric, once reduced to style, becomes "mere" technique). Serving her medical master, the audiologist becomes tester of the ears, an audiogram administrator, a glorified sort of secretary assisting the "serious" work of the doctor who really fixes the problem (usually with invasive surgeries).

And by and large, she is not happy here either. She is, as my audiologist says with scorn, the "technician and not clinician"—stuck in "a model where you're in the medical school, where you're trained in the medical school, [and] you may just see audiograms, where you may just be cranking out audiograms . . . going through the motions."[9] Indeed, a group of second-year audiology graduate students that I interviewed—all due to receive their master's degree at the end of this year of their training—placed medical doctors high on their list of "threats to our authority": "I have another thought about what threatens our authority, and that is because they have more authority, they are given more authority in society than we are, but as a profession, the audiologist's authority is often threatened by M.D.'s. And really only because they're given more authority, not because they have more knowledge about—because they know jack about what we do."[10] And although they may, in fact, know only "jack" about audiology, hearing loss, and the daily lives of people with hearing loss, physicians and an odd assortment of others—including educators, rhetoricians, inventors, institutional administrators, and eugenicists—have long been interested in people's ears and what they do or don't do.

Many believe that the "science of hearing"—audiology—was "invented" long before World War II soldiers brought home bombed-out ears. As early as 1799, during the Enlightenment fervor about the nature of language, Jean-Marc Itard was appointed resident physician at the Institute for the Deaf in Paris at the same time he was handed over one "Victor of Aveyron"—the famous "Wild Boy" found in the woods outside Paris who was mute, unkempt, "savage." The impetus for Itard's appointment to this position was a savage one: he was to civilize (to rehabilitate) Victor, to restore him to language—and in doing so, Itard and others hoped, to make stunning discoveries about the "nature" of language.[11] Although Itard's ten-year-long "experiment" with Victor failed—the boy never learned to speak and shamelessly shunned clothing, company, and civilization at large every chance he got—Itard did gain skills at a rather systematic, if not outright sinister, medical study of deaf ears there at the Paris school. Beginning modestly enough with examinations of cadavers, Itard disappointingly discovered "nothing from this . . . except the old finding that the ears of the deaf are free from visible lesions."[12]

So, he set out to *make* lesions. Thinking that the ear's inability to hear might be like the paralysis of a limb, and encouraged by the dramatic effects recent demonstrated when the legs of dead frogs were electrically stimulated, Itard applied electricity to some of the students' ears. Here he was following a model established by no less an authority than Count Alessandro Volta, the Italian physicist who contributed much to the study of electricity and for whom the volt is named.[13] Perhaps a little more humanely than Itard's experiments on the deaf residents of the Paris school, though not necessarily more sanely, Volta conducted most of his electrical auditory experiments on himself. One recent book on cochlear implants describes Volta's work as "the first daring experiment in applying electrical stimuli to a man's auditory nerves."[14] Volta's "daring" was so great that it is worth recounting his own description of his work in this area, as it was read aloud to the Royal Society of London on 26 June 1800:

> It remains for me to say a word about hearing. On this sense, which I had vainly tried to stimulate with two single metal plates, although the most active of all conductors of electricity, namely, one silver or gold and the other zinc, I finally managed to achieve some effect with my new apparatus composed of 30 or 40 pairs of these metals. I pushed deep into each ear a metal rod with a rounded end and I had the two other ends making contact with my apparatus. At the moment when the circuit was thus complete I received a jolt in my head; and a few moments later (the circuit continuing without interruption) I began to be conscious of a sound,

or rather a noise in my ears that I can't exactly define; it was a kind of crackling, jerking or bubbling as if some dough or thick stuff was boiling. This noise continued without abating or increasing, all the time that the circuit was complete, etc. The disagreeable sensation, which I feared was dangerous, of the shock to my brain, was such that I didn't repeat the experiment too often.[15]

One *almost* wants to know how often that "too often" was. Or perhaps, one doesn't.

Itard's experiments were, without doubt, frequent. But they were also far more varied than Volta's. Beyond electrical stimulation of those institutionalized deaf ears, Itard also applied leeches to some of them, deliberately pierced some eardrums, developed a gruesome technique for "flushing out the lymphatic excrement" that supposedly blocked the ears of his deaf students, soaked their ears in a blistering agent repeatedly, fractured a few skulls, applied a white-hot metal button behind their ears, and sewed strings through their necks to create a wound for the bad humors to escape from their ears.[16] All this in the name of "science"—which he did, eventually, pronounce as fruitless here: "Medicine does not work on the dead," he is reported to have concluded, "and as far as I am concerned the ear is dead in the deaf-mute. There is nothing for science to do about it."[17]

Of course, there was still something for science to do about it—and thus, audiology was (re)born, again fathered by medical science, 140 years later at the conclusion of World War II when the vicissitudes of war had performed its own experiment and created its own lesions, in the ears of many soldiers. Although the postwar restorative techniques were not so invasive or inhumane (that would come a generation later, with cochlear implants), Itard's version of Enlightenment-spawned audiology and birth of the 1940s baby boomer version took place in similar settings and existed for similar ends: both were made possible because they occurred in institutions—a wartime military and a state school for the deaf—where the "patients" were conveniently corralled by an already-existing system and thus "compliance" (a key term in audiology, as I will illustrate later) was ensured. Additionally, both the 1940s and early 1800s versions of audiology sought compliance for similar ends—to rehabilitate ears in order to restore individuals to *speech* (usually conflated with language) and its ensuing privileges: namely, Reason. The invention of audiology, then and now, was always about speech, as much as if not even more than it was about hearing.

This is where Alexander Graham Bell, quintessential inventor, also enters the scene. Providing yet another possible point of origin for audiology, Bell must ring in our ears. At roughly the same time he is inventing the telephone—an "accidental" invention born of his attempts to develop a mechanical means of making speech visible to the deaf and hard-of-hearing by using the electrical transmission of sound—A. G. Bell is also involved in numerous deaf-related activities: opening a training school for teachers of the deaf in Boston that focuses on "Visible Speech" (1871), a method of oral instruction designed by his father, A. M. Bell (1864); standing strongly behind the campaign for imposing the oral method of instructing deaf students; becoming involved, along with other noted eugenicists of the day, in the U.S. Census (1880); delivering and then publishing his *Memoirs upon the Formation of a Deaf Variety of the Human Race* (1883, 1884), a treatise charting and graphing the marriage and progeny of the deaf in order to "prove" how abhorrent it would be if deaf were allowed to continue marrying deaf and thus increasing the likelihood of deaf children and the continuation of a "deaf race";[18] corresponding with, and endearing himself to, Helen Keller; and even using his inventive genius, borrowing the technologies put in place by the telephone, to use the first audiometer to assess the hearing of children in Washington, D.C. (1886).

Between Itard and Bell, lit by a current supplied in essence by Volta, the path was laid for a "pathology of deafness" and then a full-blown "science of hearing," christened as audiology, when another ready-made institutionalized population of deaf ears fell fortune's and technology's way at the close of World War II. My point is that it did not take a war to originate audiology—merely two men with substantial authority, access to institutions, a fear of difference, a distrust of things they did not fully understand, a patronizing passion to rehabilitate those they deemed "lesser" than themselves, and recourse to a simple (illogical, but powerfully popular) syllogism at large in the culture: *Speech is language; language is human; therefore, deaf people are inhuman, and deafness is a problem.* Audiology— offshoot of speech pathology and otology, legacy of Itard and Bell, child born from the passion of a postwar moment—would suit itself up in its scientific best and attempt to solve this problem.

Arranging and Stylizing:
the (Scientific) Audiology Text

Any science—audiology included—arranges and stylizes, establishes and normalizes itself through the education of its apprentices. Thus, textbooks become an integral, even enormous part of any scientific paradigm. Thomas Kuhn, eminent historian and philosopher of science, tells us in his classic *Structure of Scientific Revolution* that the priorities of a scientific paradigm—its "accepted rules" and "loci of commitment"—can be revealed most readily by an investigation of its educational apparatus: "Close historical investigation of a given speciality at a given time discloses a set of recurrent and quasi-standard illustrations of various theories in their conceptual, observational, and instrumental applications. These are the community's paradigms, revealed in its textbooks, lectures, and laboratory exercises." The power of these educational applications—the power of a textbook, for example—in "normalizing" a view of things, people, and approaches as they intersect any scientific field has great and often overlooked significance: "Scientists work from models acquired through education and through subsequent exposure to the literature often without quite knowing or needing to know what characteristics have given these models the status of community paradigms."[19]

A textbook not only offers a current model or paradigm for that field, training new scientists in a particular way, but it often erases the previous paradigms. This, as I have already suggested, is how it is that current audiology texts have come to locate their origins in World War II rehabilitation efforts and not in the work of Volta, Itard, and Bell. What is more, the paradigm presented not only dictates the past but also attempts to ensure its own future by authorizing, within its parameters, the standards and limits for future research in that field. According to Kuhn, this backward-erasing and forward-casting double move of a scientific paradigm as it is presented in educational apparatus to newcomers in the field is just what makes scientific *evolution* virtually nonexistent: it is only through the sudden and violent overthrow of paradigms—through a scientific *revolution*—that a new paradigm takes shape and gains hold. And once a new paradigm is in place, the forward and backward process occurs anew.

So it is that Itard, Volta, and Bell are all but forgotten in present-day audiology textbooks—relegated to footnotes and "vignette" boxes or alluded to briefly to set the stage for the "historical development of audiology": for example, "Although instruments (audiometers) used to measure hearing date back to the late 1800s, the discipline of audiology essentially evolved during World War II."[20] For the most part, Volta's and Itard's savage experiments are not even mentioned; thus, they ironically constitute a history and origin both literally and figuratively beyond speech, outside the range of the paradigm.

As documented in audiology textbooks, speech itself is squarely within that paradigm, constructing audiology's pitch, tone, frequency, and volume. Speech originates. Or rather, the *pathologies* of speech originate, founding the field of audiology today: "Interestingly, it was a prominent speech pathologist, Robert West, who called for his profession to expand their discipline to include the area of audition."[21] In a piece of some historical significance, published fittingly in the *Volta Review*, this founder spoke strongly of the sense behind "the mechanical ear" (the hearing aid) and made his argument mostly by building connections between "speech correction" and "those defective in the perception of speech": "Many workers in the field of speech correction do not realize that the time has come for those interested in this field to expand the subject so as to include . . . problems of those defective in the perception of speech. Our job should include . . . aiding the individual to hear what he ought to hear."[22]

Speaking in 1936, Robert West might well be echoing Prosper Ménière (who was Itard's successor at the Paris School for Deaf-Mutes) in 1855; just as he determined the necessity of "aiding the individual to hear what he ought to hear," so Ménière admonished that "whatever they believe, deafness is an infirmity and we should repair it whether the person who has it is disturbed by it or not."[23] What *ought* to be heard, of course, is speech; the "infirmity" of deafness is that it severs the individual from speech. This paradigm anchors all audiology textbooks and drives the organization of their typical table of contents.

Most that I have looked at begin, however, outside "pure" speech: they begin with sound. From Nanci Scheetz's introduction for undergraduate students in speech-language-hearing sciences and for laypersons and professionals "who come in contact with the hearing impaired community," to Fred Bess and Larry Humes's slim "introduction" at a more advanced level, now in its second edition within a decade, to the six chunky editions of two obviously popular textbooks designed for the M.A. student entering the field of audiology, sound is where "the audiological perspective" begins.[24] Each starts with a fairly detailed and scientific explanation about the nature of sound.

In doing so, they provide a scientific base for their field and their later chapters. To master the nature of sound, the apprentice audiologist will need to engage not only new and complex terminology but also neurology, physical anatomy, mathematics, and physics. These first chapters are heavy going. Figures and tables crowd the pages in an effort to acquaint and assist the apprentice with this complex subject.[25] "You are entering science," these texts seem to say, "and the going will not be easy. Beware! Audiology is challenging! It is not just about hearing aids and Miracle-Ear clinics for your grandfather!"

Frederick Martin's sixth edition of *Introduction to Audiology* professes to simplicity with almost stuttering regularity in its first three pages, as we are told that we will first encounter an "elementary look at the anatomy of the auditory system," leaving many "oversimplifications" to "be clarified in later chapters." We will begin with "simplified explanation" and learn "basic vocabulary," and "the more sophisticated" stuff will come later. But for now, "some of the statements have been oversimplified." And please note (again) that "these basic concepts are expanded in later chapters in this book," while here we begin with "a simplified look." Still, the weight of this text's illustrations and repeated material in these first two chapters about "the nature of sound" adds up to more than just simplicity.

Bess and Humes do not simplify so much in their "introductory" text, *Audiology: The Fundamentals.* Scanning the illustrations alone makes this obvious: the figures are more challenging, representing "the movement of air particles" (their figure 2.1), "sinusoidal waveforms" (figures 2.3 and 2.5), and "constructive and destructive interference of two sound waves" (figure 2.4), among others. And while their opening chapter on the nature of sound also attempts to salt the bland and heavy scientific fare with a number of vignettes about the people behind all this—Hertz, Pascal, and Newton, for example—it is also heavily peppered with mathematical equations, physics problems, and scientific abbreviations. Whether the student of audiology is served the more "simplified" fare of Frederick Martin or the heavy meat-and-potatoes of Bess and Humes, this much is clear: he or she will have to chew long and hard. Audiology is science. Not to be digested easily.

Indeed, the graduate students in audiology that I have interviewed tell me that the scientific difficulty of the field both drew some of them to the field in the first place and makes them proud of becoming audiologists—it even grounds a good part of their authority (a point I will dwell on in the next section). One of the first-year students said, "That's a source of pride for me . . . there's some really hard courses, and conquering that, and completing all those courses, gives me a sense of pride. And then all the knowledge that you have about how the ear functions, and how all the equipment functions, the decisions you make when you are fitting someone for an aid." Another both echoed this pride in becoming a scientific authority and invoked a second aspect of audiology: "One of the things that was so appealing to me about the field in particular was that it incorporates caring as well as the science and all that kind of thing. For so long women really haven't been encouraged that often [in science], that much, I guess I should say. But this field allows that, promotes the combination even."[26]

It will be a while before the textbooks get to any of the "caring" part of the combination, though. They tend to become even more scientifically serious after explaining sound, when medical science, and particularly pathology, generally enters the picture. Rippling out from the waves of sound, they tend either to turn directly to "the nature of the problem" as it exists physiologically in "otologic," "neurologic," and "general medical" considerations connected to deafness, to "pathologies of the auditory system," and to "disorders of the auditory system," or to consider the "family dynamics" in "dealing with a diagnosis of deafness," in which deficits and difficulties in "cognition and intellectual functioning" as well as "moral reasoning and values clarification" are sure to lurk.[27] Regardless of the angle—physiological or psychological—the view remains much the same: hearing loss is a problem because of the way it inhibits speech. That culturewide syllogism Bell and Itard operated under still rings "true": *Speech is language; language is human; therefore, deaf people are inhuman, and deafness is a problem.*

Listen, for example, to Katz in his 1,100-page tome that some consider "the bible of audiology," *The Handbook of Clinical Audiology,* as he introduces "the nature of the problem":

> Like all other senses, we cannot fully appreciate hearing until we have lost it. One can begin to realize the profound effect of hearing loss on the individual as we read the chapters in this book. The potential losses are friendships, explanations, kind words, corrections, and spontaneous give

and takes. These form some of our most human, day-to-day experiences without which we might feel completely isolated, unwanted and a burden to others. Audition is also our key to oral language, which in turn forms the basis of our written communications. Despite the complexity of the issue, it is hard to imagine any sensory defect more devastating then [*sic*] deafness. Blindness even from birth does not create the educational, vocational and social problems that are experienced by the hearing impaired.[28]

In cataloguing the "potential losses" Katz again chants that syllogism—the "friendships, explanations, kind words, corrections, and spontaneous give and takes" missing when one's hearing is amiss are predicated on speech. And this speech, as Katz goes on to complete the equation, "form[s] some of our most *human, day-to-day* experiences." Finally, to total his points in a grand sum, much as does eminent language and literacy scholar Eric Havelock (see my second epigraph), Katz concludes: "Audition is also our key to oral language, which in turn forms the basis of our written communications."

This paradigm preoccupies audiology. It drives the daily work of the clinical audiologist—the testing, measurement, evaluation, and subsequent rehabilitation of "the hearing impaired."[29] From here, in most audiology textbooks—having now scientifically assessed the "nature of sound" and set up "the nature of the problem" along pathological, disordered axes—the audiologist has her epistemological bearings and is ready, with compass in hand, to begin trying out her beliefs. She is ready to test hearing. And she will do so with an ear toward speech.[30]

The paradigm of the field, as it plays out in the textbooks, points ever more definitively in that direction: toward the harmonious "acoustics" that so govern human relationships, delivered in speech and then, wave-like, in writing—as in Havelock's own meta-acoustical glorification of an oral/aural ontology in *The Muse Learns to Write.* So it is that audiologic assessment will begin, typically, with "pure-tone" measurement; once that scientific, objective baseline is established, it proceeds to an evaluation of "speech audiometry," measurements of dimensions such as the patient's speech detection threshold (SDT), speech reception threshold (SRT), cross-hearing tendencies, most comfortable loudness level (MCL), and word-recognition skills (WRS) that are far less objective and are fraught with problems of "reliability" and "interpretation" at every turn and test.

The thorns get thick, the path twisted and unclear—the science often gets lost in the woods here.

Finally, most audiology textbooks turn from testing to rehabilitation as they reach for closure. If hearing loss is the problem, particularly in how it intersects culturally with speech, then audiological measurement of pure tones *but especially of speech* is the certification and spelling out of that problem. Rehabilitation becomes the answer. For the most part, too, it is an answer in the same pure tones as the posing of the problem: AMPLIFI-CATION ABOVE ALL. In the audiology textbooks I have seen, "amplification" (which translates into "hearing aid") or "hearing aid" itself is the first item to appear in the closing chapters, which are headed by titles such as "Management Strategies," "Overview of Aural Rehabilitation," "General Rehabilitation Model," and "Management of Hearing Impairment."[31]

The rehabilitative weight—bearing the status of the "last word" and the hopes for homing in on speech—that is placed on that tiny little technological device is nowhere more evident than in the opening words of "Hearing Aids and Modern Technology," the final chapter of Scheetz's textbook, which is intended to provide an "orientation to deafness" for undergraduates. We are told there that "statistics indicate that there are 22,000,000 hearing impaired people in the United States." Yet, "within this population, only 1,000,000 wear hearing aids." Scheetz goes on to unilaterally assume that this 21 million difference (now there is a difference that matters) "can be attributed to limited economic resources, perceptions of self-image, and the lack of accurate information."[32]

Let me dwell on this statement for a moment, since it represents well the power of a "normalizing" (scientific) paradigm at work in a textbook. Certainly, hearing aids are anything but cheap—most of the latest digitally programmable ones average $3,000, and they are almost always *not* covered by one's health insurance; nor are financing plans readily available. And yes, a fair amount of stigma still lies in being perceived as "deaf and dumb" in our culture. Undoubtedly, in our culture more education about hearing loss always remains to be done. I might add, though, numerous other "attributes" of the hearing impaired that Scheetz does not consider: lifestyle; belief in how the responsibility of communication should be shared; skills and comfort levels with sign language and/or Deaf culture; skills at other kinds of communicative "coping" (lipreading, tuning out background noise, reading body language and context carefully, writing, etc.); sensitivity to having things stuck in one's ear; sensitivity to the severe limitations of even the most technologically advanced hearing aids in a wide range of listening situations; comfort with "silence" and "isolation," especially insofar as these are terms imposed by others; and even distaste for one's patronizing audiologist. These are only a few possibilities not offered in the textbook: I have no doubt that there are more. Just as the etiologies of and adjustments to hearing loss are infinitely diverse, so are the ways in which people choose to communicate and relate with others in general. To provide a list of but three attributes to account for a 21-million-person difference is irresponsible at best, abhorrent at worst.

But paradigms can be like that. They "gain their status," Kuhn tells us, "because they are more successful than their competitors in solving a few problems that the group of *practitioners* has come to recognize as acute" (my emphasis).[33] If there are three reasons for not wearing hearing aids in the paradigm of current audiology, solving the problem—gaining the compliance of those 21 million—might become easier. This narrow approach to problem solving is typical of what Kuhn calls the "mopping-up operations" of a normalized paradigm—an "enterprise [that] seems an attempt to force nature into the preformed and relatively inflexible box that the paradigm supplies."[34]

Here is Scheetz mopping up: whatever their reasons for abstaining from hearing aids, she claims that "the majority of individuals exhibiting some type of hearing loss can benefit from some form of amplification such as hearing aids, assistive listening devices and systems, and/or medical/surgical treatment."[35] This wide-sweeping summary—again, she is applying it to 21 million people—of how best to "rehabilitate" the "hearing-impaired" individual represents the normalizing paradigm of audiology, so prevalent and pervasive in audiology because it is, in fact, so prevalent and pervasive in our culture at large.

When I interviewed one second-year audiology student who was planning to continue his career and earn a Ph.D. in the field (most audiologists are women who earn master's degrees and then engage in clinical practice), he ended our interview by telling me a story of a recent exchange he had with his own mother over the announcement of President Clinton's slight hearing loss and fitting for hearing aids. Apparently Clinton had made public the results of his latest audiological assessment and had also declared that he would be wearing his hearing aids when he "needed them." The student was quite distressed: "My mother and I talked about this," he said. "And I told her how frustrating this was: 'You see,' I told her, 'now people are going to listen to the president and take him as an example. They'll think, *See, you don't need to wear your hearing aids all the time.* And that won't do them any good.'" Suddenly, though, the student realized who he was talking to. A bit sheepishly he looked directly at me and queried, "You wear your hearing aids all the time, right?" Never one to fit the paradigm, I smiled back, "Well, no, I don't."

I went on to explain why I didn't: they didn't serve me well in many situations (although I like them in the classroom, at meetings, attending lectures); my pattern of loss made it hard to fit me "perfectly"; they tended to drive me crazy—both in the noise level and the sensitivity of my ears to having things inside them—after a maximum of six hours; and, too, I was still pretty much an old dog trying to learn new tricks after thirty-odd years of coping on my own without hearing aids.

"Oh," he said.

And then I asked him a question from a different paradigm: "Have *you* ever worn a hearing aid?"

He was smart. He understood right away why I would ask that question, and he even confessed, shifting paradigms beautifully, that it might be a good idea for all audiologists to try wearing one for a while. "It might help us understand more," he concluded. And with that, I think we went beyond the textbook, past the paradigms, into learning and testing new territory.

COMMITTING TO MEMORY:
TESTING (AND) THE AUDIOLOGIST'S AUTHORITY

This young audiologist-apprentice does not serve a wicked sorcerer-master: audiology is not some evil, oppressive, autocratic entity. Audiology—again, like most science and the technology related to it—exists dynamically with and within the larger social sphere. And it is in that dynamic relation between science and society that the voodoo, if there is any, gets performed and the chants take on a powerful mnemonic force of their own: here is where rhetoric, reverberating between the public sphere and the professional one of scientists, plays a powerful, paradigm-sustaining role as it transforms a scientific hypothesis into a social *given* or, conversely, as a social norm becomes the grounds for generating scientific research. Thomas Farrell, a rhetorician of the late twentieth century, calls this rhetorical transformation "magic": the "ability of rhetorical transaction gradually to generate what they can initially only assume appears to possess a rather magical ambience."[36] Following Farrell (and Aristotle, Thomas Kuhn, Clifford Geertz, Chaim Perelman, and Victor Turner as well), in *The Rhetoric of Science* Alan Gross analyzes this magical ambience as it occurs in several scientific-social dramas: the development of the British Royal Society, the Copernican revolution, Newton's "rhetorical conversion," Darwin's "self-persuasion" in his journals leading to *The Origin of the Species,* and the more recent controversy over recombinant DNA.

Thus far, I have been arguing that the development of audiology as a full-blown field since the 1940s represents yet another such scientific-social drama. Furthermore, not only is this a drama full of the usual magical ambience that rhetoric makes, but it is also a drama *of* and *about* rhetoric. For it is not the single audiologist testing, interpreting, and rehabilitating her patient's hearing in thousands of clinics across the land who comes to believe, on her own, that *Speech is language; language is human; therefore deafness is a problem.* Nor has she simply learned this from her textbooks and teachers. If audiologists come to believe (as does Scheetz in her undergraduate textbook) that "the majority of individuals [22 million of them, remember] exhibiting some type of hearing loss can benefit from some form of amplification such as hearing aids, assistive listening devices and systems, and/or medical/surgical treatment," they have first yoked hearing loss with speaking loss and then mental loss—invoking the tradition of "deaf and dumb"—and have wedded their notion of "human" with the acoustics of orality that echo, eerily, even in writing.[37] And those connections are made because they are part of the magical ambience of our culture and, more pertinently, of our Western rhetorical tradition.

I will be concerned in this section with issues of *authority* and *audience,* two key rhetorical concepts, in what I am calling "the audiological moment"—a moment of substantial crisis, a rhetorical moment in which larger social dramas are played out, a moment when deafness is diagnosed. For if there is an audiologist present, you can be fairly certain there is a crisis at hand. And in a crisis, rhetoric almost always enters as part of the larger social drama. In this particular crisis—interchangeably referred to here as the audiological moment or the diagnosis of deafness—the audiologist is the *authority;* the person with hearing loss, in addition to those surrounding that person in concentric circles (friends, family, teachers, co-workers, community, culture), constitutes the *audience.*

As I have been suggesting, the audiologist gains significant authority first because of the tradition of Western rhetoric. She enters in a moment that signifies our sacred tradition of "speaking well" and represents just how naturalized speech has become—a moment where someone might be deaf, or even worse "mute," and thereby stripped at the outset of any real chances to become Quintilian's *vir bonus dicendi peritus,* the "good man speaking well." As it is important to keep repeating, the Western tradition of rhetoric—indeed, our entire Western culture—has been dominated by "the will to speech." We are innately suspicious of silence (and we only have to look as far as how we regard those students who are typically silent in class for verification of that); from at least Hellenistic times forward, we have valorized speech. This is the principal logos in the rhetoric of diagnosing deafness, the crux of the crisis in the audiological moment.

This long-standing emphasis on valorizing speech can be witnessed in the centuries-old communications debate surrounding the education of deaf students: whether to educate deaf persons *manually,* using a language that is, if not simply more natural, certainly considerably easier for them—or whether to educate them, as is usually the case, *orally,* spending inordinate amounts of time teaching them how to speechread, make sounds, impersonate spoken language (something that not too many of them ever get very skilled at).[38] Speech consummates all efforts; never mind the other knowledge that deaf students might miss in endless speech "therapy," while other students their age are at recess, reading *Charlotte's Web,* feasting on multiplication and division tables, memorizing state capitals.

This will to speech, and its relation to the audiological moment, is clearly revealed in those audiology textbooks. For example, in her "orientation to deafness" Scheetz tells us that one's social adequacy is related to speech; deafness is related to cognitive deficit in individuals; deafness often represents a state of deprivation and marginalization from community and culture; deaf individuals tend to have lower expectations of themselves and others, fewer opportunities in the world, increased social isolation, and unhealthy avoidance of conflict; and, finally, deaf people are typically under- or unemployed.[39] But it does not take an audiologist, psychologist, or sociologist to echo *that deafness is inhuman and a problem,* deduced from the propositions that *speech is language* and *language is human.* Scholars of literacy and language will parrot those propositions as well.

Sounding much like Eric Havelock in the epigraph, Walter Ong tells us in his classic text *Orality and Literacy* what all good rhetoricians know—that "oral communication unites people in groups." That unity is the basis for the following passage, a particularly damning declaration for those who are deaf, for whom sound does anything but incorporate. Ong argues that "sight isolates, sound incorporates. . . . You can immerse yourself in hearing, in sound[;] . . . sound is thus a unifying sense. . . . The auditory ideal . . . is harmony, a putting together. Interiority and harmony are characteristics of human consciousness. Knowledge is ultimately not a fractioning but a unifying phenomenon, a striving for harmony. Without harmony, an interior condition, the psyche is in bad health."[40] It is this harmony that the contemporary poet Richard Ryan must imagine his deaf sister to be without—and not so much because she cannot hear "Mozart, / some birds, the scraping / of wind through pine," but because, as he pines, the loss of her hearing indicates more than "the mere / being without, but the not / knowing, at all."

To be sure, our culture has a long tradition of isolating those who do not hear or speak (or know or see or look or walk or act) like us or at all—from old people to young children to minorities to the insane to the deaf tucked away in state institutions. We have places for them all. And this placement is the largest rhetorical context surrounding the audiological moment and creating the audiologist's authority, whether she wants it or not. This will to speech and the suspicion of both silence and otherness provide the context that so empowers an audiologist as she diagnoses deafness. The ways in which *not* hearing (and thus, it is assumed, *not* speaking) is so pathologically represented invoke "the politics of disablement" that Michael Oliver writes about: everything "in the issue . . . [is] seen as essentially a medical one and the experience of disability [here, deafness] as being contingent upon a variety of psychological adjustment processes."[41] In the medical marking and consequent rehabilitation (call it psychological adjustment) of deaf or hard-of-hearing persons to fit better as rhetorical presences, speaking bodies, their "degraded or attainted . . . former privileges, rank, and possessions" might, to repeat the *Oxford English Dictionary*'s terms, be restored along with their "good name or memory" through an act of "authoritative pronouncement" —this is a move approved, even ensured, by both audiology and rhetoric. It grants the audiologist her authority.

But there are still other ways she comes by her authority, some of them quite closely connected to this larger context. The audiological moment is preceded by the deaf/hard-of-hearing individual's losing authority—giving it up to the audiologist and others—even before stepping into a clinic. We don't have our hearing checked like we do our eyes—or indeed like we do any other physical part of us. The audiologists I have interviewed tell me that there are two rather standard scenes in their clinic: one involves parents with their young, often just-entering-the-school-system child in tow, while the second involves senior citizens, often towed like a child by their spouse or their own children. In both scenes, the person doing the towing usually starts the conversation: "Something is wrong with _____. Can you take a look?" Or, perhaps less directly, "It has been recommended that _____ see an audiologist for an evaluation." Always someone else, you see, is the authority that instigates an audiological exam. Almost always the one to be examined is brought in by others. Almost always the "patient" is "childish" in not having entered this clinic by choice.[42] Others are "looking out for them," and others, then, are given the authority. Then those others turn to the audiologist . . . and the moment is ripe for the turn to ethos, the ethical appeal that is centered on the character of the speaking authority.

It is in scene number one, when parents bring in their young child (the "infant"), that audiologists have told me they most feel the uncomfortable weight of their authority and when they start questioning ethics—their own, their culture's, the parents'. One of the clinic supervisors at my university audiology clinic puts it this way:

And the reason I dislike working with children is because I don't want *that* authority. When you're working with children, there's an added something, responsibility or whatever that goes with that authority, and I really don't want to have anything to do with that. I love kids, but I don't want to work with them and it's primarily that [the authority issue]. You just have so much of an effect on their whole life. With an adult, you're much more sharing the authority, and you're not with a kid. You might be sharing it with a parent, but not with a kid. And I just don't like that.[43]

The parents in this scene, the ones being more or less *forced* to take and share authority whether they want to or not, are no doubt scared. Even if they can't voice it, they know inherently our culture's premium on hearing and speech; they sense already that a deaf child may bring a separation within the family, and so many others—a canyon in education, culture, communication, and language so large that the family may not be able to bridge or traverse it. Another clinic supervisor, who has been an audiologist for over ten years, tells me of a memory that matters: "You know my first experience in graduate school with a hearing-impaired child was a little boy who was eight months old that I identified. And I remember my supervisor saying to me, you have to tell this family that their child is hearing-impaired. And I thought I would rather die right now than do this, if the ground could just swallow me up right now I'd rather do that. And that's never gotten any easier for me."[44]

Some of this same fear appears in scene number two, when a spouse or children bring in an older family member, almost always voicing grave concerns about the person's withdrawal, isolation, silence—even hostility or depression—of late. Often these patients are administered a questionnaire, whether along the lines of the lengthy ninety-item "Hearing Performance Inventory" that assesses their self-reported ability to understand speech, with and without visual clues; the intensity of their daily interactions; their response to auditory failure; and their personal, social, and occupational communication needs or the briefer "Client's Assessment of Communication" (CAC); whoever has brought in the patient is given the "Significant Other's Assessment of Communication." When these two measures are compared, the patient's handle on reality—that is, grasp of hearing loss and adjustment, appropriate or not, to that loss—is recorded as part of the audiogram. The admission to "something wrong" that motivates this moment must surely burn in the patient's memory. As one graduate student training to become an audiologist explains it:

> For a lot of people, it's a big step to come in. So I think once they finally decide, all right, my wife's been harping on me, I'm an eighty-year-old guy, I'm finally going to go in, I'll get a hearing aid or something. And then they come in and they find out, well, you've really got a high-frequency sensorineural hearing loss, you're fine through this part, hearing aids will help you here but they're not going to make it easier, so you're still not going to hear in restaurants so well and you still need to make

sure to keep your back to this side of the noise. And we're telling them things like that and they're thinking: "I went through a long time to get up the nerve." A lot of people spend a long time debating whether they even want to come and see us, and I think a lot of people once they get in the door feel like somebody's going to hand them the fix-it tool. And we can't.[45]

In both scenes, the emotions are thick, the stakes high, the questions many, the unknowns vast, the options really very few. The audiologist, they all hope, has the answers. She *is* authority; it is often given to her even before she takes it, well before that patient enters her clinic.

She authorizes here because she tests and certifies, commits records to state and social memories. Before children or adults can receive the "social services" to help them "survive" our speech-saturated environment, an audiologist will have to assess and attest. Without that audiogram—the recorded product of the audiological moment—a deaf or hard-of-hearing person would not be able to move toward the "meaningful access with dignity" in any public space guaranteed by the Americans with Disabilities Act, they would not attain education in "the least restrictive environment" advocated in the Individuals with Disabilities Education Act, they would not be able to bring a discrimination suit for injustice related to their hearing loss, and they would not receive any disability or social security benefits from their changed work circumstances—to name a few of the services available to those with a "certified" hearing loss. The power of medical judgment, as it is given here by and through the audiologist, cannot be underestimated. In her history and cultural critique of "the disabled state," political scientist Deborah Stone attempts to sort through some of the intricate entanglements of medicine, the state's social welfare system, and the disabled individual. Medical judgment serves to certify "disability" for entry into the social welfare system, Stone suggests, because it is perceived (historically and at present) as proceeding from objective technologies, as being "nonintrusive" on disabled lives, and as being politically neutral.[46] All three of these qualities are assumed of the audiologist as well.

The audiologist authorizes on "neutral" grounds because she represents resources and support; she sees herself as a "case manager and as a resource person . . . willing to hook families up with whomever they need to go to," in an environment that looks formidable and unsupportive of, if not ignorant of and apathetic to, her patient's daily struggles in a

culture saturated with speech.[47] If such characterizations—"unsupportive," "ignorant," and "apathetic"—seem a bit strong here, I need only
point to the lack of insurance or monetary resources for things audiological. Except for the screening of newborns, audiograms are rarely covered
in insurance plans (although, alas, speech therapy regularly is); moreover,
the technologies for "assisted listening"—hearing aids, FM systems, special phones (TDDs or enhanced volume controls), light alarm systems to
warn of everything from doorbells sounding to phones ringing to babies
crying—are generally *not* covered on otherwise adequate health insurance
plans. In a culture that so valorizes speech and listening, there is little
money where our mouths are. There is only the audiologist, her authority, her caring, her attempt to help find nonintrusive and politically neutral answers with her objective technologies as she reintegrates (i.e., "re-
habilitates") her patient into a "normal" life.

And this facet of her authority—her characteristic caring and assistance in finding answers—marks her most distinctly in the eyes of her
patients and her profession. Oddly enough, the textbooks never approach directly the issue of the audiologist's ethos and certainly never address even implicitly her *caring* character. But among the audiologists
themselves, this appeal has tremendous rhetorical force; it is central to
what they do and what they believe themselves to be. In interviews I have
conducted, long-practicing audiologists, "master" audiologists who teach
those in training, and apprentice audiologists at both entry and more advanced levels all repeatedly emphasize how the art and skills of listening,
caring, and sharing constitute the core of their authority.[48] "I think it's
critical that you listen first," one of them tells me at the outset of an interview, responding to my question about what the characteristics of an
audiologist are. And others offer such qualitative comments as "we are
people-oriented"; "[I became an audiologist] because I wanted to help
people"; "I had much more authority when I gave up that authority and
it became an interactive process between me and the patient . . . sharing
the authority actually gives me more authority in the long run"; "in general, we [as both women and audiologists] are caregivers." Another remarked on her entry into the field: "I felt like that was the *one* thing I
could do [caring]; maybe I didn't have all the knowledge, or I couldn't
work all the equipment, but the one thing I could do was try to make
them feel comfortable and feel like I could listen and I felt like that was
the only strong point I had."[49]

These "caregiving" qualities—and a whole host of others that these audiologists have revealed to me—help us understand why audiologists are, by and large, female.[50] And while it is not appropriate here to dwell on that gendered "authoritative" space, we should note that the strength of her ethos—the ethical, rhetorical appeal of her character as it connects with her audience—is highly significant for understanding how the audiologist comes by her authority in the audiological moment. To put it simply, the stereotypical characteristics of women as nurturers, caretakers, "assistants"—a stereotype these audiologists simultaneously revel in and reject—gain her rhetorical ground in establishing an ethos. In caring, listening, being people-oriented, and offering what are often perceived as nonintrusive and politically neutral "answers" to her patient's various questions, in what they describe as "sharing the authority," "slid[ing] your authority in the back door," "knowing your client," being "flexible [and] able to go with the flow," and above all just being able "to listen to what they tell you," an audiologist is exhibiting the three elements that constitute ethos, named by Aristotle as "the three things we trust other than logical demonstrations": "practical wisdom [*phronēsis*], virtue [*aretē*], and good will [*eunoia*]."[51]

Still, ethos only goes so far. And so, too, the pathos surrounding the audiological moment—the near-hysterical Western fear of nonspeaking subjects—is limited. In the end, Aristotle always assures us (somewhat idealistically) that logos will carry the day, win the argument, make the point more effectively than the other two appeals. This is where science comes into play. Science, as our master-myth, our cultural logos, does its fair share in also constructing the ethos and pathos of the audiological moment.[52] Science solidifies, fixes the memory.

As Alan Gross illustrates quite provocatively in his chapter in *The Rhetoric of Science* on the origin of Darwin's *Origin of the Species,* self-persuasion is the first step both in rhetoric and in most scientific discoveries that lead to scientific discourse. An audiologist, too, must first convince herself—even as she is convincing her client (who, you will remember, isn't likely to sense that anything is really "wrong" in the first place—it is others who are indicating that). She does this above all by administering the audiological exam with its various technologies, the same "objective technologies" that Deborah Stone claims "the disabled state" is so attracted to as a means of both expanding and restricting the entrance of an individual into the social welfare system. Here she is after producing an audiogram, recording "precise observation and prediction," which Gross claims are the special topics of science, the "unique sources for [science's] arguments."[53]

After noting some of the patient's history and specific "complaints," an audiologist moves to soundproof chambers and typically begins by measuring hearing in pure-tone frequencies. These are sound frequencies (measured in hertz, Hz), generally ranging from 250 Hz (low sounds) to 8,000 Hz (high sounds), that are played at varying decibel (dB) levels. The patient listens for the beeps and boops and indicates to the audiologist, usually sitting outside the soundproof chamber, on the other side of a one-

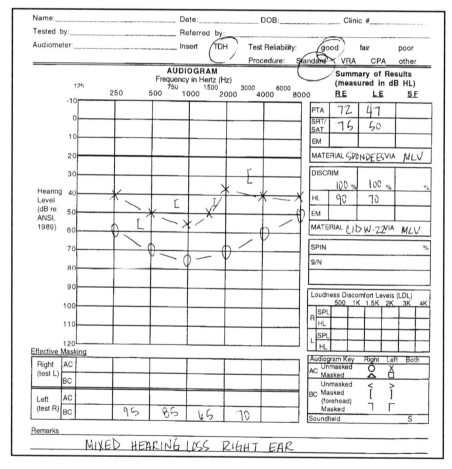

Figure 4.1 Audiogram Reflecting a Mixed Loss. Courtesy of The Ohio State University Speech-Language-Hearing Clinic.

way mirror in a room that contains all the testing equipment, what she has heard by raising her hand or pressing a button. Pure tones constitute a precise ideal; about the only time a human being will ever hear a pure tone is in an audiological exam. Most of the sounds we hear—including, most significantly, speech—are far more complex. But measuring pure tones will tell what a person can and can't hear in a way that can be easily plotted, charted, graphed, categorized—in other words, the procedure gives *precise* information.

The necessity of such scientific precision becomes all the more clear when the audiologist turns to the second major portion of the

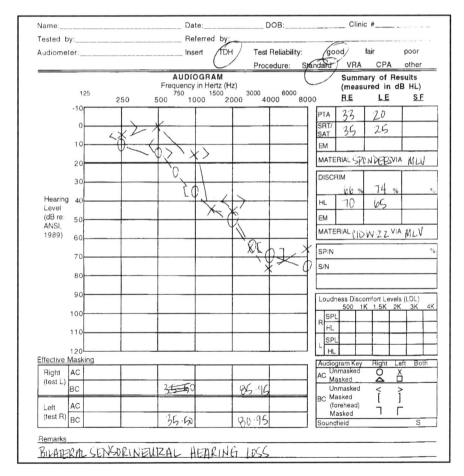

Figure 4.2 Audiogram Reflecting a Sensorineural Loss. Courtesy of The Ohio State University Speech-Language-Hearing Clinic.

audiological assessment: speech audiometry. Here the plotting is not so thick, the charts are less pure, and the categories are less capable of capturing what is really happening with the patient's hearing. Sections of textbooks that deal with speech audiometry are riddled with the problems of adequately assessing how well the two ears function independently (determined by a complicated procedure known as "masking"), how well the client discerns speech from background noise, how well the client recognizes words and speech at certain decibel levels, how well the client tolerates background noise, or even how much "interference" from tinnitus the client suffers. To take only one illustration of the remarkable imprecision

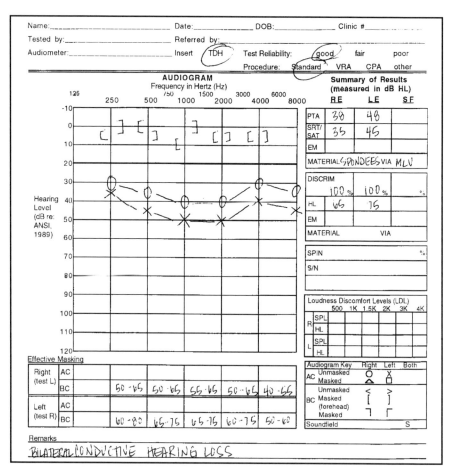

Figure 4.3 Audiogram Reflecting a Conductive Loss. Courtesy of The Ohio State University Speech-Language-Hearing Clinic.

in assessing speech: two different audiograms, collected almost a year apart and both giving "reliable" results and indicating precisely the same pure-tone loss pattern, show a difference in my own speech recognition threshold—that is, my ability to assess a series of spondees ("baseball," "hot dog," "cowboy," "ice cream") at the end of a "carrier phrase" ("you will say . . . ")—of 20 percent. In one year, I could "hear" 65 percent of those spondees and repeat them; in the next, I was down to 45 percent.

Such a difference, which is undoubtedly statistically significant, makes the measure seem anything but scientific. And had my audiologist asked about the 20 percent difference, I probably would have been able to give

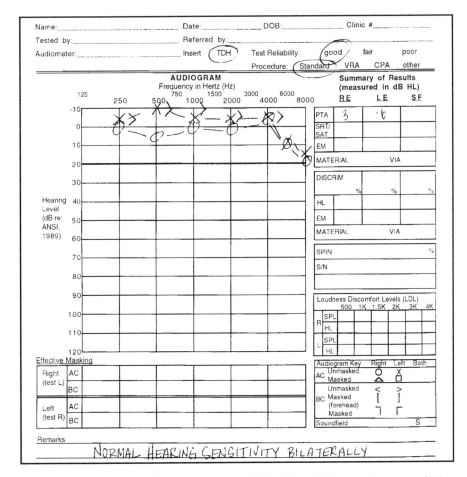

Figure 4.4 Audiogram Reflecting Hearing within Normal Range. Courtesy of The Ohio State University Speech-Language-Hearing Clinic.

her a sufficient (although perhaps not scientific) answer: the stress of my communicative life had increased considerably over the year, in both the home and workplace, and my bouts of tinnitus had also increased. But there was no science here—just the social and the subjective. In fact, my audiologist paid no attention to the discrepancy.

Instead, and perhaps even because of the inherent difficulties of speech audiometry, the audiologist turns her scientific ear elsewhere, hoping to gain logic—and to effect persuasion of self and client—from other "places." One such literal location is the soundproof, one-way mirrored room in which the exam takes place and which makes up part of the "precise observation and prediction" required by the audiological moment. Like the use of pure tones, the absence of any other sound and of recourse to sight certainly gets rid of those confounding variables and back-ups—methods of "cheating," I actually heard one audiologist call them—that we might otherwise rely on to help us hear. "Protected" from competing factors in the soundproof, viewless room, the patient cannot depend on the context of other sounds and the other components of discourse—cannot read lips, watch expressions, or note body language. Once those variables are weeded out, the measurement is rendered more "reliable." Stripping away other sounds, sights, and contextual clues simplifies the testing and its results; it works to rule out "error," establishes clearer cause and effect, and, in the end, conveys more convincingly the diagnosis of deafness. But ironically, this situation in no way approximates most of the hearing and listening that any of us does.

Likewise, when an audiologist comes ready to convince a client to wear a hearing aid, the standard "trial" for the aid is back in that soundproof room. And it's often very effective. (Precision is as precision does.) Many patients, one audiologist told me, get quite "choked up" over how much more and better they can hear in this trial. They leave the clinic full of hope—pathos born of logos. But a year later many, if not most, have stopped wearing their aids most of the time. There are many complicated reasons for this attrition but one of the most important, my audiologist explains, is the breach between the hope gained in that trial and the frustrating reality of negotiating a vast range of listening situations that are anything but pure tones and single words from a clear voice in a soundproof room. Thus, while the enormous expectations often set up in an audiological exam contribute greatly to the audiologist's authority in the audiological moment itself, the gap that widens later between expectations and realities tends to reduce future authority: "People when they walk in also, a lot of them, have unrealistic expectations about what we can do. Because of things like eyeglasses that fix the problem or having bone spurs [that are easily medically treated], people think that eventually someone will find the answer and take care of it. And so these people come in, and I think that kind of robs us of our authority because we have to start right off by saying, 'We might not be able to help you much.'"[54] So much for precision.

Still, audiology seems to go to great lengths to gain what precision it can. The plotting of one's hearing in *x*'s and *o*'s on a grid represented by measurable elements—sound frequency in hertz and decibels, percentages for this, more numbers for that, and a reassuring multiple-choice checklist at the top that certifies the degree of the audiogram's "reliability"—all these and more constitute scientific rhetoric. Finally, as the trump card, the most common of science's characteristic rhetorical topics, there is classification—the stock-in-trade of the scientist-nomenclator. To taxonomize is to approach truth; this is the creed most scientists live by,[55] and Aristotle himself was certainly no exception to the rule.

An audiologist will wind up her audiological assessment with a written evaluation that is sure to label the patient with "mild," "moderate," "severe," or "profound" losses across frequencies taken both singly and then as a whole. And even though textbooks and living audiologists alike will advise us all to be wary of such labels, they persist. Scheetz, for example, tells undergraduates: "Although these classifications have been established to aid the consumer [note that there is no 'patient' here] and professional in understanding the severity of the varying degrees of loss, one must be careful not to 'pigeonhole' or label someone based on this information."[56] And my own audiologist laments about parents and educators who want to live by the labels: "They see it as an all or none phenomenon. They want to know the cookbook. And I've never met a child that you could cookbook, you know."[57] Finally, one audiologist-in-training tells me of the first and most important lesson she has learned from working in the clinic with real patients: "the patient doesn't read the textbook, so they get different results than we might expect them to because we've been taught certain things. And then they come in and give us a whole different line of reasoning . . . they didn't read the textbook."[58]

Still, the textbooks persist in categorizing, for they are arranged and stylized in accordance with a certain scientific paradigm. All the classifications proceed from a normative master category, and they go beyond

questions of ability to hear sound.[59] A glimpse at a few of the classifica-
tory charts in these books reveals, once more, how bound the field is with
speech—both Scheetz and Bess and Humes (following on Katz's defini-
tive *Handbook of Clinical Audiology*) lay out hearing loss on the grid of
speech (see figures 4.5 and 4.6). The audiologist's authority, again, is
locked in this grid and tied to her "scientific" ability to classify, especially
insofar as she relies on sophisticated technologies to measure and reach
conclusions about what categories her client ought to fall into. These labels, these taxonomies, carry an enormous weight; yet, we have to keep reminding ourselves, they only designate, quite simplistically, decibel loss
and not speech reception—they say nothing about discrimination capabilities, ability to "read" context, or adaptability to various situations.
They are used to mark children for certain educational services, to procure
disability and social services, to enable one to enter and exit what Deborah Stone calls "the disabled state" and perhaps to bring a discrimination
suit, and to specifically designate one's abilities not only with "listening"
skills but with speaking ones as well. The scientific stone of classification
is heavy indeed, and tossed in the cultural waters the circle widens, the
ripple continues outward, as such labels also apparently paint profiles of
one's cognitive, social, employment, relationship, and "adjustment" capabilities. Classification speaks volumes.

Hearing Threshold Level[b]		Descriptive Terms
1981 ASA reference	1964 ISO reference	
dB	dB	
−10 to 15	−10 to 26	Normal limits
16–29	27–40	Mild hearing loss
30–44	41–55	Moderate hearing loss
45–59	56–70	Moderately severe hearing loss
60–79	70–90	Severe hearing loss
80+	91+	Profound hearing loss

[a]After Goodman, 1965
[b]Average of hearing threshold levels for 500, 1000, and 2000Hz.

Figure 4.5 Scale of Hearing Impairment. From Scheetz, *Orientation to Deafness*,
p. 46.

Hearing Threshold Level, 1951 SAS Reference	Hearing Threshold Level, 1964 ISO Reference	Probable Handicap and Needs
Less than 30dB	Less than 40dB	Has difficulty hearing faint or distant speech; needs favorable seating and may benefit from lip reading instruction. *May also benefit from hearing aid.*
30 to 45dB	40 to 55dB	Understands conversational speech at a distance of 3 to 5 feet; needs hearing aid, auditory training, lip reading, favorable seating, speech conversation and speech correction.
45 to 60dB	55 to 70dB	Conversation must be loud to be understood and there is great difficulty in group and classroom discussion; needs all of the above plus language therapy and maybe special class for hard of hearing.
60 to 80dB	70 to 90dB	May hear a loud voice about 1 foot from the ear, may identify environmental noises, may distinguish vowels but not consonants; needs special education for deaf children with emphasis on speech, auditory training and language; may enter regular classes at a later time.
More than 80dB	More than 90dB	May hear some loud sounds, does not rely on hearing as primary channel for communication; needs special class or school for the deaf; some of these children eventually enter regular high schools.

[a]After Goodman, 1965. From *Handbook of Clinical Audiology* by Jack Katz, Copyright 1972 by Williams & Wilkins Co. Reprinted with permission.

Figure 4.6 Relations between Hearing Threshold Level and Probable Handicap and Needs. From Scheetz, *Orientation to Deafness,* p. 49.

CODA: DELIVERING THE CYBORG, CREATING THE COCHLEAR IMPLANT

The point at which the weight of this classification becomes almost too much to bear, I would argue, is when it invokes the ultimate hope for delivering speech to the deaf—the cochlear implant. Often presented as simply an amplified version of a hearing aid (see figure 4.7), the cochlear implant is a device with one part surgically implanted into the head so that twenty-two electrodes can be placed in the cochlea, thereby replacing some 22,000 auditory nerve fibers that enable hearing.

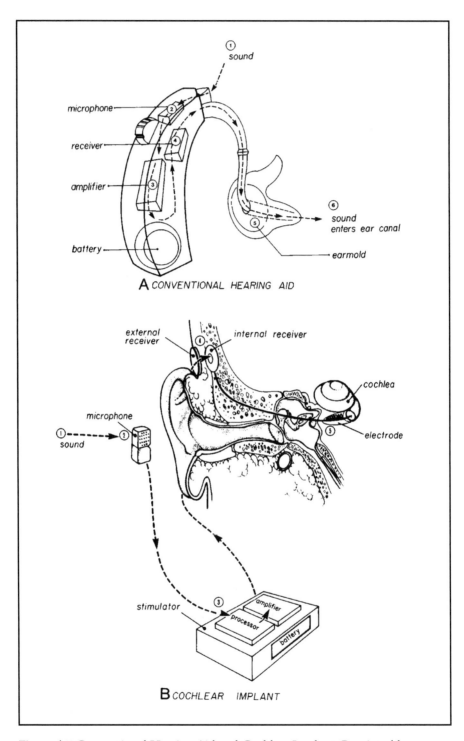

Figure 4.7 Conventional Hearing Aid and Cochlear Implant. Reprinted by permission from Bess and Humes, *Audiology,* 2nd ed., p. 260. ©1995 by Williams and Wilkens.

As one textbook explains the concept behind the implant: "the electrical fields around these implanted wires are of sufficient magnitude that they can electrically stimulate any remaining auditory nerve fibers and can create an auditory sensation."[60] The book goes on to outline the connection between the implanted portion and the microphone mounted, like a hearing aid, behind the patient's ear; the microphone is also connected to a box the patient wears, "about the size of a pack of cigarettes," known as either the "stimulator" or "processor." But most texts, including this one, do not dwell on or even mention the business of those *remaining* auditory nerve fibers—most of which are known to be destroyed in the process of implanting the device in the patient's head and cochlea—and how the *auditory sensation* that is created seems rarely to be very speechlike.

Yet the impetus behind the cochlear implant, as with all of audiology, is undoubtedly speech. The technology was first developed in the hope that those profoundly deaf persons who had lost their hearing after they had already developed language and had a remaining "memory" of sound would be able once again to process speech. That hope has rarely been fulfilled, and meanwhile the patient profile has changed: cochlear implants are now performed on very young children, after age one, who were born profoundly deaf. The logic remains, the hope hovers: perhaps with early implantation these children will come to know language (translation: "speech"). Yet none of these dreams has ever really been manifest in the light of day.

Listen, for example, to just two audiology textbooks on the subject:

There are examples of so-called "star" patients who perform remarkably well with the device by itself; however, the majority of people fitted thus far appear to derive the greatest benefit from the device when it is used as an aid to speechreading. Its primary usefulness as an aid to speechreading appears to lie in making gross cues of timing and voicing available to the patient. At a minimum, the cochlear implants appear to provide an awareness of sound to the once-silent world of the deafened patient.[61]

A cochlear implant is largely a *rehabilitative* procedure for improving *speech perception*. . . . Based on the performance of *some* of the children implanted so far, a cochlear implant *should be* expected to provide *at least some* of the following: perception of stress patterns across words, perception of the number of syllables, perception of syllable boundaries, closed-set word-recognition ability, and in a few cases, open-set word-recognition ability. These benefits are only *summary* statements, *however,* as there is much variability across children. *Some* children gain no speech perception benefits from a multi-electrode cochlear implant, and *some* gain *some* open-set word-recognition ability with a single-electrode cochlear implant. . . . [*S*]*ome* believe that a cochlear implant will *at the least* provide an awareness of environmental sounds and that perception of these nonspeech sounds is a significant advantage[;] . . . at the present time it is not possible to predict the expected benefits for an individual child with any certainty.[62] (my emphasis)

What is the sum of all this "some"-ing? As I see it, two possible results coexist: there remains no proven pattern of success for performing the cochlear implant, and yet the will to speech haunts that operating room with a frightening power. Even in these passages we hear speech subliminally: the cochlear implant device serves best "as an aid to speechreading," and various successes have been measured principally in terms of the elements of speech—things like "gross cues of timing and voicing," "perception of stress patterns" and the number of syllables, and perhaps even a little "open-set word-recognition ability" if the implantee is really, really lucky.

It pains me to point out the obvious here, yet as these books seem to ignore it, I will: All these elements of speech are *not language*. All the recognition of syllable boundaries in the world does not make one a communicator, does not qualify one as a capable language user. It is as if the already-quoted words of Prosper Ménière, resident physician of the Paris School for Deaf-Mutes in 1855, come floating forward, unchanged through the centuries, unaffected by any experiences in the intervening time: "But whatever they believe, deafness is an infirmity and we should repair it whether the person who has it is disturbed by it or not."

A rhetorical analysis of cochlear implants and the discourse surrounding them, as well as a consideration of the implanted body within the frame of the recent rage of academic and cultural critiques of "the cyborg," though deserving of attention, lies beyond the scope of this book.[63] But the will to speech asserts itself so strongly—and the audiologist's authority in that initial diagnosis of deafness comes to matter so much—in the case of the cochlear implant that it demands mention here.

The group of second-year audiologists-in-training that I interviewed ended their discussion with me, appropriately and without my prodding, on the subject of cochlear implants. We had been discussing the particularly ethically fraught territory of the audiologist's authority in diagnosing deafness in children, when one young woman, Kate, remarked: "I just recently watched a cochlear implant surgery. I'm really glad I watched it because now I have a better understanding of what a serious procedure that is. You can talk about it, but if you actually see it. . . . I have such a better awareness now of what a big deal it is . . . how invasive it is . . . and how many things can go wrong during it." Another student, providing what became the final word for that group interview, added: "Well, forget about the surgery, the thing that bugs me about them is that we don't know if they're actually ———. I mean, they're damaging what structure is there."[64]

What stunned me on reviewing this interview—what perked my ears up—were those unspoken words: "we don't know if they're actually ———." What goes in that blank? Speech, I think. What Kate wanted to say, I suspect, but couldn't—and it doesn't really matter if her reasons were deliberate or subconscious—was that we don't know if they are actually aiding *speech,* or, more important (and not the same thing), getting people to *language.* And if she did say that, what then would be the grounds of her own authority? If the will to speech were no longer the paradigm she practiced under, what might replace it? And where would she stand in that replacement? What would she deliver?

How then would audiology—and for that matter rhetoric, too—be reinvented?

NOTES

1. Juan Luis Vives, a fifteenth-century Spanish rhetorician, and Francis Bacon, a philosopher and founding father of the British Royal Society for scientists, both opined that "speech *is* reason." Elocutionary interests in gestures were fanned by the work of rhetoricians John Bulwer in the seventeenth century (*Chirologia*), Thomas Sheridan in the eighteenth (*On Elocution*), and Gilbert Austin in the nineteenth (*Chironomia*). Emphasis on voice qualities gained rhetorical favor with Benjamin Rush in the nineteenth century (*Essays*) and earlier, with Joshua Steele, at the end of the eighteenth (*Essays*). The role of women in the speaking, privileged world enters the rhetorical tradition through the writings of Christine de Pisan (*"City of Ladies"*), Laura Cereta ("Letter"), Mary Astell (*First English Feminist*), Margaret Fell ("Women's Speaking Justified"), Sarah Grimké ("Letters"), and Mary Wollstonecraft (*Political Writings*). And the movement of rhetoric into the popular sphere was a project of Giambattista Vico

(*Study Methods*) and of A. S. Hill (*"Principles of Rhetoric"*); the popular province of rhetoric is also the subject of Nan Johnson's book *Nineteenth-Century Rhetoric in North America.*

2. See, e.g., Bess and Humes, *Audiology;* Katz, *Handbook of Clinical Audiology;* F. Martin, *Introduction to Audiology;* McLauchlin, *Speech-Language Pathology and Audiology;* and Newby and Popelka, *Audiology.* These are the textbooks I will work from and with throughout most of this chapter.

3. Newby and Popelka, *Audiology,* p. 1.

4. Ibid., p. 2.

5. Hosford-Dunn, Dunn, and Harford, *Audiology Business and Practice Management,* p. 9. The addition of "language" to the title of the organization is surely a syllogistic slip of the tongue.

6. One textbook, for example, outlines the "primary issues discussed in ASHA Presidential Addresses" from 1960 to 1984. Telling of the tensions between speech-language pathology and audiology are the concerns that surface in these annual addresses—concerns about "professional boundaries," "single level of certification," "heterogeneity and specialization," "unified professional image," "common core of knowledge, "single vs. two professions," "establishing common goals," "autonomy vs. interdependence," "need for developing and maintaining an integrated common core of knowledge," "single certificate for speech-language pathology and audiology," and "a single core profession" (McLauchlin, *Speech-Language Pathology and Audiology,* pp. 51–55).

7. The popular Newby and Popelka textbook reiterates audiology's "family" connections with other fields and "philosophies": "many living relatives exist on both the medical and nonmedical sides of the family. Among the medical relatives are pediatrics, gerontology, psychiatry, and neurology and neurosurgery. . . . Among the nonmedical relatives of audiology are psychology, physics, and education" (*Audiology,* p. 2).

8. Gwen, 13 March 1996.

9. Ibid.

10. Liz, 2 October 1997.

11. Note here how "language" is yet again conflated with "speech"—a fusion that is foundational to much of the Western tradition of both philosophy and rhetoric.

12. Itard, quoted in Lane, *When the Mind Hears,* p. 132.

13. This is the same Volta whose name was given to the prestigious "Volta Prize" in science—a prize Alexander Graham Bell was himself awarded for the invention of the telephone. Consequently, the Alexander Graham Bell Associa-

tion for the Deaf in Washington, D.C., is housed in a building known as "the Volta Bureau," and the one of the oldest (and perhaps most oral in its emphasis) journals on deafness is named the *Volta Review.*

14. Epstein, *The Story of the Bionic Ear,* p. 34.

15. Quoted in ibid.

16. Lane, *When the Mind Hears,* pp. 132–34.

17. Quoted in ibid., p. 134.

18. Bell wrote an important eugenics treatise in 1914, "How to Improve the Race." The irony of all his efforts at eradicating sign languages and "a deaf race" is that both his wife and mother were deaf—his wife, Mabel Hubbard Bell, was postlingually deafened from scarlet fever at the age of twelve and his mother underwent early and substantial hearing loss that progressed as she aged.

19. Kuhn, *Structure of Scientific Revolutions,* pp. 43, 46.

20. Bess and Humes, *Audiology,* p. 8.

21. Ibid.

22. West, "Mechanical Ear," p. 345.

23. Quoted in Lane, *When the Mind Hears,* p. 134.

24. These textbooks that trumpet sound are Scheetz, *Orientation to Deafness;* Bess and Humes, *Audiology;* F. Martin, *Introduction to Audiology;* Newby and Popelka, *Audiology.*

25. There are forty-one illustrations, tables, graphs, etc., in the first fifty-five pages of Martin's first two chapters about sound in *Introduction to Audiology.*

26. Amy, 2 October 1997; Liz, 2 October 1997.

27. See the table of contents for Katz, *Handbook of Clinical Audiology;* Bess and Humes, *Audiology;* Newby and Popelka, *Audiology;* and Scheetz, *Orientation to Deafness.*

28. Katz, *Handbook of Clinical Audiology,* p. 4.

29. The term *hearing impaired* is purely audiological. As I have remarked elsewhere, it is not a term that d/Deaf people tend to use on or for themselves or others like them. If it is used—as it was by Anna, the subject of my case study in chapter 3—it derives from audiologically driven educational placements of students in the "mainstream."

30. I know that many audiologists—some of whom I have come to think of as friends and colleagues by now—will no doubt flinch at my tone and directness here. I do not mean to be sarcastic or merely flippant, or to hit below the

belt. What I do intend is to illustrate just how pervasively—and often implicitly, subversively, and deeply—the paradigm of that syllogism runs throughout the field of audiology, saturating the apprentice in ways that leave her little chance to think about how or how much she is, in fact, being saturated. I might say the same—and perform the same kind of analysis with this same syllogism as my center—on the history of rhetoric and rhetoric textbooks. It is worth repeating here once more: the will to speech commands rhetoric as much as it does audiology.

31. See respectively Bess and Humes, *Audiology;* Katz, *Handbook of Clinical Audiology;* Newby and Popelka, *Audiology;* and Newby, *Audiology.*

32. Scheetz, *Orientation to Deafness,* p. 255.

33. Kuhn, *Structure of Scientific Revolution,* p. 23.

34. Ibid., p. 24.

35. Scheetz, *Orientation to Deafness,* p. 255.

36. Farrell, "Knowledge, Consensus, and Rhetorical Theory," p. 11.

37. See the chapter epigraphs as well as Katz, *Handbook of Clinical Audiology,* and Scheetz, *Orientation to Deafness,* most profoundly among the textbooks I analyze, for the perspective that to be human is to engage the acoustics of orality.

38. I dwell more critically on trends in deaf education in chapter 2.

39. Scheetz, *Orientation to Deafness,* pp. 50, 137–38, 145, 175, 146, 175, 214.

40. Ong, *Orality and Literacy,* pp. 69, 72.

41. Oliver, *Politics of Disablement,* p. x.

42. As befits this particular scene, the word "infant" derives from the Latin *infans* (by way of the Old French *enfant*), which literally means "unable to speak."

43. Laura, 2 October 1997.

44. Gwen, 13 March 1996.

45. Helen, 2 October 1997.

46. Stone, *The Disabled State,* pp. 104–7.

47. Gwen, 13 March 1996.

48. In another research project in progress, "Women, Authority, Deafness," I dwell on the nature of the *female* authority of the audiologist (and sign language interpreters, deaf educators, and deaf women professionals as well).

49. These comments were made by audiology students Stacy, Laura, Amy, Laura, Kate, and Helen (all interviewed 2 October 1997).

50. The "feminine" and "authoritative" qualities audiologists have discussed in interviews include having good listening skills, "people" skills, and interactive skills; paying attention to "gut" feelings; trusting the patient over the textbook; being flexible; using "backdoor" types of authority; adapting self to the patient; borrowing authority from one's "master"; meshing all forms of authority to create one's own; giving up authority in order to gain it; adopting a confident persona (regardless of one's actual feelings); working well on a team; being able to "read" relationships; avoiding confrontation; desiring to help others; and not requiring one—or *the*—answer for a given problem. In addition, these female audiologists also spoke candidly of the threats to their authority, many of which they claimed were related to their sex.

51. Aristotle, *On Rhetoric* 2.1.5; translated in Bizzell and Herzberg, *The Rhetorical Tradition,* p. 161.

52. For a provocative critique of science as master-myth, see Donna Haraway's *Simians, Cyborgs, and Women,* especially chapters 8 and 9: "A Cyborg Manifesto" and "Situated Knowledges: The Science Question in Feminism and the Privilege of Partial Perspective."

53. Gross, *Rhetoric of Science,* p. 11.

54. Stacy, 2 October 1997.

55. For a discussion of the rhetoric of science as it exists in "taxonomic language," see Gross, *Rhetoric of Science,* pp. 33–53.

56. Scheetz, *Orientation to Deafness,* p. 47.

57. Gwen, 13 March 1996.

58. Kate, 2 October 1997.

59. These long-standing classifications—mild, moderate, severe, profound—mirror with remarkable faithfulness the classifications for mental retardation so popular in the 1940s and 1950s (just as audiology was developing as a field). So, too, the audiogram looks much like a map drawn of intellectual capabilities in order to assess one's degree of retardation; normalcy is the baseline here as well. These similarities seem far from coincidental.

60. Newby and Popelka, *Audiology,* p. 454.

61. Bess and Humes, *Audiology,* p. 259.

62. Newby and Popelka, *Audiology,* pp. 455–56.

63. The academic discourse on "the cyborg" and "the body and/in technology" has begun to flow freely from numerous academic presses. While this scholarship is exciting, meaningful, nuanced, and even fascinating, it oddly—time and time again—neglects the "obvious" cyborg, that of the disabled body. See, e.g., Hables-Gray, *The Cyborg Handbook;* Wilson and Laennec, *Bodily Discursions;*

Terry and Urla, *Deviant Bodies;* Terry and Calvert, *Processed Lives;* Balsamo, *Technologies of the Gendered Body;* Cranny-Francis, *Body in the Text;* Rogerson, "Clockwork Oranges"; and Featherstone and Burrows, *Cyberspace/Cyberbodies/Cyberpunk.* Finally, Owen Wrigley's critique of the cochlear implant (*Politics of Deafness,* pp. 203–11) serves as a fitting counter to the growing number of "scientific" collections on the cochlear implant, to the corporate materials (and rhetoric) explaining and advocating the device (particularly from the Cochlear Corporation, chief developers of the technologies behind the implant), and to such popular books as Epstein's *Story of the Bionic Ear.* But still, a significant rhetorical analysis of all three of these kinds of scientific-public discourses is needed to carry Wrigley's account further.

64. Kate, 2 October 1997; Liz, 2 October 1997.

Interlude 2

Interpellations

Call to A. G. Bell

Got a quarter
so I call you up on the telephone
ring-ring-ring
but only your wife and mother are home,
so no one answers.
You out charting and graphing
marriages and progeny
of the deaf,
while only your wife and mother
—deaf—
are home. (ringed in)

So I leave a message
after the beep—
but actually,
it's before the beep because
the beep
I cannot hear.

So, you miss
half of it.

I start again.
This time, I mouth the message—
so you can lipread.
But you don't get it,
can't tell my b's from my p's,
my f's from my v's.

145

So I try again
slowing . . . down . . .
emph-a-siz-ing
each
W-O-R-D,
my face contorted, clownlike.
Still,
that won't do.
(What are you, dumb?)

I try signing,
hands across space
in your face,
but you are horrified
by the spectacle of my body
moving
beyond speech,
and you avert your eyes.

Too late.
I have burned your retina,
salt-pillared you,
left you speechless.
And oh, the time is up,
message too long.
(It's taken 120 years to
get this call through.)
Sorry.

No, wait—
I'll fax you the facts;
I'll send a video,
documentary of my life,
caption and all,
interpreter on standby;
or perhaps TTY or relay service;
an e-mail even,
coming through.

Let's "talk."

But oh—
now that I've gotten my medium,
I've forgotten my message.

∽

An Assessment of the Speech-Recognition Threshold
You will say . . .

Bad day—
soundproof
gray room.

No hear
"cowboy,
baseball,
hot dog."

Feel dumb.
Don't cry.
Be numb.

Want out—
go home.
Feel dumb.

Lip read
these words:
deaf girl.

NOTE: A. G. Bell, inventor of the telephone, was also a foremost and formidable advocate of oralism for educating deaf people. As one of the premier eugenicists of his day, he conducted "research" that sought to prove his argument against allowing deaf people to marry other deaf people—fueled by the fear that they would only have more deaf children and thereby pollute the human race. His own mother and wife were deaf.

PART 3

Deafness as Culture

CHAPTER 5

The Coming Out of Deaf Culture:
Repeating, Reversing, Revising Rhetorics

in which I consider the fortunate deaf

the language palpable,
their palm prints folded around
the names of the things.
seasons like skin
snuggled against fingerbone
and their wonder at loving
someone like you perhaps,
even your absence tangible,
your cold name fastened
into their shivering hands.

—LUCILLE CLIFTON, *"in which I consider the fortunate deaf"*

Deafness is less about audiology than it is about epistemology.[1]

—OWEN WRIGLEY, *The Politics of Deafness*

Old arguments die hard; rhetoric repeats itself; what looks like a new story is often only the old slightly retold.[2] Deaf people are not really so fortunate in this framework, although as is the case with most master narratives and colonial conditions, those who are positioned as fortunate are themselves deaf to less fortunate others. Deafness thus becomes not so much a sensory condition, not so much a literal loss recorded by testing pure tones in a soundproof booth on some quasi-scientific chart, as a way of thinking and knowing the world. Deafness, and even little "d" deafness, as a rhetorical, epistemological story situated in one postmodern rhetorical situation—that of the 1988 "Deaf President Now" (DPN) protest—will serve as my point of origin in this chapter.

151

DPN—an act of Deaf culture's "coming out"—serves as a rich resource for rhetoric. In this chapter, I argue that lending an ear to an event like DPN, even situating it rhetorically at the center of Deaf history, illuminates some of the ways that rhetoric can (and does) repeat itself, reverses (and thereby rejects, even as it reifies) itself, and finally suggests ways in which it might revise itself. Its story provides one variation on an origin myth: the coming out narrative. My analysis of DPN's rhetorical situation views the linguistic awareness and redefinition of literacy accompanying the acceptance of American Sign Language as a real language as constituting the primary ingredients for such an uprising and the cultural recognition of Deaf culture that has followed.[3] But I will begin by providing more context for DPN, both as a coming out story and as a literal and rhetorical event.

QUEER CONNECTIONS

The analogies between queer culture and Deaf culture abound. Considered bestial, savage, sinful, "unnatural," perhaps insane, and most likely immoral for most of their post-Enlightenment histories, deaf and gay individuals share a history of "stigma" like that outlined by sociologist Erving Goffman: their bodies are "marked"—though not necessarily visibly—by both medical and religious institutions and they become "blemished person[s], ritually polluted, to be avoided, especially in public places."[4] Deaf people have often been curiosities, "queer" in their "strange" and "silent" ways; gay people have just as often been silenced, speechless in dominant heterosexual histories and discourse.[5] From these positions, deaf and gay individuals "pass"—playing out and through a politics of passing, balancing borders of (non)existence in their daily interactions and relationships. They are not only different in "mainstream" culture at large, but they are often as not different and "nonnative" even in their families: most gay and deaf persons are born into families heterosexual and hearing, respectively.

Their differences are often "hideous"—beyond the imagination of dominant heterosexual and hearing lives—and yet they are hidden. Hearing, like one's sexual orientation and relationships, cannot readily be seen. Thus, these bodies are different, but the danger lies in their deceptive pos-

> Your belief that Paul is caught between cultures is half right:
> he is ingrained in the hearing establishment (through educa-
> tion), but seems to have a deaf cultural vacuum. It's as if he
> senses something's wrong or missing, but he doesn't know what.
> (The connections with gay identity *are* remarkable.)
>
> > —Carl Zaks, Ohio State University undergraduate, comment-
> > ing on several conversations he had with Paul, a twenty-
> > year-old "hearing-impaired" OSU undergraduate
>
> I think deaf people, and handicapped people in general, have
> come out of the closet.
>
> > —Rick, history/government professor, Gallaudet University

sibilities. You can stand in line next to, even bump elbows with, a gay or deaf person all day and *never know*. Hearing and heterosexual people hate it when that happens—when a presence is not entirely palpable, when difference is not totally tangible. It seems so queer, these bodies so closeted.

But now, their "coming out"—deaf and gay, individual and collective—concerns hearing and heterosexual cultures alike. Eve Kofosoky Sedgwick begins *Epistemology of the Closet* by "axiomatically" noting the categorical contradictions entangled in the unstable definitions connected with queerness in the past century:

> In arguing that homo/heterosexual definition has been a presiding mas-
> ter term of the past century, one that has the same, primary importance
> for all modern Western identity and social organization (and not merely
> for homosexual identity and culture) as do the more traditionally visible
> cruxes of gender, class, and race, I'll argue that the now chronic modern
> crisis of homo/heterosexual definition has affected our culture through its
> ineffaceable marking particularly of the categories secrecy/disclosure,
> knowledge/ignorance, private/public, masculine/feminine, majority/
> minority, innocence/initiation, natural/artificial, new/old, discipline/
> terrorism, canonic/noncanonic, wholeness/decadence, urbane/provincial,
> domestic/foreign, health/illness, same/different, active/passive, in/out,
> cognition/paranoia, art/kitsch, utopia/apocalypse, sincerity/sentimentality,
> and voluntarity/addiction.[6]

These same binaries axiomatically mark differences between "hearing" and "deaf," between "Hearing" and "Deaf," in our culture, and I would add "adult/infant" to the list. Deafness, as Lennard Davis argues in *Enforcing Normalcy: Deafness, Disability, and the Body,* is no stranger to binaries: "That binarism [deafness/hearing, disabled/abled], like so many others—straight/gay, male/female, black/white, rich/poor—is part of an ideology [or is it 'audiology'?] of containment and politics of power."[7]

The coming out narrative—for both deaf and gay individuals—seeks a way out of containment, an airing of the closeted self, and a self-transformation of identity reidentified, power repoliticized. "Coming-out stories," writes sociolinguist, sign language interpreter, and literacy instructor Kathy Wood, "like all self-transformation stories, are rhetorical attempts to justify one's life, to realize acceptable selves by creating coherent identities." In parallel analyses, Wood searches for linguistic "coherence" in the coming out stories of deaf and hearing lesbians and in the literacy life stories of Gallaudet students enrolled in her English classes.[8]

My concern here is less with coherence per se than with the "rhetorical attempts to justify one's life" represented in a coming out narrative. Moreover, I find the possibilities for applying the concept of coming out to the whole of Deaf culture(s) provocative, if not also original.[9] In this chapter, I examine not so much individual stories as they explain individual lives (as I did in chapter 3 in telling Anna's "passing" story), but instead a whole social movement—"Deaf Awareness," "Deaf Pride," and "the Deaf Way" coming of age.[10] The story of the Deaf President Now protest (re)centers Deaf origins, represents a rhetorical attempt to justify Deaf Life (and deaf lives), and thereby counts as a cultural coming out narrative as its characters celebrate their "cause," defy oppression, hiss at hegemony, and cast the chains of colonialism aside. To be sure, there is melodrama here. Most good stories are like that. Most true ones, too.

Why Begin Here?

I take my cues for situating DPN as my rhetorical-historical center from Michel de Certeau, who writes in *The Writing of History* of the reasons, places, ruptures, and desires that begin any history. I begin with this current (1988) event because "in fact, historians begin from present deter-

I explained about two very important things [in a paper written in class the previous day]. One was the Deaf President Now, and everything that's happened since then. And it makes me more proud to be deaf. And of course deaf pride is involved. It helped me to get through. It was really key, really important. I didn't have a lot of pride, deaf pride, before that [DPN], so . . . if that hadn't happened, I would have stayed the same. So, I noticed those kinds of things. And other people in general have also noticed the same thing. They've noticed that they can. "Remember what happened? Hey, do you remember what happened?" we used to say to each other. And they'd say, "I missed that." And then, we'd fill each other in, and they'd become more aware of that.

—Mike, twenty-year-old "deaf" Gallaudet student

Junior year [in college] I was thinking about graduate school, and I enjoyed psychology so much, that I was thinking about that. Junior year was 1988 when DPN happened. And that just clinched it. I thought, this is civil rights, this is something I believe in that is important. . . . Yeah, I didn't just see it as for deaf or for . . . but as a civil rights movement for people who are considered disabled by society, who don't have the same easy access to society as we who can hear do. The majority is set up around the majority, good or bad. So that convinced me to call Gallaudet and ask about their graduate programs and specifically in psychology.

—Scott, school psychologist, "hearing" graduate of Gallaudet University, sign language interpreter, and school counselor

minations. Current events are their real beginning." Although I count myself not so much a historian as a rhetorician—and thus one who is always concerned with the historicity of any piece of discourse as I might investigate the persuasive elements and outcomes of its past, present, and future—I do understand that history might begin virtually anywhere, that "each historian situates elsewhere the inaugural rupture . . . that is, at the borders demarcating a specialization within the disciplines to which he or she belongs."[11] Since my specialization, rhetoric, sends me to the borders of argument, searching (with Aristotle) for "all the available means of persuasion," I find myself looking at DPN in the near-present because of its substantial rhetorical impact not only on the Gallaudet Board of Trustees but also on the Deaf community worldwide, the disability rights movement, and even the able-bodied and Hearing world at large as it "captured the attention and imagination of millions of people in the United States and, indeed, throughout the world."[12] My epigraphs for this section aim to illustrate some of DPN's appeal.[13]

I choose to begin at DPN, too, because I believe it marks a shift in literacies. And literacy, as I argued in my second chapter, weaves into and perhaps is even the weaver of the fabric of both rhetoric and deafness. How an act of rhetoric like DPN marks a literate shift and identifies, even as it justifies, a culture will be what I most want to illuminate in my rhetorical analysis later. As the previous two chapters on deafness as disability and pathology have shown, as the institutions of education and science (through biomedicine, audiology, and speech pathology) have dominated the discourse and provided the persuasion about deafness, the "illiterate" deaf body has stood in the way of much of Western culture, threatening quite ominously our rhetoric—our will to speech—and thereby our understanding of what is human, the nature of language, how the world works. In choosing here to color in my earlier drawings from the palette that is DPN, I again follow Certeau, who illuminates the "rift" between dominant literacies and "unknown languages" and the role that such a rift plays in historiography:

> Modern medicine and historiography are born almost simultaneously from the rift between a subject that is supposedly literate [the hearing body, the speaking subject], and an object that is supposedly written in an unknown language [the deaf body, the signing object]. The latter always remains to be decoded. These two "heterologies" (discourses on the other) are built upon a division between the body of knowledge that *utters* a discourse and the *mute* body that nourishes it.[14] (my emphasis)

DPN occasions these two divisive heterologies; it helps Hearing history decode deafness even as it brings vision to and nourishes that deafness.[15] In DPN we see (far more than we hear) deaf individuals and Deaf community seeking to anchor in certain moments of the rhetorical-historical past even as they float free from such anchors of argument. Thus, in DPN we see rhetorically how "history is played along the margins which join a society with its past and with the very act of separating itself from that past."[16] Put yet another way, we see how (both Deaf and Hearing) rhetorics repeat, reverse, and revise themselves. And it will be these "three Rs" that I will most want to teach in this chapter as I explore how DPN still recapitulates deaf history as "hearing history"—in a move Owen Wrigley keenly critiques in his chapter "Hearing Deaf History"— and yet recasts Deaf history as its own even as it fruitfully offers ways to recreate rhetoric in and of itself by lending an eye to the "unknown language" of the other who "utters" differently but persuades powerfully.

That DPN took place on educational grounds (literally and figuratively) also signifies in my choosing to make it my rhetorical-historical center in this chapter. First, the history of deafness—or rather, the history we "have" following the "discovering" of deafness in the Enlightenment— has been more or less handed down through schools, principally in residential deaf institutions throughout the world.[17] The transmission of Deaf culture is often argued to occur in these very institutions where, since "Deafness is a culture characterized as an incidence ratio, its 'natives' are colonized [institutionalized] anew with each generation."[18] But as they are institutionalized anew there also occurs a regeneration of the culture from (deaf) peer to (deaf) peer, instead of from hearing parent to deaf child— the "enculturation" rather than "acculturation" process that Linda Ross documents in her recent ethnography of one state residential institution for deaf children.[19]

Second, the histories we have of Deaf communities almost always feature deaf education at large, deaf schools more particularly, and often even more particularly the state-funded residential institutions. So it is that in the prologue of Jack Gannon's *Deaf Heritage: A Narrative History of Deaf America,* deaf education comes to America (in the form of the deaf and French man, Laurent Clerc, and the hearing American, Thomas Hopkins Gallaudet) in a rather chilling "Columbus comes to the New World" narrative:

> The wind billowed, filling the sails. The rigging snapped taut as the little wooden ship, the *Mary Augusta,* alternately floundering and plowing the seas of the Atlantic Ocean, made its way westward to the city of New York. Several days before, at high tide, on the afternoon of June 18, 1816, the

Mary Augusta had left Le Havre on the northern coast of France. To the deaf people of American, this was a historic journey.

The vessel carried six passengers, a crew of twelve, and the ship's captain. Four of the passengers were Americans and the other two were Frenchmen, one of whom, Laurent Clerc, was traveling with one of the Americans—the Reverend Thomas H. Gallaudet.

In the beginning of the voyage, 30-year-old Laurent Clerc was something of an oddity to the other passengers. He was a deaf teacher of the deaf, coming from the National Royal Institution for the Deaf in Paris on a unique mission. He and his friend Gallaudet hoped to start a school for the deaf in America.[20]

This "New World journey" passage echoes "Hearing Deaf History"—the narrative frame of deaf history represented in the conqueror's "conversion" code—that Wrigley critiques when he calls Harlan Lane's near-definitive history of the deaf, *When the Mind Hears,* "a 'pious biography,' a work infused with the saint-making language of religious hagiography."[21] In treatments of the key figures and moments most often cited in such history—Abbé de l'Epée, Abbé Sicard, Laurent Clerc, Thomas Hopkins Gallaudet—the trope of conversion controls the narrative. "That which is now called 'history,'" writes Wrigley, "begins with the first efforts at conversion; what precedes is only 'prehistory.' This conversion was not only religious, sought by a priest [l'Epée, Sicard, Gallaudet], but linguistic, as he [l'Epée] tried to create the first manual code of the written language—a far more significant conversion, which is still being contested."[22]

The conversion-driven history of deaf people—and the entanglements of education and religion in this enterprise—goes far beyond this moment in American deaf history. Two Spanish priests, Pedro Ponce de León and Juan Pablo Bonet, often count as key figures in deaf chronologies. Ponce de León was one of the first documented teachers of the deaf (ca. 1550), and Bonet was the first credited with publishing a book on education for the deaf. In *The Silent Minority: Deaf Education in Spain, 1550–1835,* Susan Plann documents the bridge between mid-sixteenth-century monastic communities, where the monks under vows of silence established significant systems of sign communication, and deaf students: these systems were transferred in part initially through private tutoring and through public teaching. Thus, while education on the one hand helps transmit "Deaf culture," on the other hand (dirtier) hand it converts through the viruslike transmission of Hearing Deaf history.

Nearly every major moment chronicled in Deaf history involves education (see the "(Partial) History of Deaf Education" in chapter 2). Even before the "discovery" of deafness in the Enlightenment, when organized deaf schools were first established, the literate life of deaf individuals is what principally occupies deaf "chronologies" such as those offered by Gannon in *Deaf Heritage:* ten of his sixteen entries before 1700 concern the "teaching" of deaf persons, from condemnatory conjectures on the "reasoning" capacities of deaf persons by Aristotle (355 b.c.e.) to Pedro Ponce de León's role in teaching the deaf (ca. 1550) to Juan Pablo Bonet's publication of the first book on educating the deaf (1620) and finally to developing and publishing methods for teaching speech and lipreading to the deaf, based on his medical observations, by the father of speech pathology, Dr. Johann Amman (1700). Philosophers, explorers, clergymen, doctors—hearing all—had a hand in educating the deaf and therein in shaping (Hearing) deaf history.

And this history seems predominantly to have been shaped with a close correlation between deaf education and deaf community. In *Language in Motion: Exploring the Nature of Sign,* Jerome D. Schein and David A. Stewart turn specifically to the coterminous connection of deaf schools and deaf organizations:

> It is illuminating to correlate the emergence of organizations of Deaf people with the establishment of their schools. In the United States there is no record of any organization of deaf adults before 1817. The New England Association of the Deaf was founded in 1837, twenty years after the first permanent school for deaf students opened in Hartford, Connecticut. The U.S. Congress chartered the National Deaf Mute College (later renamed Gallaudet College and later still Gallaudet University) in 1864. Springing up in the same vicinity just sixteen years later was the National Association of the Deaf.
>
> These two instances illustrate the general pattern of the emergence of organizations of deaf people. A school for deaf children is erected. Deaf children are drawn to it from all over a state or region, as are deaf people seeking positions as teachers, residential staff, kitchen staff, and the like. The presence of a growing number of deaf persons leads to the call for some sort of mechanism to organize gatherings and exchange information.[23]

Beyond forging deaf communities and deaf organizations (and perhaps largely because education leads to such forgings), the link between
deafness and education occurs in the location of individual deaf identities:
within Deaf culture, conversational social etiquette traditionally requires
introducing yourself by naming, after your birth name, the school you attended. To be sure, this etiquette is becoming fast outdated as state residential institutions for the deaf disappear entirely or are severely under-
enrolled in the wake of the Individuals with Disabilities Education Act's
"mainstreaming" of deaf children into public schools.

Gallaudet University is foremost among the surviving deaf institutions, the pinnacle of presence in deaf education—the world's only liberal
arts university for the deaf and hard-of-hearing. As one student I once tutored there signed to me:

> Gallaudet seemed important to me, it really did. I felt connected to Gal-
> laudet, yeah . . . but it was also an emotional time for me [first coming to
> Gallaudet], because for a long time this was my goal, to finally get here.
> Because at that time, what I knew was at that time Gallaudet was the only
> school in the whole world for deaf people, you know? And . . . I felt like
> it was a very big, very special university, you know what I mean? It was, I
> know there were other colleges, but this place, Oh wow, I just feel that
> this place, I feel a real connection, you know, everybody's the same as me,
> they're deaf.[24]

And echoing the enormous appeal of Gallaudet's identity connection
for deaf people—especially young adult, formerly mainstreamed, deaf
people—one history professor who has taught there for two decades told
me that the chance for "common bond" was what Gallaudet's education
offered most powerfully:

> With more opportunities available, with the ADA making interpreters re-
> quired, why should they come here [Gallaudet] if they don't want a "deaf
> experience"? If they don't want to learn to be deaf, culturally deaf, if they're
> not already "Deaf"? . . . They [i.e., primarily mainstreamed "hard-of-
> hearing" students] come here not signing very well, not feeling very com-
> fortable, [and] are so strongly taken with, perhaps, the feeling that finally
> they are with people who are like themselves, and who have been so alien-
> ated or felt so unaccepted in other environments, that when they come

here they feel that, "Wow, these people are like me, even though I can't sign as well as they do, I'm going to do everything I can to get like that."[25]

DPN magnified and magnifies that common bond. Nor is it mere coincidence that it took place on the "Deaf world's" premier educational stage, Gallaudet University.

More generally, I turn to DPN because it turns us toward education and that in turn places us back in rhetoric. Perhaps the point is best made by one of the more important contemporary figures in my own rhetorical education, James Berlin:

> On the one hand are the material and social conditions of society, on the other are the political and cultural. It is rhetoric—discourse—that mediates between the two, forming the core of a society's educational activities. The ability to read, write, and speak in accordance with the code sanctioned by a culture's ruling class is the main work of education, and this is true whether we are discussing ancient Athens or modern Detroit [or Gallaudet University, for that matter]. These rules are of course inscribed in a rhetoric, a systematic designation of who can speak, when and where they can speak, and how they can and must speak. Educational institutions inculcate these rules, determining who is fit to learn them and who has finally done so—in other words, who is authorized to be heard.[26]

While this passage is uncannily hearing-heavy, Berlin's argument that education inculcates rhetoric also reminds me that where there is the power of force, there is also the power of counterforce, and therein the power to free. We will see how DPN became counterforce—not only how rhetoric's rules were in force (and enforced) in DPN's educational setting at Gallaudet (rhetoric repeated), but also how they were counterforced (rhetoric reversed) and, finally, how they were also freed (rhetoric revised).

And I also have personal reasons for turning to DPN. It lands close to my own point of origin and entry into "deafness" and "Deaf culture." It was in 1988, the year of DPN, that I left "home," went back to graduate school after years of teaching high school, sought out a sign language class (far away from the university—in the basement of a Baptist Church), and began pondering the consequences of my "coming out" as "deaf." It was DPN—and yes, strong-willed, smart, sexy Marlee Matlin as Sarah Norman in *Children of a Lesser God,* too—that swung that closet door open for me. This was the rhetoric I learned how to be d/Deaf from.

And a lot of it goes back to DPN. It was one of those defining moments when the frustration that had been here for two hundred years, about not having a place at the table, when they were able to make themselves known in a very effective, intelligent, clever way. I think that was exactly as it should have been. I remember trying to come on campus not knowing that it was closed. And the gate where I normally would have come in, they had put a bus and let the air out of the tires. And there were a bunch of students hanging around. And one of my students . . . was there in battle fatigues. And I said, "you're really going to stop me?" And they said, "No, we're not going to stop you if you really want to come on campus. But we wish that you wouldn't." I thought, at this point, "we'll respect it." . . . And I think it paved the way for a lot of other organized activities that wouldn't have come without this kind of thing. I think the desire was there for along time, and I think DPN was the defining moment for a lot of people.

—Rick, history/government professor, Gallaudet University

consciousness razing—n. That remarkable week-long phenomenon in March 1988, where the entire world woke up to the clamor at Gallaudet University.

—Ken Glickman, *More Deafinitions for Signlets*

WHAT HAPPENED AT DPN?

In March 1988 deaf students at Gallaudet University in Washington, D.C., rose up, some two thousand strong, and spoke with a single "voice" that was not heard but rather was seen by the world. In an uprising now known as DPN (Deaf President Now), these deaf students formed a community with a cause. Communally they affected pedagogy—abandoning classes, closing the gates to the school, and refusing to budge until their demands were met. Communally they affected politics when Jesse Jackson and several members of Congress came to their aid, spoke in their defense, and all of Congress talked of cutting into Gallaudet's huge federal funding if the students did not get what they asked for. Finally, they affected power structures and widened their own community: they rejected their newly appointed president and got many of their faculty—and their janitors, too—to join them. And soon even deaf schools in Canada and West Germany closed on their behalf, the American Postal Workers Union donated $5,000 to their cause, and the media swarmed in, fumbling in its attempts to get interviews from students who didn't speak and to record rallies in which the protesting "voices" were a sea of silent hands waved above 2,000 heads.[27]

What happened? What was it these students wanted? Well, they had a vision—a dream, you might say. They wanted an end to paternalism; they wanted a voice and ears like their own to represent them in matters of power, politics, and pedagogy. They wanted, quite simply, a Deaf president.

For 124 years Gallaudet's president had been a hearing person (and male); for 124 years these hearing presidents had been elected by a principally hearing board of directors; thus for 124 years d/Deaf people had held no power, had no real representation at the very place they should most have power and representation—their exclusive, one-of-a-kind Deaf university. So, when on 9 March 1988 their hearing board, led by Jane Spilman (who did not even know the most basic sign language), elected yet another hearing president over the other two candidates, who were fully qualified and deaf, Gallaudet's students got a little rowdy, formed a powerful community, made themselves very visible in the news, and increased Deaf awareness worldwide about a dozen times over. By the time the week was up, the short tenure of the hearing president, Elisabeth Ann Zinser, had ended with her resignation, as she was "'zinsered' (censored) by Deafies";[28] their hearing, ASL-ignorant board chair, Jane Spilman, had resigned; they had a new Deaf president, Irving King Jordan, who was himself d/Deaf and a graduate of Gallaudet, and who currently taught there;[29] they had promises of a restructured board that would be at least 50 percent Deaf in the future; and the world had not only "heard" deaf people, but had, judging from the rash of newspaper stories and editorials across the country, shouted along with them, echoing support for their cause. "Deaf Awareness," "Deaf Power," and "Deaf Pride"—slogans now often emblazoned on the shirts of deaf students at Gallaudet—had come of age.

But before this new age dawned, before this highly rhetorical moment, deaf education in American schools had historically and principally gone by the hearing world's agenda: oral communication, based on print-centered literacy and the rhetorical imperative of "the good man *speaking* well," has always been strongly insisted on in deaf education; manual, visual communication—the use of the hands and the body—has been discouraged or forbidden outright. If deaf people are to function and communicate at all, the argument goes, they must do so *as if they can hear;* if they can't get along in the hearing world, then they can't get along at all. Knowing the dominant (hearing) culture's language, doing well with its print-powered literacy, is the key to "getting along." End of argument.

By now, we recognize this argument, built on the will to speech and empowered by the false syllogism, already cited, that echoes throughout our cultural history (*Language is human; speech is language; therefore, deaf people are inhuman, and deafness is a problem*). It is an argument that even now many current "literacy" and rhetoric studies are taking up, whether to refute or support—an argument constructed from the power, politics, and pedagogy of a dominant and privileged culture and meant to keep that culture in power primarily through its language and rhetoric, its "social grammar," as Henry Giroux would have it. Schools, Giroux maintains, both implicitly and explicitly serve the dominant culture, teach the dominant social grammar.[30] The dominating social grammars that most concern me here are oral and written Standard English; the language of the less dominant and, until recently, barely recognized Deaf culture is visuospatial American Sign Language.

ASL relies primarily on vision, on seeing the world and language *enacted;* English (like all modern spoken languages) arrives and arises primarily from hearing— even when we read silently to ourselves we tend to read "aloud," the small muscles of our jaws and tongues twitching out the words. As Walter Ong unfortunately makes all too clear throughout his seminal work *Orality and Literacy,* the modern emphasis on hearing sound is much preferred: "sight isolates, sound incorporates," he argues.[31]

One large factor that kept deaf people from a strong and unified sense of their own culture was the very isolating and isolated status of their unique visual language: sign languages are unable to be distributed widely in disembodied print; until recently, they have not been recognized as "real" languages by the hearing world, by the dominant discourse. Now, however, thanks to the pioneering work of numerous sociolinguists and psychologists, sign languages are, for the most part, considered legitimate languages, and subsequently Deaf culture, Deaf communities, and deaf individuals everywhere share a new sense of worth as the hearing world grows increasingly aware of the not-so-silent Deaf minority.[32] I believe that growing awareness of Deaf culture and its visuospatial language, ASL, will provide fertile ground for studies in rhetoric, literacy, and culture since it is an awareness advanced and marked by issues that researchers in those areas pay particular attention to—issues of power, politics, pedagogy, persuasion, literacy, language use, and the social and cognitive construction of knowledge and culture.

Because ASL finally gained acceptance linguistically and, therefore, was being used more openly and proudly to shape Deaf cultural identity, the students at Gallaudet could use it to form their own power, to establish their own political and pedagogical agenda, to declare themselves to be members of a culture and not just "disabled" individuals. Furthermore, the *social* success and freedom gained for all of Deaf culture from that event has increased awareness and identity redefinition among and within many deaf *individuals*. Thus, the legitimation of ASL, together with an event like DPN, has led to the coming out of a culture and its individual members. This coming out is precisely the dynamic that gives studies in Deaf culture, language, and literacy a provocative value for rhetorical studies at large.

To make and support these arguments and to carry out my analysis of DPN, I first need to lay out the social and linguistic groundwork of some history—to locate the exigencies out of which the rhetorical situation of DPN grew. A "rhetorical situation," as first defined by Lloyd Bitzer, is "a natural context of persons, events, objects, relations, and an exigence which strongly invites utterance"; the "exigence" in a rhetorical situation is "an imperfection marked by urgency; it is a defect, an obstacle, something waiting to be done, a thing which is other than it should be." Moreover, "an exigence which cannot be modified is not rhetorical[;] . . . further, an exigence which can be modified only by means other than discourse is not rhetorical."[33] The exigencies that I believe invited the "utterances" of DPN were a *repetitive* history of tensions between Hearing dominance and Deaf ways in deaf education; a *reversal* of attitudes and knowledge about American Sign Language in the United States that fostered, both internally and externally, Deaf cultural awareness and growth; and a *revisionary* cultural climate, tuned to the struggles of civil rights and women's movements, that would listen favorably to arguments of "rights" and "representation" among nondominant groups—that would be likely to translate what it heard as "an imperfection marked by urgency . . . a thing which is other than it should be" into a "persuasive situation, which exists whenever an audience can be changed in belief or action by means of speech [*sic*]" as *revisionary rhetoric,* "a mode of altering reality."[34] What is more, on arriving at this last exigence, we will see that the rhetorical situation of DPN revises the very nature of rhetoric and certainly, in being both rhetorical *cause* and *effect,* revises as well the concept of "the rhetorical situation."

Troubles at the Deaf Residential Institution

Louisiana School for the Deaf and the Deaf community have been a part of this state's history for 141 years. Like many other residential schools, we have had to deal with paternalistic attitudes and the generational inbreeding of state workers, their families, and local educational talent who have always worked for the deaf, not with them. Hearing people have their own culture and for the most part only work in ours. Those who "just" work here but do not really live the Deaf experience or contribute to its growth are not too far removed from the personnel of a prison—they only work there.

—Open letter, Louisiana Association of the Deaf (1993)

Troubles at the "Mainstreamed" Public School

Leo Jacobs, a prominent deaf educator and author of *A Deaf Adult Speaks Out,* fears mainstreaming will result in "a new generation of educational failures." Mervin Garretson, deaf educator and past president of the National Association of the Deaf, warns that deaf children could be "educationally, vocationally, and emotionally mutilated." Patrick Graybill, a deaf actor and former member of the National Theater of the Deaf, worries that mainstreamed students will be "lost between two worlds," unable to speak well enough to be understood by hearing people and unfamiliar with ASL and deaf culture.

—Douglas Baynton, *Forbidden Signs: American Culture and the Campaign against Sign Language*

A Repetitive Exigence: Deaf Education in the United States

Deaf people—usually seen as "disabled," in terms of what they *lack*—have been variously defined and educated by the more dominant hearing culture throughout U.S. history.[35] In all of his work, Henry Giroux reminds us of how significant schools are in the social construction of our society and selves. For Giroux, following the famous Brazilian educator Paulo Freire, power, politics, and pedagogy are always inextricably connected. In *Schooling and the Struggle for Public Life,* Giroux specifically outlines the power of schools and the role they play in how we construct "citizen" and "community," the ways in which "all [school] interaction contains implicit visions about the role of the citizen and the purpose of community."[36]

For almost two hundred years now, the oral (and written) traditions of deaf education have contained such "implicit visions about the role of the citizen and the purpose of community"; those visions, seen by the hearing people usually in charge of deaf education (as they remain today, even at Gallaudet), usually portray the possibilities of deaf citizens as fully functional, literate members of society, "saved" from their "deaf and dumb" existence by the dominant hearing culture (by the likes of Ken Glickman's *hearo*). The assumption that deaf people inherently need to be "fixed" or "saved" is criticized as the "pathological view of deafness" by scholars such as Timothy Reagan and Harlan Lane, and it is part of what Owen Wrigley points to as the hearing-dominated "conversion" narrative that comprises (and compromises) so much of "deaf history." In these pathological and conversionary views, it matters little that deaf citizens often never achieve the vision held out to them: our oral and written tradition of literacy keeps on demanding that they should, that they can, that they *will.* Our tradition of literacy—with its focus on mastering increasingly complex, and often abstract, pages of print—and our rhetorical "will to speech," which insists on ascension to Quintilian's *vir bonus dicendi peritus* ("good man speaking well"), have tended to devalue Sign—the complex of all native sign languages—as languages in and of themselves.

And our dominant print and oral-/aural-centered literacy has achieved that devaluation in various ways. One way has been by keeping alive the age-old oral-manual debate that Richard Winefield outlines so well in *Never the Twain Shall Meet: Bell, Gallaudet, and the Communications Debate* and that Douglas Baynton historically and culturally critiques more recently in *Forbidden Signs: American Culture and the Campaign against Sign Language.* In this debate, the dichotomizing of mind-body and language-communication (as analogs and echoes of oral-manual)—binaries on which the history of rhetoric itself is unfortunately built—repeats itself. At issue, most fundamentally, is whether it is best to teach a deaf child—or, more accurately, to *attempt* to teach a deaf child—to read lips, vocalize, and read and write in English (i.e., to communicate), or whether it is best to teach a deaf child sign language from the outset (i.e., to offer language, even one that is not dominant). Note, too, that the debate plays out on the *body* of a deaf person—whose sign language is embodied—but in the *mind* of the "naturalized" speaking subject. In its long embarrassment over the role of the body in argument and persuasion, rhetoric has struggled in both theory and practice with the canon of "delivery" at large; named as the fifth part of rhetoric by Aristotle and other classical rhetoricians (who name the other four canons as invention, arrangement, style, and memory), delivery is mostly absent from rhetorical history. In response to the intermittent bubbling up of small pockets of "elocutionary" interest in the seventeenth, eighteenth, nineteenth, and late twentieth centuries, where delivery and the body reappear at the center, rhetoric has usually marginalized such texts and figures, thereby repetitively reminding us (quite philosophically) that speaking well is a thing of the mind, yes; the body, no.[37]

Yet performance keeps popping up; bodies keep getting in the way, coming out of closets. So, too, the debate over oral versus manual methods in deaf education never seems to get entirely settled. The rhetoric repeats itself. Even now, when most child psychologists and linguists would agree that the deaf child desperately needs immersion in a language *as early as possible,* and that sign language is the most natural and logical option, the argument for taking up endless, valuable hours of language learning with lipreading and speech skills still remains strong. The ludicrousness of the so-called logic in such an argument seems never to become obvious in a culture in which the will to speech overpowers common sense, if not ethics, at every turn. In *The Politics of Deafness,* Owen Wrigley uses a comparison with education of the blind to make the case poignantly:

> Education for blind children focuses heavily on verbal communication, on speaking to and eliciting speech from the blind child. Education for deaf children is, likewise, focused heavily on verbal communication, on

speaking to and attempting to elicit speech sounds from the deaf child. For the blind child, the policy concentrates on the sense and modality present: hearing and speech. For the deaf child, the concentration is exclusively on the sense and modality absent: hearing and speech. Imagine a school for blind children in which a majority of the learning day consisted of teachers shining very bright lights into blind eyes, while saying little more than "Think color? What color?" Though that seems odd, it is a rather accurate portrayal-in-reverse of mainstream deaf education.[38]

The colors of this portrait come from the repetitive rubbing and binary binding of mind-body, communication-language, oral-manual. And this is the same rubbing that has marked the entire rhetorical tradition, painted boldly in the trademark syllogism brushed on the canvas of the will to speech. In this mural, while some like Lucille Clifton may marvel at "the fortunate deaf," the deaf students placed in our educational system and surviving in our "literate" culture are mostly viewed as problems at best, inhumane at worst. They are smudged out in those hyphenated spaces.

Rhetoric, like deaf education, prefers the binaries, thrives on opposition. And both rhetoric and deaf education, too, tend to stay locked in those oppositions, afraid to engage the hyphens and enter into the gap between the binaries and in doing to consult deaf persons on the very matters concerning them most). "Hyphens connect, but they also keep apart," muses Paul Preston in his qualitative study of CODAs (children of deaf adults), *Mother Father Deaf.*[39] So—connected but separate—the arguments over mainstreaming versus residential institutions, integration versus separation, assimilation versus accommodation, language versus communication, and social versus academic emphases for deaf education volley back and forth. Tide in, tide out. The rhetoric repeats itself.

In one illustrative conversation I had with a deaf literacy researcher who studies emerging literacies in deaf children ages three, four, and five, three variations on the social versus academic theme played themselves out, as she spoke of three different children caught in the net of the mainstreaming or residential institutions choice.[40] First, Charlotte narrates a "social" choice story:

> The family has two deaf children. Their first child, a girl, was born deaf, and when they found out, they learned sign language (and I would say they used a pidgin). When their second child was born, they signed to

him as well, and they found out later that he was also deaf. For both of the children, language acquisition was very normal, particularly for the second child. So when they went to school, they were not language delayed, as many of our kids are [referring to the deaf children she often works with], and so academically they did really well. And so the parents decided to mainstream them. . . . But the issue has always been social. They were the only two deaf children in the whole school, the only ones who have an adult following them around all day [their interpreter], and it creates a unique phenomenon. Even though other children in the school have learned sign language and they offer sign language classes in the school, both of the deaf children frequently complained about the loneliness, the isolation. . . . Even though she's academically very capable [of public school mainstreaming] and probably should be in a regular classroom in terms of academic challenge, she doesn't want to be alone any more, to be the only deaf girl in the school, alone.

Then Charlotte quickly counters with another social story of a mainstreaming choice made for a young deaf student, running quite in reverse:

On the flip side, there's a little girl who I'm working with now, who goes to the school for the deaf here in town. But in her neighborhood, she's with all hearing kids. So, it's a completely different context. Her parents are going to mainstream her next year so that her schoolmates will also be her playmates. Right now her schoolmates are not her playmates—they don't live nearby—and so, she feels isolated in the neighborhood. Instead of keeping her at the school for the deaf, which may be better for this child at this point in her life, they're going to mainstream her because of the social implications.

To be sure, these two counternarratives both emphasize the "social" answer to the question, "What is the best education for a young deaf student?" And in doing so, they make evident how any one answer—a sure foot planted on one end of the usual dichotomized options in question— is only one foot, and hardly sure. But the picture becomes even more complicated with a third story, in which the problems of hyphen-hopping are all the more evident as Charlotte relates how deaf individuals can spend their lives in those hyphens:

This one little guy was mainstreamed only two days a week, so I saw him at the school for the deaf and then in the regular kindergarten classroom [i.e., the mainstreamed public school environment]. At the school for the deaf, this child was a leader, but in the regular classroom he was very reticent, very quiet, not at all the leader. His personality changed tremendously because, I think, of the social context.

Beyond the hyphenating tendencies that repeat themselves throughout deaf education, a second, and related, devaluing debate rages repetitively around the use of sign language, particularly in educational contexts: the question of its capabilities for displaying abstract and formal thought. Stemming from the work of Helmer Myklebust and Hans Furth in the 1960s, the perception still persists that sign language somehow limits its user to concreteness and informality—that it cannot achieve what we so value in the hyperliterate, abstract, formal environment of the academy. While I tutored and completed case study research on deaf student writers in "basic English" classes at Gallaudet in the early 1990s, I heard this debasing argument more than once from the very lips of some of those who teach in the English Language Program.

Likewise, I found it reverberating in a recent spirited exchange between eminent deaf studies scholars Peter Paul and Harlan Lane, as they volleyed—sometimes viciously—over the value of a field, "the psychology of deafness." Their debate takes place in four issues, spanning a year from March 1996 to March 1997, of *BRIDGE,* the newsletter published by the American Educational Research Association's special interest group on "Research on Education of Deaf Persons." Peter Paul, well-published deaf education researcher, who at that time was the editor of *BRIDGE,* argues *for* "a psychology of deafness." Although he asserts that "there is no Myklebustian psychology of Deaf individuals, especially when one is referring to the cultural behaviors (beliefs, attention-getting actions, etc.) of members of the Deaf culture," he goes on to "forgive Myklebust and the early pioneers for their now inaccurate or incomplete assertions regarding the use of signs and deaf individuals' difficulty or inability to understand abstract entities." Invoking Thomas Kuhn's theory of scientific revolutions, he blames not them but their faulty paradigm. "Nevertheless," he looks favorably on what he calls Myklebust's studies of the "compensatory strategies that individuals with hearing impairment used in the acquisition of knowledge" and locates the "psychology of deafness" there, in studies of "compensation" for one's hearing loss.[41]

Harlan Lane, author of several culturally sensitive though also contro-versial books on deafness, answers by pointing out that "overwhelmingly, the studies in the literature on the 'psychology of deafness' purport to be about the psychopathology that results from growing up deaf." He objects to the Myklebustian tradition of a "psychology of deafness" principally on grounds that turn away from "deficit" and "disability" perspectives of deaf-ness and instead look to deafness as a cultural difference: "There is a big difference between the psychology of an activity, such as reading [Paul's specific area of expertise in deafness research], and the psychology of a cul-tural group, such as Hispanic-Americans." It is because of the group's shared language, ASL, that Lane claims Deafness to be a cultural marker, not a psychological condition—there can be no "psychology of deafness," just as there can be no "psychology of Hispanic-Americans."[42]

Despite Lane's arguments, and despite the pioneering work of lin-guists like Ursula Bellugi and the powerful prose of "hearies" like neur-ologist-author Oliver Sacks, all of whom claim that ASL is indeed capable of abstraction and formality, sign language still tends to be seen as limited—as merely gestures or mimicry. As "mere rhetoric." In this frame, sign language can never be philosophical, critical, intellectual. Only speech can go there.

This was the stage upon which the DPN players had to act. And like Hamlet's players within a play, the DPN protesters had to find ways to re-peat the dominant discourse, to reverberate the rhetorics, even as they raised consciousnesses beyond that repetition. Two sociology professors at Gallaudet, John Christiansen and Sharon Barnartt, analyze in some depth in *Deaf President Now!* the "factors we feel contribute to the success of all protests and which contributed to the success of DPN."[43] Most notable for my own argument here are the factors involving what Christiansen and Barnartt call "availability of cultural 'frames,' with precedent for 'frame ex-tension'" in the political and cultural climate as a whole and making "frame extension possible" here.[44] DPN was framed principally within the civil rights movement, a move I'll return to in considering DPN's revi-sionary rhetoric; the students even borrowed the symbolic "We still have a dream" banner from the Crispus Attucks Museum in Washington, D.C., for their historic March on the Capitol that ended a week of protest. This was the same banner displayed by civil rights leaders when they sought to have Martin Luther King Jr.'s birthday declared a national holiday. In this way, available culture frames—that is, available rhetorics—set precedents and were extended. Civil rights rhetoric reverberated throughout DPN. Indeed, as the box at the beginning of this section shows, it even echoed in the reasons given by one hearing student for coming to Gallaudet University to do graduate work in psychology.

The type of issue involved at DPN also had a frame that could be extended, and it was. The DPN supporters secured, repeated, and extended the frame of the Civil Rights movement: at least the Martin Luther King version of it—the one, significantly, most familiar to and most preferred by white American culture). They did so in at least four rhetorical frames: (1) they focused on the culture-language issue and the need to have leaders "of the people, for the people, by the people"; (2) they repeatedly foregrounded the "natural" necessity of sign language at the world's only university for the deaf and hard-of-hearing; (3) they illustrated both the uniqueness and "naturalness" of their language; and finally (4) they protested peacefully and creatively.

"It's time," declared an early Deaf President Now rally flyer for 1 March (the protest actually began on the seventh): "timeliness" ticks here. The sophistic, rhetorical concept of *kairos* rings through as DPN rose to fulfill what Isocrates named as crucial to rhetoric, addressing the "fitness for the occasion"; DPN redressed the repeated rhetorics of deaf education's binding binaries even as it rode forward on the repeated rhetoric of the Civil Rights movement.

A REVERSING EXIGENCE:
ASL, THE POWER OF A REAL LANGUAGE

As a rhetorical situation, DPN arises from yet another exigence. Following on and yet entangled with the rhetoric of sign language being historically oppressed and discredited as a "natural" language, DPN presented, for hearing and deaf alike, deaf people with a very different view of their language. Deaf author Carol Padden writes that the "all-important value of the [Deaf] culture is respect for one of its major identifying features: American Sign Language."[45] In fact, she goes on to explain, Deaf culture deliberately disassociates itself from speech and writing. Such a disassociation is a rhetorical reversal. And instances of this kind of rhetorical reversal abound: since DPN is not just a rhetorical situation (an "effect" of

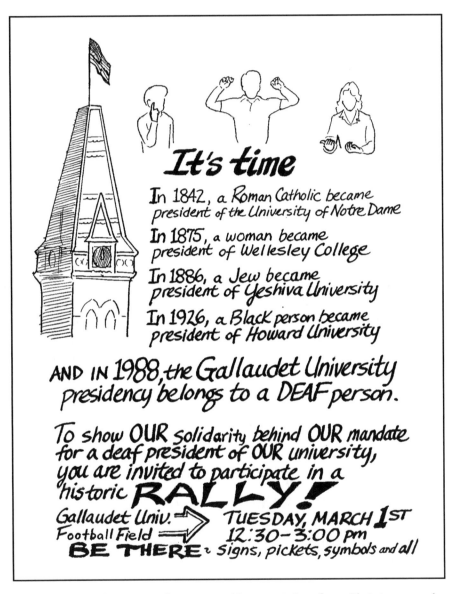

Figure 5.1 Flyer for DPN Rally. Reprinted by permission, from Christiansen and Barnartt, *Deaf President Now!* p. 22. ©1995 by Gallaudet University Press.

exigencies, as Bitzer argues) but a rhetorical "cause" as well, they have flourished in the post-DPN Deaf world. After considering how the reversal of ideas about sign languages lead to DPN, helping to generate that

In the final analysis, it seems to me that there are two com-
pelling reasons to advocate for academic acceptance of ASL. One is
what the language has to offer. Languages are tools, not only for
communicating ideas but for exploring ideas. ASL is, in my opinion, a wonderful pedagogical tool for sharpening the intellect, exploring the world, and testing research hypotheses.

The second reason concerns what academia has to offer the
language, its culture, and its speakers [*sic*]. We must not lose sight
of the fact that ASL is a minority, suppressed language, and that its
speakers and their culture historically have been oppressed and
poorly understood. The recent appointment of a hearing candidate
[i.e., Zinser] with no background in ASL or Deaf culture to become president of Gallaudet University, the subsequent galvaniz-
ing of the nation's deaf communities [in DPN], and eventual selection of Gallaudet's *first* deaf president, are eloquent testimony
to this.

—Sherman Wilcox, introduction to *Academic Acceptance of*
American Sign Language

rhetorical situation, I will then turn to how DPN itself seems to have
launched further reversals.[46]

After ten years of ASL research at the Salk Institute, linguist Ursula
Bellugi, in "How Signs Express Complex Meanings," discusses (and dia-
grams) in great detail various morphological features of ASL: referential
indexing, reciprocity, grammatical number, distributional aspect, tempo-
ral aspect and focus, manner and degree, derivational features such as
nouns created from verbs and predicates created from nouns, extended
meanings, and compounding. In other words, Bellugi discusses the many
identifiable linguistic features of ASL. She concludes that "the visual-
gestural communication system of deaf people has been shaped into an independent language with its *own* grammatical rules" and that, furthermore, "the human capacity for building complex linguistic systems is the
same—whether we speak or sign."[47] In other words, ASL is a natural
language—it is similar to yet different from all other languages. And in
those similarities and differences, it illustrates the universality of language

The second big impact on me [in my life] was the "structure of ASL" in a course I took. It finally hit me that ASL was a language. That was 1979. I felt more proud, I felt proud of myself . . . and I was less disgusted. My identity became positive after that, and that's how I came to do sign language teaching. And that's how I came to this organization, ASLTA [American Sign Language Teachers Association]. That's my organization.

—Ellen, Gallaudet graduate and ASL teacher

My mother and father were hearing. They didn't sign at all. My father, he didn't worry about me and my communication at all. But mom, she got scared, she got concerned. She read a book somewhere and she thought that if I couldn't learn lipreading it meant my mind would be messed up. That was wrong information. But my mother believed that idea for a long time. In fact, my mother would stop me and make me speak and lipread and slap my hands, "Don't do that. If you do that, your speech is going to go way down." But I didn't get the concept of speech and lipreading. When I got into the residential school [at the age of six], wow! That [ASL] was my real language, my first language. . . . I have too much pride in my first language, ASL. I think it's a beautiful language and it's easy to understand and communicate with. And English? It's hard. I have no concept or no way for me to understand it. ASL, it's very easy for me to function and to understand. My mind works that way in that language.

—Charlie, Gallaudet graduate and ASL teacher

even as it evidences the "palpable" particularities that a poet like Lucille Clifton finds so interesting.[48]

First, its similarities. Because it is real and natural, like spoken languages, ASL has a wide range of forms, including SEE (Signing Exact English), Signed English, PSE (Pidgin Sign English), SimCom, and the true language of the American deaf shared only with the American deaf, ASL. Like speech, sign languages, of which ASL is only one, are not the same in different languages: there is French Sign Language, Spanish Sign Lan-

guage, Chinese Sign Language, and so on. And finally, as James Woodward has shown, ASL, like American speech, comes in a wide variety of
ethnic and regional dialects—blacks sign differently than whites, males
often differently than females, midwesterners differently than southern-
ers. Additionally, there is a continuum between ASL and signed English,
just as there is one between spoken and written English.

Because of this continuum, Woodward has argued that ASL is
inherently "diglossic." Its more "literary" variety (approaching SEE)—
essentially a one-on-one signed translation for each and every word
spoken—is used in formal conversations, in places such as churches and
classroom lectures; its more "colloquial" variety is used in smaller, less formal settings, for intimate conversations.[49] This diglossia illustrates how
much ASL is community- and culture-oriented, how much it is a language
of the Deaf. As Woodward explains: "When a Hearing person enters a conversation where Deaf people are using ASL, the Deaf people will automatically switch from ASL to a more English-like signing. This 'code-
switching' [while it accommodates the hearing, English-speaking person]
prevents the Hearing person from seeing and learning to use ASL and
thus, from being able to participate in intimate interactions with Deaf
people."[50] In this way, diglossia serves ASL as both an inclusive and exclusive gate into the culture and community of Deaf people. There is even
a certain social etiquette to signed conversations that differs substantially
from the etiquette for spoken conversations—and because of these differences, it is often easy for native signers to tell who is a relatively new signer
in a conversation. They have not yet learned how to be polite.[51]

But the differences between ASL and other languages is all the more
important to me, at least for the purposes of my argument here, because
they mark the territory for reversing rhetorics. Oliver Sacks makes a
poignant argument for the reality and power of ASL as a unique language.[52] In *Seeing Voices: A Journey into the World of the Deaf,* he supports
ASL from virtually every angle. He lauds it as the *only* language that incorporates the unique dimension of space, making it a "four-dimensional
channel of expression" (using three spatial dimensions plus the dimension
of time), and he places it above and beyond speech in its capacity to "simultaneously evoke a concreteness, a vividness, a realness, an aliveness,
that spoken languages, if they ever had, have long since abandoned." Likewise, he marvels over the personal, physical power of sign language;
though "one can have or imagine disembodied speech, one cannot have

disembodied Sign."[53] More scientifically, he points to what he sees as evidence for the biological, innate grammar of sign language: it, like speech, is processed in the left hemisphere, despite its strong use of spatial figurations, which are typically a right hemisphere function.[54]

Finally, and most important for my own argument here, Sacks maintains that for deaf people, sign language is "an embodiment of their personal and cultural identity":[55] a visual, enactive embodiment. Indeed, as many Deaf history, Deaf studies, and ASL scholars have claimed, sign language provides entry—it is the admission ticket—into Deaf culture.[56] And if sign language forms the basis for and entry into Deaf culture, little wonder then that its validation might lead to the increased strength of Deaf culture, to a growing awareness of Deaf culture among both deaf and hearing populations, and eventually to the empowerment of deaf people at places like Gallaudet University.[57] Little wonder that students at the world's only liberal arts university for deaf people, armed now with a language at last granted full sociolinguistic status, should call for a reversal and a "voice" in matters of power, politics, and pedagogy concerning themselves. In the momentous DPN uprising of March 1988, the students at Gallaudet had come of age through language, because of language. Now that they had a language to call their own, a language that even the dominant hearing culture could no longer refuse to recognize as "real," those students had something to stand on. Language cannot be separated from power—as Michel Foucault and, more recently, Norman Fairclough (in *Language and Power*) have reminded us.

Before the linguistic acceptance of a language they called their own, deaf people—either culturally or individually—had no wedge against the dominant "social grammar," no way to persuade and empower outside their own communities, no way to flip the switch and reverse the dominant rhetoric. Persuasion and power, definition and acceptance of both self and society, begin with language—in all cultures. And such socially and individually constructed beginnings among deaf people, such issues of literate and linguistic (re)definition by the use of ASL, such successful displays of power and persuasion as occurred at Gallaudet during DPN in 1988 form the core of studies in rhetoric, literacy, and culture.

In DPN, rhetorics of reversal occurred in various ways. Some students, for example, cleverly decked their dogs out in sheets that proclaimed "I know signs better than Spilman"—thereby emphasizing the natural and "simple enough" nature of sign language, a language that even dogs (but not Jane Spilman) were willing to learn. Throughout the event, the question was asked over and over again: "Do you, ———, know sign language?" The Board of Trustees president, Jane Spilman, was put in the blank, as well as the nominated hearing president of the university, Elisabeth Zinser; even the members of the Gallaudet University Board of Trustees were placed there. By and large, they all drew blanks when asked the question; purportedly only three of the fifteen board members could respond affirmatively. In this way, the tables were turned by deaf students who have always been questioned on their English literacy. This time, ASL was at a premium—the language that one ought to know.

And throughout DPN, signs drowned out voices in a dramatic reversal of the usual "silencing" of languages. When the media stuck microphones in the faces of the deaf protesters with no interpreter in sight, they were forced to fumble through an aural vacuum. When they panned cameras out to capture a dramatic protest moment, they were often met with a silent sea of deaf hands waving above heads. No journalism school had prepared them for this. Yet to their credit, as Christiansen and Barnartt make clear in their account of DPN, "reporters quickly learned that they could get the information they needed if the camera was focused on a deaf person while the microphone was placed in front of a hearing interpreter."[58] In perhaps one of the most dramatic reversals of the whole event, what one DPN participant described as "the turning point of the whole protest week," came Spilman's figurative assassination, her literal silencing. The scene is worth recounting in full. On the afternoon of the first official day of the protest, Monday, 7 March, Jane Spilman took to the platform in the Gallaudet field house and

> addressed the crowd by saying, "Good afternoon, everyone," and "Tim Rarus [one of the student leaders], I don't know where you are." As she was saying this, Harvey Goodstein [a Gallaudet professor] walked onto the podium and stood directly in front of her, facing the audience. While Spilman was waving her arm trying to get the crowd's attention, Goodstein calmly said (signed sans voice) that they had met the board and the board refused to meet "our" demands, "so," he asked, "should we leave?"
>
> After this unexpected interruption [an interruption, significantly, without speech and in sign language alone], Spilman attempted to regain the floor. . . . Before she could proceed any further, hundreds of people got out of their seats and headed for the exits. Spilman stopped talking

and simply stood behind the lectern [ah, silenced], looking a bit bemused by the events taking place in front of her. . . .

Spilman watched for a few moments as most of the crowd marched out and as many others left their seats and milled around near the lecterns. She asked those who were left to be quiet, saying it was difficult to talk above the noise. The decibel level did not noticeably decrease . . . and one of the Ducks [alumni supporting the protest] added to the noise by setting off the fire alarm. Spilman tried again, saying several times that she couldn't hear above the noise. The students predictably responded: "What noise?"[59]

The rhetorical reversal of languages in power, of "voices" recognized and "noise" rendered meaningless while literal and figurative gestures stole the stage, characterized the events of the DPN week at Gallaudet University. And such reversals have openly abounded since then.

While deaf people have certainly always subversively—and sometimes openly—resisted "the Hearing world" (especially when they gathered in community and cultural events), I believe the rhetoric of reversals has run all the stronger since DPN. As one consequence of these events, in 1989 Gallaudet hosted an international week-long conference and cultural event, "The Deaf Way." The video that recaps some of its highlights opens with ten people from ten different countries signing their "hellos" and ends with interludes from the dramatic productions of deaf theater groups from eight countries. Billed as the ultimate international celebration of Deaf culture, the Deaf Way certainly reversed Hearing world notions about the illiteracy, isolation, or lack of rich cultural and artistic heritage in d/Deaf lives.

So, too, in Nicolas Philibert's award-winning French documentary, *In the Land of the Deaf* (1994), hearing and deaf alike are treated to a feast of the richness of sign languages and deaf lives. In key contrasting moments (call them reversals) in the film, we see the struggles and tears of deaf children trying, again and again, day in and day out, to get speech "right" from the lips of their hearing teachers and parents; juxtaposed to their trials are the ease, smiles, and obvious enjoyment of hearing adults learning sign language from a deaf teacher. Likewise, scenes of tension and estrangement from their own families (usually hearing) are played against scenes of laughter and much physical contact with their deaf peers. Other scenes are more painful in their dualized realities: the hearing children are laughing and playing at recess or taking a break from their lessons with choir practice—their harmonized voices floating out through the open window, through the billowing curtains, but falling finally on the deaf ears of those other (deaf) children who are not at recess but are still, as always, practicing their speech lessons.

While these scenes surely and accurately capture some of the essence of "the land of the deaf," I do not believe we have seen their like in a major screen production until now. Nor have we seen, in either quantity or quality, scenes like these that have occurred since DPN:

- deaf videos in sign language *not* being voiced-over yet offered for public consumption (a rhetoric of reversal against all the years of videos without closed-captioning)
- the policy of having no voice operators to handle the phones at some deaf organizations—calls are taken in TTY or relay services only
- the demands made since 1988 at nearly every state residential school for the deaf that echo the four demands made at DPN (especially during the 1992 protest at the Wisconsin School for the Deaf)
- the radical reclaiming (reversing) of terms thought taboo by Hearing culture—"deaf" and "hard-of-hearing"—while the mainstream-minded and hearing-assigned term "hearing-impaired" falls into extreme disfavor, disappearing even from most academic journals
- deaf individuals deliberately choosing to remain "d/Deaf"—shunning hearing aids or cochlear implants when they are offered to "fix" the patient—or even wishing openly for a deaf child, favoring only deaf-deaf marriages
- the increased demand for ASL-only instruction at many deaf schools (a definite swing away from oral-with-interpreter or even "SimCom" or "Total Communication" approaches that combine English and ASL, signing and speaking)
- the ratcheted-up standards for sign language proficiency not only among instructors at places like Gallaudet University, but for the students as well
- even the privileging of "language" over "communication" as manualists and oralists alike are dismissed in the "bicultural-bilingual" (Bi-Bi) approach to deaf education[60]

These are all instances occurring with notable frequency in the post-DPN Deaf milieu; and each exemplifies the "reversal" of a previously dominant ASL-oppressing rhetoric.

Of course, reversed rhetoric stands dangerously close to the original. Those who were oppressed can easily become oppressors; the slaves can become insensitive masters themselves as they internalize the plantation mentality, causing further division among themselves. This is the bind of binaries, the tangle of essentializing tendencies, the quandary and indeed quagmire of rhetorics that *only* reverse themselves. Caught in the terms of the same rhetoric it seeks to refute, "Deaf culture" can all too quickly and completely become "Deaf cult." In such a cult, militancy commands and the "deaf" are excluded by the self-appointed elite "Deaf"; the rhetoric of eugenics practiced by Alexander Graham Bell is replaced by the equally genocidal rhetoric of those who believe that only the DOD—Deaf children born of Deaf parents—are "fit" to rule the race. These positions, sadly, are also part of the post-DPN rhetoric of reversal. In a brief book published in 1994, *A Child Sacrificed to the Deaf Culture,* Tom Bertling examines these "cultish" tendencies, as does Owen Wrigley repeatedly, and with sensitivity and depth, in *The Politics of Deafness.* I share Wrigley's concern with the "constables of cultural purity" that have reinvented Hearing colonialism as "Deaf colonialism" and have dangerously made the demarcation between "deaf" and "Deaf" into a distinction that "*is now used primarily to exclude those who have failed to select the politically correct coping strategy.*" Like Wrigley, and as a rhetorician, I am inclined to believe that "in effect, the d/D dichotomy plays into the strategies of domination by pitting Deaf people against themselves over labels assigned to alternative strategies for coping with the dominant Hearing cultures."[61] Here again, I do not find deaf people so fortunate. Rhetorics that reverse often rub too close to rhetorics that repeat.[62]

Of Exigence: Revising (with Vision) Literacy, Culture, and Rhetoric

Where I find the most fortune is in the revisionary rhetoric made all the more possible by an event like DPN. The post-DPN scene has left us with more than a rhetorical situation, more than just Bitzer's "exigence which strongly invites utterance" or "an imperfection marked by urgency." The situation has engendered infinite, echoing questions that, if asked, might

The past two decades have witnessed an explosion of a new kind of knowledge concerning deaf communities, their cultures and their languages. The new knowledge represents a revolutionary shift in the perception of Deaf people from a pathological to a cultural perspective. This positive and affirmative point of view on their language and culture has fostered a social revolution amounting to a new empowerment of Deaf people.

—"Deaf Studies Mission Statement,"
Gallaudet University (1992)

Well, the reason I got involved in social work, in spite of my father's protests (he felt like they were a dime a dozen, and even though we do some pretty important work, our pay is not exactly high). But the reason I got involved in social work is because I felt that after my experience being mainstreamed and growing up in a hearing environment, and then going to Gallaudet, I felt my ability to speak well, my ability to understand the hearing culture and the deaf culture as well as being able to communicate within these two cultures, that I could serve as a bridge between the two, and I felt that there was a lot of education that needed to be done. Both with hearing and deaf to overcome that barrier that existed between the two. I felt like I was in a good position to be able to relate to the experiences of being deaf in a hearing world.

—Kathy, Gallaudet graduate (B.A.),
Ohio State University graduate (M.S.W.)

send us revisiting not only "deafness" but our entire notions of literacy(ies), culture(s), and rhetoric(s), as well as the relations among them.

Although I have only scratched the surface here, my arguments and examples addressing Deaf culture, Deaf education, issues surrounding ASL and English, and the Gallaudet DPN protest show how deep and complex the connections between language, literacy, and power are. When

At the beginning, most of my works are not related to Deaf Culture or deafness. My intention was to talk about the language oppression in the deaf community, but the works can be easily symbolized for any cultural group that experiences paternalistic oppression. The audience can decide for themselves. I do not force them to focus on my issues. I rather let them think about it and compare with their experiences. . . . I believe that myself as a Deaf person who is playing with the language is a good example for the Deaf community. A Deaf person who can create stories or poetry hold[s] a powerful place—a powerful voice. The Deaf community looks at them highly because they use ASL (the strongest product of Deaf culture) as a weapon or tool for building self-esteem, pride, strengths, and independence in the community. I feel that works about Deaf issues [oppression, specifically] are cliché by now unless there is a new way to show old themes. . . . No need to have pity here. Enough of that. Let's move on. What I start to focus on is the traditional techniques that Deaf people tend to play with such as ABC story, Handshape story, Number story, etc.

—Peter Cook, poet (Flying Words Project)

we question and explore our attitudes toward deaf people—toward their culture, language, education, "rights," and representation—we explore as well our own attitudes and conditions regarding these issues, in the critical move that Lennard Davis calls "deafness as insight." I will end this chapter by considering some of the revisionary questions that I—and I hope others, both deaf and hearing—may explore in the near future as we investigate Deaf culture, language, and literacy use and thereby further illuminate central issues in literacy, rhetoric, and cultural studies. Although DPN may seem to have disappeared from the discussion here, I feel its "absence tangible"—as Lucille Clifton characterizes the language of "the fortunate deaf"—its "name fastened" still into my "shivering hands" as I write of the revisionary possibilities of late-twentieth-century "deafness." And because I consider revision here, my analytical gaze is far less fixed as I scan the horizons for possibilities (for all the available means of persuasion); most of the "certainty" I have about the revisionary possibilities of a moment like DPN, marking as it does the coming out of Deaf culture, comes in the questions which that coming out raises.

Revising Literacy

In exploring, more specifically, the realm of literacy, deafness might enlighten us. Most deaf people, particularly those who have come as far as Gallaudet University in their own educational and career struggles, do indeed recognize the need to learn Standard Written English (SWE); but at the same time they need to be recognized as functional, competent, and literate in ASL, particularly if it is their native language. The conversations I have had with Gallaudet graduates, both those explicitly drawn on in this chapter and not—with Charlie, Anna, Ellen, Kathy, Mark, and David— reflect this need for double recognition. Ken Glickman and Peter Cook, the two deaf artists (comedian and poet, respectively) that I have had the pleasure of interviewing, echo these sentiments, and they reverberate in my many conversations with those in deaf education, both hearing and deaf, throughout the last ten years.

Yet the difficulty of undertaking such simultaneous tasks—of recognizing and retaining, let alone excelling at, these two very different languages—is staggering; for such a double recognition requires its users to become not only in effect bicultural and bilingual but "bicognitive" as well. I cannot emphasize this point enough: *English and ASL represent not just two very different culture and languages, but entirely different ways of thinking and seeing the world, manifesting epistemological and ontological (as well as ideological and audiological) distinctions that resound to their very cores.* The cognitive and existential differences come, in part, from the differing modalities of the two languages: modern English, though arising from an oral tradition, has long since been dominated by texts, by print; ASL, in contrast, is still an "oral" language in that it has no written forms and can only really exist when two living beings are communicating with each other in the immediate present. Thus, in our late-twentieth-century print-immersed culture, sign language locates "locution" uniquely, provocatively, *in body.*

It is clear that ASL uses time and spatial concepts quite differently than does English. For example, its structure relies primarily on narrative and parataxis, while written English relies more on argument and subordination. ASL is thus bound more tightly to the present tense, lacking past tense verbs entirely; it does, however, have "establishing" signs—usually occurring at the beginning of a signed "utterance"—to communicate action taking place in the past, present, or future. We might wonder how a narrative, present-tense language like ASL continues to influence its users as they attempt to become literate in English. How does a linguistic and cognitive dependence on narrative, on body, on visuality affect the (English) literacy development of deaf students? And if ASL, according to Walter Ong's famous (and perhaps infamous) criteria in *Orality and Literacy*, is inherently "oral," to what extent is the writing of deaf students oral as well? How might this change our understanding of orality?

In one of his most provocative and important arguments in *Enforcing Normalcy*, Lennard Davis considers "the deafened moment": "a dialectical moment in the reading/critical process that is defined by the acknowledgment on the part of the reader/writer/critic that he or she is part of a process that does not involve speaking or hearing." Davis aims, in illuminating this moment, to "place deafness next to 'textuality,'" to point out how "print narratives are actually surrounded by silence," and thus to place sign language right next to (if not, in fact, within) writing.[63] In this placement, sign language might then be seen as *not* oral, or even anti-oral. But I am not entirely convinced. The parallels between writing and sign language that Davis plots in "Deafness and Insight," his book's central chapter, make perfect rhetorical sense to me: the history of rhetoric, from Plato forward, is one in which writing (like sign language) is "othered," while speech reigns. But still—"orality" rings in my ears when I consider sign language. Writing removes us from the present. Writing disembodies. Writing provides a synonym for literacy. Orality does not; sign language does not. In these ways, then, sign language is the "same but different" in its relation to our two dominant locations for locution—orality/speech and writing. An understanding of that relation, and thus our investigation of sign language itself, can radically revise our thinking about literacy.

In addition to its unique oral and narrative roots, ASL relies primarily on vision, on seeing the world and language *enacted;* "I listen with my eyes" is a phrase deaf people use often. For Ong, as for most authorities throughout the academic tradition of literacy, the inability to perceive the world in a sound- and print-centered way is linked to cognitive deficiency, if not outright mental illness. As Ong explains it: "you can immerse yourself in hearing, in sound[:] . . . sound is thus a unifying sense[.] . . . [Such] interiority and harmony are characteristics of human consciousness[;] . . . without harmony, an interior condition, the psyche is in bad health."[64] From this angle, and from many others I have already discussed, deaf people are once again left with the burden of using a language and perceiving the world in a certain way that is, according to such derogatory accounts, deficient. But what if this difference were not defined as lack? What if, instead, we turned toward revision and asked ourselves just what this "visual literacy" might mean—particularly in a such a visual age as ours?[65] What if, in considering deaf literacy(ies), we asked ourselves—squarely—what other literacies lie beyond the print-centered, will-to-speech, dominant-discourse-only ones that are always and already apparent?

Past and present debates over the use of Black English Vernacular (BEV) and "Ebonics," various regional dialects, and other "foreign" languages within American public schools are implicated here, as are issues of the authenticity of one's "voice" and the validity of one's own language. I do not think that we, deaf and hearing alike, can ignore the dominant social grammar—the student protesters at DPN surely did not. Students, both deaf and hearing, need to be able to use Standard Written English. But for me, the more crucial question is how to legitimate the students' native language, whether spoken or signed: how to affirm the senses of both individual worth and social belonging that arise from their native language at the same time they might be learning the conventions of SWE and therein, too, the ways—epistemological, ontological, ideological, and audiological—of the dominant discourse. This is but one more question that deafness might help us answer; we might look, for example, more carefully at the ways that students involved in the DPN protest balanced and blended their double consciousnesses, making use of both dominant and suppressed literacies.

In turning to such a double consciousness, we might then consider how the cultural "constraints" of Deaf culture might be related, negatively and positively, to the development of deaf people's reading and writing abilities in English. In trying to answer this question we would also need to explore what the social and individual purposes and uses for literacy are among deaf people, along the lines of Shirley Brice Heath's *Ways with Words*. How are these literacy purposes and uses similar and dissimilar to those of hearing people in similar situations? How does DPN qualify as what Heath calls a "literacy event"—"any action sequence, involving one or more persons, in which the production and/or comprehension of print plays a role"[66]—and how does it also perhaps revise the print-dominated nature of that definition?

And in another revisionary move, these kinds of questions and revisionary considerations would need to be addressed by listening to deafness, by letting the deaf "speak" (even write) for themselves, and by pursuing ever-more fruitful scholarly exchanges between deaf and hearing alike. As I remark at the beginning of this book, and as Owen Wrigley emphasizes: "The exclusion of deafness and deaf people is as direct as it is exemplary," because "like the 'Indians' before them, the Deaf have routinely been dismissed as a possible source of accurate information, in addition to being routinely rounded up and excluded for administrative convenience."[67]

Revising "Culture"

Looking at literacy uses and purposes among deaf people would also connect us with cultural studies. An area that as yet remains virtually uncharted is that of the social and cognitive commonalities and intersections, as well as difficulties and points of diversion, between ASL and English, both cultural and linguistic. What happens between deaf and hearing, between ASL and English, in what Mary Louise Pratt calls "the contact zones"? What are the rhetorics involved between deaf and hearing, ASL and English, in what Gayatri Spivak names as "the politics of translation"?[68] Specifically, if we want to consider the interactions of culture(s) in our classrooms, we might use the "contact zones" of deaf students working toward English literacy—particularly at places like Gallaudet University, where their skills in sign language are also honed—as a way to determine how the commonalities between two languages and cultures might be emphasized and drawn on, while the difficulties are de-emphasized, as we teach students to become literate in *two* languages: both their native and the dominant culture's language. How does or can American deaf education revise itself into "bicultural" education? How does or can it maintain bilingualism, while accommodating the vastly different modalities of English and ASL (speaking and signing, oral/aural and visual)? How does or can it create a bicultural consciousness?

How a newly emerging culture or discourse, one that is engaged in coming out, tells its own story of identification, transformation, self and other finding, relationship formation, and community and culture building can also be heard in lending an ear to the coming out of deaf individuals and Deaf culture. This story is, I would wager, substantially different than the dominant discovery narrative—the tale commonly told by colonial discourses (what Wrigley calls "Hearing Deaf history"). As we have seen in this chapter, the rhetorical strategies of the two stories differ, and the revisionary rhetoric of the culture that is coming out marks its boundaries.

But exactly how are those boundaries marked? And how can the emergent culture revise and not essentialize? How can it answer the dominant discourse in a new way, beyond simple anger? This question has plagued other nondominant discourses and emerging theories—feminist, African American, and queer theory come immediately to mind—just as it now beleaguers deafness. One well-educated university ASL interpreter draws directly on such analogies:

> I view a lot of what's happening in the deaf community as being motivated by anger. And I remember that when I became involved in the women's movement. All of a sudden becoming aware of centuries of oppression, and being mad at all those centuries. Not just mad about my contemporary situation, but what's been happening since dirt, and I'm mad at all of that. I had to work through that, find a balance, choose my battles and where to focus my energy. And I'm looking at the whole deaf empowerment movement as a lot of anger. They have a lot to be angry about. . . . They are also finding their voice, just as women are finding their voice and after the Harlem Renaissance, African Americans are again finding their voice, and people with disabilities are finding their voice.[69]

In finding their voice, they must rephrase a central concern of African American history and theory once so powerfully expressed by Audre Lorde: Can deafness tear down the (hearing) master's house without using the master's tools?

And how does "attitude" figure as such a tool? What exactly does "attitude" mean in demarcating the boundaries between "deaf" and "Deaf"?[70] Can you constitute a culture on coping strategies or temperament alone? (And didn't Helmer Myklebust already make such an attempt with his politically incorrect "psychology of deafness" fashioned in the 1960s?) How is such a constitution rhetorically similar and dissimilar to audiological, biomedical, or educational assessment—the three linchpins of the "pathological view of deafness," as Harlan Lane, among others, argues?

What are the epistemological, ideological, ontological grounds of a cultural construction of Deafness? Can the center hold on these grounds? Does rhetoric hold it? Does rhetoric pull at it, move it? What, for example, are the grounds of logos, pathos, and ethos in this culture? How do logic, emotion, and character look and act differently—and similarly—in arguing about deafness from various positions *inside* and *outside* the culture?[71] And what portrait do we have of "precarious placements"— those who sit the fences in matters of d/Deafness? For example, in speaking of her own precarious situation, one interpreter I interviewed spoke of the intense "come here, go away" dynamics between deaf people and interpreters, particularly in our post-ADA era; she primarily blamed the "big issue about interpreters making money off of deaf people." She recognized the rhetorical predicaments of her own representational dynamics: "Because of my work, I'm placed in this precarious situation, and I'm not just going to start spilling my guts [to her deaf client]. I realize there's an unequalness, but that's just the nature of my job."[72] We might consider then, what logic and emotion reside, culturally and rhetorically, in the bodies and minds of the CODAs, the "hard-of-hearing," the late-deafened, the sign language interpreters—the whole motley crew. What is the rhetorical and cultural space they occupy?

And in what space, at what sites, and in what ways does passing happen? We should tune our ears to listen to the role of passing in/between Deaf and Hearing (deaf and hearing)—to consider how passing matters. We might look at when deafness is "given up," when it is "withheld," and why these retreats and advances, maskings and outings occur. We might chart the tropes of passing, measure which frames fit and which are broken by coming-out-as-deaf stories: how do these match other cultural rhetorics and frames we already know of? So, too, we might note how Deaf culture regenerates itself, and also degenerates—how certain rhetorics are learned, how its own dominating discourses, epistemologies, and ideologies are passed on. Thus we might ask: What rhetorics remain in the enculturation process? And which have disappeared or are in the process of being rubbed out? Was one long-practicing interpreter right in telling me, "When that generation of people who I learned sign language from, and who I learned about deafness from [a pre-DPN and pre-ADA generation]—when they're gone, I think that culture will be gone. It's evolving into something else"?[73] Is this really an *evolution*—or is it a Kuhnian, paradigm-shifting revolution? Can we trace the rhetoric of evolution—or the rhetoric of revolution—in Deaf culture's regeneration and degeneration? What does it mean that a rhetoric, a culture, is passed primarily from school-age peers to school-age peers instead of from parent to child?

How, if Deaf rhetoric stays so culturally contained in its encultura-tion and regeneration process, how do we—if ever—come to know deaf-ness, come close to the culture? (Or should we?) Are the rhetorics between Deaf and Hearing—the arguments, and therein the ways of knowing and being in the world—no more or less than those Kuhnian "incommensu-rate paradigms"? If a Deaf person signs in the forest, can we hear her? I believe that these questions of understanding across incommensurate par-adigms particularly plague, even as they paradoxically energize, Deaf "lit-erature." I will return to them at length in the following chapter on sign language poetry.

Revising Rhetoric

Because I believe in Kuhn's incommensurate paradigms, but because I also believe in the possibility for signification—be it in signs or speech—across those spaces, and finally because I also believe that it is rhetoric ("mere" or "all") that makes even as it erases that significant little prefix "in-" when we consider cultural commensuration—I end here(in) with rhetoric. The available means of persuasion uncovered and offered in the coming out of Deaf culture, in relocating a moment like DPN at the center of d/Deaf history, are as qualitatively rich as they are quantitatively numerous.

DPN and the coming out of d/Deaf culture enter on a stage set for "rights" and, like the actors in *Hamlet*, perform a play within the larger play that "by the very cunning of the scene . . . struck so to the soul." The rhetoric of rights fixed DPN in the American consciousness—repeating and capitalizing, as is the American way, on the rhetoric of the civil rights and women's movements as it set the stage further for disability rights, paving the way for the American with Disabilities Act that would come in 1990. In fact, DPN was invoked more than once in the congressional de-bate surrounding the passage of the ADA. In producing what John Chris-tiansen and Sharon Barnartt characterized as a "spiral of mobilization" that "contributed to future such events through its continued symbolic visi-bility," DPN transcends being just a rhetorical situation;[74] not merely the effect of an exigence, it becomes a generative cause as well. And what is further (re-)created is a rhetoric of rights.

Both Owen Wrigley and Lennard Davis, authors of what I believe to be the two most provocative critical works on deafness today, go to the issue of rights and the intersection of deafness in that arena in closing *The Politics of Deafness* and *Enforcing Normalcy.*[75] The rhetoric of rights has undergone some substantial revision in the hands of deafness and on the threshold of Deaf culture's coming out. DPN arrives as part of a rhetorical situation, as an effect of other events, ushered in by exigencies, entering the scene at a point where "rights" have been made part of the daily discourse (part of the common rhetoric of the times) due to precursor movements. But it also *causes* a rhetorical situation in the "rights" arena, engendering exigence in several ways.

First, as Christiansen and Barnartt argue in their account of the effects of DPN, this event substantially reframed disability as a "minority" rather than a "medical" issue. This was necessary for setting up the passage of the ADA: "a new frame had to emerge that viewed persons with disabilities as a minority group, whose members experience discrimination."[76] DPN, as Deaf culture's coming out moment, somehow flipped the rhetorical switch, turned deafness and by extension disability as well into an issue of rights rather than a medically certifiable, pathologically correctable thing that happens to *some* people. This is no small revision: for rights concern us *all.* That key rhetorical move continues to echo throughout the disability rights movement; it is shouted through the pages of the *Disability Rag* (the principal American disabilities-oriented newspaper), murmured throughout the halls of the annual Society for Disability Studies meetings, overheard in the recent development of several national institutes for disability studies—and this very moment it is bubbling even on the lips of some university administrators as those students who have been "righted" by the ADA now are coming to their colleges.

But some things are still hard to speak about. Some rights are still silenced. In lending an ear to the revisionary rhetoric of Deaf culture's coming out, we see (perhaps even hear?) more clearly now the literal injustice of deaf citizens and others who cannot speak for themselves in court, who must be represented through interpreters or, more troubling still, who are virtually alingual, unable to express themselves well in either sign language or spoken English. They remain jailed, literally and figuratively. As Lennard Davis recounts the exemplary story of one Jose Flores, whom he calls in his article in the *Nation* a "prisoner of silence," he meditates on the huge crack in our system of "rights" that swallows a languageless citizen:

"[Flores's] uneasy position is not so quickly made easy because the judicial system [in which, as Davis himself points out, law itself 'is really a highly elaborated form of language'] cannot allow for the idea that it may not be possible to try a whole category of people fairly, and because the Deaf community has largely shied away from its nonlinguistic brothers and sisters, since they represent an otherness to the notion of Deaf people as a linguistic minority."[77] In order to address the rights of citizens like Jose Flores, in order to create a space for his rhetorical body, we will obviously need to continue revising the rhetoric of rights. But how? How do we envision a rhetoric beyond the speaking subject? How can we fit a citizen like Flores into the polis?

As we approach such questions, we will also need to continue on the revisionary path of the rhetoric established by the so-called multicultural agenda. The first and crucial step has been to reenvision deafness, and indeed all disabilities, as something other than a negative, as *not* on the multicultural agenda. Deafness, like disability more generally, is a "difference that matters."[78] But we certainly would not know that from examining any of the multitudinous "multicultural" textbooks, readers, courses, or even entire school programs that have drawn so much positive and negative attention across the American educational scene today. Disability still does not figure here. Likewise, the current academic fetish with "bodies" and "body discourse" makes no place for disability or deafness. This absence speaks ironic volumes; unfortunately, few are listening. How can we tune our rhetoric of multiculturalism to this different frequency?

We need to look at it all differently and employ the powerful can-do rhetoric that, as Kathy Jankowski rightly claims, characterizes "deaf empowerment" in an event like DPN.[79] We might revise our dominant cultural rhetoric—the one driven by the will to speech—to see deafness as insight. We might consider somatically relocating our rhetorical sensibilities to perceive "visual rhetoric" and "visual literacy" such as that presented by sign languages—a move that should not be all that difficult, given our late-twentieth-century immersion in visual culture and media. And finally, we need to take long looks at our own cages of reason. After centuries of being corralled by Plato and his fear of anything but speech, after being so deeply branded by Enlightenment philosophers who rode for the "speech is natural" ranch, how can we run with, rather than chase after, what Wrigley calls the "outlaw ontology" of deafness?

NOTES

1. Amusingly enough, however, my spell-checker does not recognize "audiology" and always suggests that I change it to "ideology."

2. Like most stories, this chapter does not have only one author. In fact, although I have had these ideas in mind for eight years and have expressed them elsewhere (see "Coming Out of Deaf Culture" and "They've Got Power"), I believe this version to be so strongly influenced as to be nearly "coauthored" by three others—Owen Wrigley, Lennard Davis, and James Fredal. It was my recent reading of Wrigley's provocative *Politics of Deafness* that "slightly retold" this particular version of my thinking about contemporary Deaf culture and potential intersections with rhetorical theory, the rhetoric of historiography, and the historiography of rhetoric. It was my reading of Davis's equally provocative *Enforcing Normalcy* that turned my thinking about using rhetoric to read deafness on its head, encouraging me to conceive of ways to use deafness to read rhetoric. My long "collaboration" with my husband, James Fredal, evinces itself most fruitfully here in his shared (and considerable) knowledge of the philosophy of language, the Enlightenment, and rhetorical theory at large. "The will to speech" is principally his brainchild, and I have tried to nurture it well here.

3. For a few recent and powerful mass media examples of the new Deaf culture's visibility in the 1990s, see Edward Dolnick's provocative essay on "Deafness as Culture" in the *Atlantic Monthly;* Russ Rymer's and Lou Ann Walker's front-page reviews of two recent "deafness" books, Cohen's *Train Go Sorry* and Merker's *Listening* in the *New York Times Book Review;* and David L. Wheeler's "Lessons in the Signs" in the *Chronicle of Higher Education.*

4. Goffman, *Stigma,* p. 1.

5. To be sure, there are "differences" between queerness and deafness, between gay culture and Deaf culture, and between gay/lesbian/bisexual individuals and Deaf/deaf/hard-of-hearing/hearing-impaired individuals. As William Connolly so powerfully observes, "The definition of difference is a requirement built into the logic of identity, and the construction of otherness is a temptation that readily insinuates itself into that logic" (*Identity/Difference,* p. 9). Part of my intent in un-queering these two identities by weaving them together is to call into question the often unquestioned "othering" that drives the "logic of identity." While "differences" surely exist, neither "deaf" or "queer" identity constructs (either individually or collectively) are so queer as to be unique, nor unique and thus totally queer.

6. Sedgwick, *Epistemology of the Closet,* p. 11.

7. L. Davis, *Enforcing Normalcy,* p. 4.

8. Wood, "Coherent Identities," p. 1. Wood also cites a colleague, Tina Neuman, in arguing "that the coming-out-as-lesbian process was similar to the coming-out-as-Deaf process" (p. 27).

9. Like Owen Wrigley, I am no believer in the secure monolithic entity of "Deaf culture" nor of the stability of d/Deaf identities, individual or collective; "Deaf identity," writes Wrigley, "and the money in your ATM are connected. Neither is secure" (*Politics of Deafness,* p. 270).

10. These are slogans I have sighted—on bumper stickers, T-shirts in the Gallaudet University bookstore, and even as the title of an international conference in 1989—since DPN in 1988.

11. Certeau, *Writing of History,* p. 11.

12. Christiansen and Barnartt, *Deaf President Now!* p. vii. In *No Pity,* Shapiro calls DPN "the closest the [entire disability rights] movement has come to having a touchstone event, a Selma or a Stonewall" (74).

13. To be sure, DPN is not at the center of attention and imagination of *all* deaf/hard-of-hearing/hearing-impaired persons. In fact, as Carl Zaks, an Ohio State University undergraduate student wrote about "one particularly illuminating conversation about Gallaudet" and "about education and vision" he had with Paul, a twenty-year-old "hearing-impaired" OSU undergraduate student, "I was telling Paul about DPN and the deaf president. He at first thought I was joking him because he thought I was talking about the president of the U.S. But I told him I meant at Gallaudet, and he said that if I had told him that in eighth grade [about the time DPN actually happened!], he wouldn't have believed me. He still seemed surprised when I told him."

14. Certeau, *Writing of History,* p. 3.

15. In an earlier version of this chapter, I had used the common Western metaphor of "voice" where I now place "vision" in this sentence. This is perhaps yet another illustration of how pervasive speech is, how totally *utterance* dominates the Western cultural landscape.

16. Certeau, *Writing of History,* p. 37.

17. The curious "discovery" of deafness in the Enlightenment—when, of course, it had long before existed—is a point that both Owen Wrigley and Lennard Davis dwell on provocatively. For Wrigley, in his critique of "Hearing Deaf history," "the history of the deaf is a 'story of discovery' much like that of Columbus and the 'New' World, in that it was partially a rediscovery, partially a conquest, and most certainly an appropriation" (*Politics of Deafness,* p. 60). This (re)discovery comes from the heads of two prominent eighteenth-century thinkers—"J. G. Herder (1744–1803), who is generally considered the originator of sociolinguistics, or, if one prefers, the key source from which later discussions of the relationship between language and identity flow," and "Abbé de Condillac (1715–80), who studied with John Locke" and "wrote an essay on the origins of language that was taken very seriously during its time" (p. 61). In *Enforcing Normalcy,* Davis makes similar observations about the odd eighteenth-century "origins" and double-serving nature of deafness: "I want to

make the somewhat preposterous suggestion that Europe became deaf during the eighteenth century. . . . I shall argue in a similar vein that deafness became visible in the Enlightenment and thus became the subject of a discourse of treatment by professionals while ironically also becoming symbolic of an aspect of the Enlightenment subject itself" (p. 51).

18. Wrigley, *Politics of Deafness,* p. 93.

19. Ross, "Re-examination of Acculturation and Enculturation."

20. Gannon, *Deaf Heritage,* p. xxi.

21. Wrigley, *Politics of Deafness,* p. 44.

22. Ibid., p. 50.

23. Schein and Stewart, *Language in Motion,* p. 22.

24. Mike, 1 November 1991.

25. Rick, 8 May 1996.

26. Berlin, "Revisionary History," p. 52.

27. Gannon's photo essay, *The Week the World Heard Gallaudet,* chronicles the entire Deaf President Now event; Christiansen and Barnartt's *Deaf President Now!* provides a day-by-day account of DPN and offers assessments as well, addressing the questions "why was this protest successful?" and "what hath DPN wrought?"

28. Ken Glickman puns on much of Deaf culture and sign language, using the form of "sniglets" in *Deafinitions for Signlets* and *More Deafinitions for Signlets.* Even his title is a pun, as his clever play with language ignores and implicitly mocks the usual stigma of "language-deprived" assigned to those with hearing loss. For "zinsered," see *More Deafinitions,* p. 121.

29. I. King Jordan gained early renown in the Deaf community—even though his "late-deafened" status (he did not lose his hearing until an accident at the age of twenty-one) has always caused some cultural concern. Playing perhaps at colonialist undercurrents, Glickman offers the signlet "*King's English*" as "the proper speech and usage of English and what got our beloved King his present job at Gallaudet University" (*More Deafinitions,* p. 66).

    In contrast, the infamy of Jane Spilman at Gallaudet University and in Deaf Culture cannot be underestimated. Humored (quite seriously) in Glickman's *More Deafinitions for Signlets,* she is sketched, broken at the waist on her pedestal, as the example of "*hearo*—n. A Hearie who mistakenly thinks he is out to 'save' Deafies" (p. 56). Likewise, she illustrates the "political jargon" version of "*profoundly hearing*—adj. phr. A term that best describes Ms. Jane Spilman" (p. 87). Her numerous paternalistic insults during DPN earn her the nickname "Mommy Spilman" (p. 73), and she even becomes, by extension, a name given to "any Hearie held responsible for "*paternalispus*—that emotional ooze of disgust that wells up from inside, such as when Deafies in the middle of protesting are told by Mommy Spilman to go home and get a good night's sleep" (p. 81). As such, she is immortalized in a signlet verb meaning "to overthrow"—*unspilmanize* (p. 115).

30.　Giroux, *Schooling and the Struggle for Public Life,* p. 158.

31.　Ong, *Orality and Literacy,* p. 72.

32.　These sociolinguistic pioneers include William C. Stokoe, Ursula Bellugi, Ceil Lucas, Jerome D. Schein, David A. Stewart, Clayton Valli, Sherman Wilcox, and James Woodward. Sociolinguistic and psychological research contributing to the validation of American Sign Language (and in some degrees, all sign languages) began with Stokoe's landmark *Sign Language Structure,* and was significantly aided by his first ASL dictionary (Stokoe, Casterline, and Croneberg, *Dictionary of American Sign Language*). Some recent significant contributions to the "validation" literature are Lucas's collection on *Sociolinguistics in Deaf Communities* (1995), Schein and Stewart's *Language in Motion* (1995), Wilcox's collection *Academic Acceptance of American Sign Language,* and perhaps, too, the *ASL Dictionary on CD-ROM* by HarperCollins Publishers (1994). While video and computer technologies are surely aiding the validation, acceptance, and awareness of sign languages, the classifications by those in charge of dominant discourses matter, too: in 1997, the Modern Language Association finally officially recognized ASL as a "natural" language by moving it out of the "invented" languages (where it stood right next to the "Klingon language") in the *MLA Bibliography* and placing it in the "natural" ones—on par with Spanish, English, and German.

33.　Bitzer, "The Rhetorical Situation," pp. 303–4.

34.　Ibid., p. 302.

35.　Some books and key articles that deal specifically with the thorny issues of deaf education's history are Dolnick, "Deafness as Culture"; Gallaudet, *History of the College for the Deaf;* Gannon, *Deaf Heritage;* R. Johnson, Liddell, and Erting, *Unlocking the Curriculum;* Lane, "Constructions of Deafness" and *Mask of Benevolence;* Mayberry and Wodlinger-Cohen, "After the Revolution"; Moores and Meadow-Orlans, *Educational and Developmental Aspects of Deafness;* Sacks, *Seeing Voices;* Van Cleve, *Deaf History Unveiled;* Winefield, *Never the Twain Shall Meet;* Woodward, *How You Gonna Get to Heaven?;* Wrigley, *Politics of Deafness.* See especially two recent examples of sophisticated critiques that illustrate the no-easy-answers dilemma of deaf education: *Train Go Sorry,* in which Leah Hager Cohen explores the larger linguistic, educational, and cultural issues surrounding deafness by also looking at the past and present of one prominent deaf educational institution, the Lexington School for the Deaf in New York City; and Douglas Baynton's sharp questioning of "the trap of paternalism" in *Forbidden Signs,* suggesting that the differences between "oralism" and "manualism" are not to so significantly different after all.

36. Giroux, *Schooling and the Struggle for Public Life,* p. 152. Freire's *Pedagogy of the Oppressed* might be required reading in any Deaf education or Deaf studies program.

37. Some key texts that do take up the body and *delivery* in addressing the "art of persuasion" are John Bulwer's manual of rhetorical delivery, *Chirologia* (1654); Thomas Sheridan's *Course of Lectures on Elocution* (1762); Gilbert Austin's *Chironomia; or, A Treatise on Rhetorical Delivery . . .* (1806); and more recently, perhaps, the contemporary feminist, performance, and body-centered rhetorics of such authors as Hélène Cixous ("Laugh of the Medusa"), Julia Kristeva ("Women's Time"), Audrey Wick ("Feminist Sophistic Enterprise"), Mary Daly, and Sonja Foss.

38. Wrigley, *Politics of Deafness,* pp. 30–31.

39. Preston, *Mother Father Deaf,* p. 202.

40. All quotations taken from interview with Charlotte, 19 April 1996.

41. Paul, "Final Reply to Harlan Lane," p. 8.

42. Lane, "Is There a Psychology of Deafness," pp. 5, 7.

43. Christiansen and Barnartt, *Deaf President Now!* p. 168.

44. Ibid., p. 169.

45. Padden, *Deaf Children and Literacy,* p. 95.

46. I do not intend here to hint at any essentializing or totalizing position for DPN—to assert that it was somehow the sole instigator of these reversals— but only to indicate that it was a key event in a complex of events that helped raise the consciousness(es), individual and collective, deaf and hearing, that could conceive of such reversals.

47. Bellugi, "How Signs Express," p. 72.

48. These universal similarities and particular differences are the subject of studies by several leading socio- and psycholinguists: Victoria Fromkin (see "Sign Languages") and Ted Supulla and Elissa Newport (see Wheeler, "Lessons in the Signs").

49. Woodward, "Sociolinguistic Research," p. 120. The formal and colloquial forms of signing illustrate yet again how much it is like *all* languages. And indeed, as ASL has gained strength as a language, those at the vanguard of "Deaf culture" (especially in places such as Gallaudet University), including Ben Bahan and M. J. Bienvenu, who are native ASL users, have increasingly used ASL in what might be considered "formal" and academic presentations.

50. Ibid., p. 121.

51. See Hall, "Train-Gone-Sorry," and Wheeler, "Lessons in the Signs," for discussions of the etiquette of sign language.

52. Admittedly, as some members of the Gallaudet Deaf community have made clear to me, in some of his arguments Sacks romanticizes and idealizes ASL; at the same time, many deaf people consider them poignant in their "impressionism." The reader of *Seeing Voices* might keep in mind that Sacks himself is a "hearie," and that his involvement in Deaf culture and interest in Deaf studies and ASL has been recent and fairly marginal.

53. See Sacks, *Seeing Voices,* pp. 87–89, 120–21, 110.

54. Ibid., pp. 46, 89, 118.

55. Ibid., p. 123.

56. For a small sampling of scholars making this claim, see works on the bibliography by Kannapell, Neisser, Padden, Reagan, Trybus, Van Cleve, and Crouch.

57. This "empowerment" through the rhetoric of social movements is the subject of a new and important book by Katherine A. Jankowski, *Deaf Empowerment: Emergence, Struggle, and Rhetoric.* One chapter focuses on rhetorical empowerment in the Deaf President Now protest, and she develops her argument principally through "an examination of the rhetoric of the Gallaudet board of trustees and administration [that] reveal[s] the prevailing ideology of paternalism" (p. 101). While I do not doubt that paternalism dominates much of the discourse surrounding deaf education—a key point for the arguments of Owen Wrigley (*Politics of Deafness*) and Douglas Baynton (*Forbidden Signs*) as well—I have sought instead to examine the rhetoric of deaf education principally through its repeated rhetorical binaries, by considering the categories that continually confine it.

58. Christiansen and Barnartt, *Deaf President Now!* p. 67.

59. Ibid., p. 78.

60. While the shift away from "communication" and toward "language" is a reversal at the hands of the Bi-Bi movement in deaf education, I will argue in the final section of the chapter that the shift to Bi-Bi itself is a revisionary rhetoric.

61. Wrigley, *Politics of Deafness,* pp. 104, 107–8, 109.

62. In the pitting of "deaf" against "Deaf," we might note another repetition: we nearly come back to those Myklebustian "compensatory strategies" that constitute a (bogus) "psychology of deafness."

63. L. Davis, *Enforcing Normalcy,* pp. 101, 104, 112.

64. Ong, *Orality and Literacy,* p. 72.

65. Ironically, in *Orality and Literacy,* Ong calls our age one of "secondary orality"—a tag that has since undergone substantial critical comment.

66. Heath, "Protean Shapes in Literacy Events," p. 350.

67. Wrigley, *Politics of Deafness,* pp. 81, 47.

68. See Pratt, "Arts of the Contact Zone"; Spivak, "Politics of Translation." These are some of the questions that guide my work in chapter 4, "Diagnosing Deafness." They are also the central questions I take up in a work-in-progress not included in this volume, on women, authority, and deafness; it addresses, among other things, the feminist ethics of care and representation in the highly gendered fields of sign language interpreting, audiology, and deaf education.

69. Cynthia, 18 August 1996.

70. I have asked nearly everyone I have met in the Gallaudet community (both deaf and hearing) how one knows if someone is "big 'D' Deaf." The answer given is delivered with quick assurance: "Attitude!" Yet when they are pressed further to define "attitude," that assurance tends to resolve to jaw-jutting arrogance, and I am left with the attitude, again and again, that if I myself don't understand "naturally" what this "attitude" is, well then, it isn't worth explaining to me. This response essentializes "Deafness" further.

71. The dire need for more ethnographically oriented studies of Deaf communities (deaf schools and the like) done from the *insider* perspective, to match and counter all the *outsider* accounts so far written, was a point made strongly by Yerker Andersson—past president of the World Federation of the Deaf, past member of the President's Council on Disability Awareness, and past chair of the recently formed "Deaf Studies" department at Gallaudet—in an interview of 8 May 1996.

72. Cynthia, 18 August 1996.

73. Ibid.

74. See Christiansen and Barnartt, *Deaf President Now!* pp. 213–17.

75. If I were to do an Aristotelian rhetorical analysis here, I might call "rights" a topos, a "commonplace," in the arguments of Davis and Wrigley.

76. Christiansen and Barnartt, *Deaf President Now!* p. 215.

77. L. Davis, "Prisoner of Silence," p. 354.

78. "Differences That Matter" is the title of chapter 6 of Wrigley's *Politics of Deafness.* In this regard, deafness fares far better than "disability" at large in the minds of most Americans. That is, I think most are now far more willing and able to conceive of deafness as "culture" than they are to consider "disability" at large as an issue beyond the direct concern of the medical or welfare systems.

79. See Jankowski, *Deaf Empowerment,* pp. 160–75.

*W*ords Another Way: Of Presence, Vision, Silence, and Politics in Sign Language Poetry

All verbal communication, written as well as spoken, involves a marriage of two elements—sound and sense. This is basic, like saying that all material entities exist in both space and time, but it's a good place to start. Indeed, we can quickly refine upon the premise by saying that all verbal communication is comprised of sound become sense. Whether it was a pressing collective need for sense that originally organized sound (out of a recognition, say, that it was a valuable shorthand for gesture), or whether sound coalesced out of some imperative of its own to make sense, is not certain. But the fact remains that the two elements are almost indissolubly bound in language. I say "almost" because there are moments—moments that I experience most intensely while reading lyric poetry—when the two seem to come apart. I recognize with a shock that these are sounds that are parading before me as meanings and emotions; I realize how thin the wall between meaning and music can get.

—SVEN BIRKERTS, *"Hamann's Bone: A Note on the Language of Poetry"*

Then must we not infer that all these poetical individuals, beginning with Homer, are only imitators, who copy images of virtue and the other themes of their poetry, but have no contact with the truth? The poet is like a painter who, as we have already observed, will make a likeness of a cobbler though he understands nothing of cobbling; and his picture is good enough for those who know no more than he does, and judge only by colors and figures. . . . Come now, and observe this point: The imitator or maker of the image

201

knows nothing, we have said, of true existence; he knows appear-
ances only.

—PLATO, *Republic,* book 10

One way we might ride with the "outlaw ontology" of deafness I referred to
in the preceding chapter—although Plato would certainly not approve—
is through poetry. Let me introduce you to sign language poetry.[1]

It is a poetry that Sven Birkerts, popular commentator on the contemporary art, would undoubtedly be puzzled—if not shocked—by as
well. For here, as we view a sign language poem, although I will grant
that meanings and emotions still parade before us, there is no real "marriage of two elements—sound and sense"; and moreover, rather than
sound becoming "a valuable shorthand for gesture," we might experience
quite the opposite—gestures becoming valuable shorthand for sound. In
this revised experience, the essential elements of Western rhetoric and
culture are remade as well—*presence, "voice," silence,* and *politics* "come
apart" as the poet not only becomes *like* a painter, but *is* the painter in
action.

CLAYTON VALLI'S "DEAF WORLD"

This poem seems sonnetlike, more particularly Petrarchan, in that it contains
what I would call "two stanzas"—one about hearing world experiences with
hearing aids, the other about discovering the deaf world. The first stanza, as in
a true Italian Petrarchan sonnet, sets up a problem (trying to comprehend
sounds with hearing aids), and the second stanza offers a solution (discovering
the Deaf world). The poem also ends with a kind of "couplet," when the poet
(or, in this case, the performer, Jed Galimore) pushes aside both deaf and hearing worlds, questioning how much he is the "same" as either, and choosing,
with a look of satisfaction, to just be himself "in the middle." An English gloss
of the poem might sound like this (with actions, expressions, signs indicated
in parentheses):

(Body turned toward the left.) "I was born in the world, began wearing
hearing aids." (Expression at putting on the aids is one of pain; his body pulls
back a little, as in revulsion and being overpowered. His signs indicate a confusion, slight pain, over the continued *boom, boom, booming* in the ears.) "I listened to music through the hearing aids." (Expression indicates this is okay,
but nothing remarkable.) "I saw movies with my hearing aids." (Eyes are

squinting, trying to concentrate, bring into focus the conversation in the film; he begins to look disgusted, distraught.)

(He turns his body to face the other way, toward the right.) "I entered the deaf world." "I saw rocks, water . . . deaf world . . . all around." (Look of wonder and interest on face, hands at normal chest level.) "I saw deaf trees." (Eyes and signing level now raised to right below shoulder.) "I saw deaf mountains." (Eyes and arms placed up above shoulders, raised again, eyes expressing wonder.) "I saw deaf sky." (Expression of peaceful fascination; signs now at eye level.) "Deaf everything, all around." (Signs and body position moved more toward midchest again and facing forward.)

(Now turns toward right/deaf side.) "Deaf. We are same, you and me." (While this is a statement, he looks a little dubious. Then turns to left/hearing side.) "Same, you and me." (Looks quite dubious now and pain returns to his face. Then his hand pushes, sweeps away the hearing world. He turns to face the right/deaf-world side. His hand pushes aside this world, too. He turns to face the middle. His hand centers on his chest, standing in the middle of the two sides. A look of satisfaction on his face.)

At the conclusion of this poem the explicator, Lon Kuntze, remarks only on the representation of "growing up" indicated through the series of raised hand signs and then says, cryptically, "Indeed, there are different patterns and hidden meanings in the poem that I hope you'll uncover."

Clayton Valli's "Hands"

This poem employs predominantly one basic handshape, the five fingers spread into the number 5. It is typical of sign poetry, particularly that by Clayton Valli, to feature a few basic handshapes or to revolve around a few repeated and sometimes re-created signs. In brief, I would say "Hands" is a simple but profound poem about all the things the hands not only do but can symbolize. The symbol pattern here is the four seasons. "Hands" reminds me of how much of the "best" poetry in even the English language is simple and involves basic "elements"—love, sadness, joy, wind, fire, earth, water, trees, sun, and so forth. I would describe it as follows:

The performer, Claudia Jimenez, begins by caressing her hands in the center space in front of her body. She holds out her hands in the sign HERE—an open palms move—with eyebrows raised (indicating an invitation, an open-ended question, and also "topic" in ASL). She then lifts her hands above her head, with eyebrows still raised, and makes the sign for "water/rain falling"—in S curves down. She moves to sign FLOWER, a flower growing out of the earth, and the hands open up here again, so that the palms are open, as if offering us something. Her hands now move to the sign for "wind blowing," wheat waving in the wind; the flowing S curves come again, but this time they flow side to side. Again, the palms are open and the eyebrows up. Now her hands become a tree, then a single leaf falling from this tree—still with open palms, and the S curve movement repeated as the leaf floats toward the ground. WORLD is signed in a large space (with full movements, going beyond the parameters of everyday signing space), with hands open and eyebrows up. From here she moves to a sign for "emoting" or GIVING-OUT-FROM-SELF—completed with large, emphasized movements. This giving-out movement ends with open hands and upraised, inviting, question-asking eyebrows.

ELLA MAE LENTZ'S "EYE MUSIC"

This poem stylistically features a common technique used in sign folklore—to create a story using letter (*a, b, c*) or number (*1, 2, 3*) signs. Here the numbers used are 1, 2, 3, 4, and 5. They are mostly signed on the horizontal plane with palms flat to the ground (rather than vertically, with palms out and away from the body). "Eye Music" begins with a brief opening in which Lentz tells of how she used to lie in her mother's lap, while traveling in a car, and watch the telephone wires whizz by. This is, she states, an experience common to many children (especially of her generation). The wires, punctuated with telephone poles, reminded her of sheets of music, and she came to think of this experience as her "eye music."

Lentz performs the videotaped poem in black and white with some sepia tones, so the audience seems to be viewing a photograph from the past. The camera shifts slightly (though not abruptly) from viewing her almost top down (from her head down) to straight on, at eye level. Remarkably, you seem to *move* while viewing the poem, as if you yourself are in the car and in the young girl's place on her mother's lap. This effect is created both through the camera and video technology and through Lentz's fast, smooth, flowing movements from one sign to the next. The poem takes but a minute to complete.

Lentz also creates an impression, fittingly, of herself as the conductor of an orchestra as she creates a lyric that is far more sensual than in any way linguistic.

The poem runs at a fast tempo, with feelings of excitement, wonder, and mesmerism. She changes tempos (one might even say that she changes tone, pitch, and volume) and intensity as the telephone wires change speeds and directions—undulating, sometimes flutelike (she signs this instrument), punctuated by the drums of telephone poles (again, this instrument is signed). All this is indicated with merely the signs for the numbers 1 to 5.

The upbeat tone throughout the poem indicates the child's peace and joy in this experience. At the end, the pace slows a bit, and she ends questioning where all the lines have gone. Poked in tubes? Her face puckering. A questioning. Slight frustration. Eyes squinted. "Where?"

FLYING WORDS PROJECT'S "I AM ORDERED NOW TO TALK"

Before signing this poem, Peter Cook, the deaf poet-performer, tells a brief story about becoming deaf at the age of three from spinal meningitis. For a long time, he thought everything and everyone else's voice was "broken"— the dog, his parents, the TV. Then one day he realized that it was *himself* that was broken. His parents sent him to the Clarke School (a famous oral institution) so that he could learn to talk and "fit into the hearing world better." He was not allowed to sign there—they slapped his hands if he did. He learned how to speak and lipread. But, as he signs, "*Bat* and *cat* look the same on the lips. So, they try to teach you the noise through vibrations as well. You have to practice. Over and over and over again." He ends by saying that he didn't learn sign language until he was nineteen years old.

At this point, Kenny Lerner, Cook's hearing interpreter-collaborator, asks for the house lights on. He explains, too, that Peter is going to sign something to the deaf people in the audience only (without Kenny to voice-interpret) and that "he will be focusing on hearing people. So, please, feel paranoid." The (hearing) audience laughs nervously. Peter Cook explains that he will be voicing, not signing in this poem—and that it is for the sake of the poem itself that he will do this. (It is not well-accepted in Deaf culture to voice at all, let alone voice without signing.)

Kenny then explains that they have distributed a poem, in writing, among the audience. This is the poem they will perform:

"So, please," Kenny says, "read along in your program book." Kenny and Peter separate to the two sides of the stage. Spotlights are on both of them. Peter begins voicing (without signing) and Kenny begins signing (without voicing). Peter stands, near motionless, with his hands by his side in the beginning of the performance. His voice is loud, monotone, wooden, "unnatural," nearly unintelligible. Kenny's signs are a bit stiff and exaggerated as well.

The poem that is spoken is the same as the one written in the program book:

I Am Ordered Now to Talk

I
here
on
wood plane with cold nails
front
of
red fake suns
well, you know
my eyes heard
with plastic smile, they said:
you
must
now
talk

the baby will cry without a tear
dried tonsil glued to
pink palate
tried to tell that a speech freako!

you
must
now
talk

freako gave me mike
plus howdy doody blast box
plug to my karma; angry at me
because I bought my lifebook for 5¢

you
must
now
talk

don't stare at me
I was on that cold metal table
that speech freako wants me
as example for the society
rip my brains with
peanuts buttered spoon
scream with blackboard trick:

B IS NOT P
D IS NOT T
S IS NOT Z

eyes fall over chair
why
that freako can't lipread a mirror

you
must
now
talk

for the sake of ma bell
nail my feet in this space
rammed my press release
to tell you

I
am
ordered
now
to
talk

In delivering this poem, Peter strongly emphasizes each refrain: "*You must now talk.*" At one point in the performance Peter and Kenny come together—with Kenny standing directly behind Peter—and mimic the popular "deaf ventriloquist act," as Kenny becomes Peter's arms (and thus, his embodied voice as well). This occurs at "that speech freako wants me / as example for the society" and continues until "for the sake of ma bell." Appropriately, this is the speech-training part of the poem: a hegemonic moment, when Kenny (the hearing man who is now signing) becomes the hearing doctors with their hands above the deaf child's head, ripping out his brain, reaching inside of him, becoming his "voice" (his arms here) to show him the difference between *D* and *T, S* and *Z.*

Ironically enough, this physical togetherness is the point in the poem when the performers seem to convey their words with the most intellectual and sensual clarity. Symbolically, too, the discourse emanates from the deaf person, Peter Cook, and the hearing person stands behind him, supporting him.

Then they separate again, and finish the poem. By the last "I am ordered now to talk," Peter's voice is dramatically strained, emphasized, painful—the "talk" stretches on, tense and loud.

Flying Words Project's "Poetry around the World"

This poem employs a poetic technique that Cook and Lerner call "transformations," in which one sign transforms subtly into another. Transformations, in fact, tend to form the entirety of this poem. Here I will only offer brief words and phrases to catalog the experiences and transformative metaphors of the poem-performance. Actual signs are in small caps. "Poetry around the World," is, in essence, one transformative string of metaphors, all fused with each other. It looks like this:

The "new" sign for POEM opens the performance (the hand throwing out things from the area of the heart) and gradually Cook begins to add in the plosive "p" as he repeats the sign for "poem"—as if performing this for an oral school exercise. Each "p" gains slightly in volume and explosiveness over the last. Speed also increases. This "p" sound with the sign POEM popped out from his chest is repeated eight times and has an effect and rhythm similar to a train gathering speed. There is a big smile on Cook's face.

The sign POEM transforms into GUN and this gun is moved all around, primarily in circular movements around Cook's body. Lerner voices: "Poetry is shot . . . orbiting, circling, revolving . . . exploding. It can open a window." And here the sign becomes WINDOW OPENING. (And from henceforth I will drop Lerner's voicing, which is minimal, and catalog only the sign transformations.)

SMOKE. SMOKING. FLAMES. FIRE. POPCORN. TASTES TERRIFIC. Back to POEM again, this time done with two hands throwing it out right and left, still a big smile on his face. PAINTER. PORTRAIT. (Here Cook has lots of fun, making the audience laugh, while he impersonates a painter, making brush strokes with varying enthusiasm on a canvas. And then, finally, painting himself.)

PAINTBRUSH turns back to GUN. And the gun brushes across him (like a paintbrush) each way. The FRAME-OF-THE-PAINTING is represented and this frame opens up, closes down, almost squishes him. From the closed-up hands of the box/frame closed almost in on itself, the sign is transformed into BUTTERFLY. It flits all around. He watches it with wonder. It lands playfully on his head. He swats it off and the hand transforms into a CANDLE. Then a LEAF-FALLING-FROM-A-TREE. Then the leaf transforms into a RIVER.

River flows back to POEM again. Repeated a few times, it then erupts into a MUSHROOM CLOUD, the NUCLEAR WIND, BLOWING, MELTING.

Suddenly, lights go off on stage. We have only Cook and Lerner's four arms and hands, blacklighted. The arms in black light perform numerous synecdochic representations: beating out various rhythms, approximating couplets and then stanzas, looking like rhyme, circling against and then with each other, punctuating each other, forming faces—some funny, some eerie—watching you, then staring even, eyes popping out of the face. The end.

In this chapter I draw parallels between (even paint) the arts of poetry and rhetoric by situating them both in Deaf culture. I would like to extend the "reach of poetry" a little further than does Albert Cook in his book of that title. There Cook seeks to "test [poetry's] 'reach' through the pressure that some poets have been able to put on the condition of their utterance and thus to attain a further range of expression."[2] The pressure sign language poetry exerts on our conceptual limits for poetic utterance, the way it furthers the range of expression for *both* Hearing and Deaf cultures, and the way it allows us to listen to and thus ride with the outlaw deafness are my stances in this chapter. As stances, though, they hardly stand still.

Rhetoric has long made clear that everything is about the stance we take—and the stance we change. Cook begins his second chapter, "The Stance of Modern Poetry," by arguing that "modern poetry establishes, like all poetry, an intimate communication that depends on the suspension of some conversational and logical rules, though it can reinvoke those rules in its own chosen ground of merely virtual utterance."[3] These conversational and logical rules, which I might simply call "rhetorical rules," their suspension, the role of "intimate communication," and the way that sign language poetry "reinvoke[s] those rules in its own chosen ground of merely virtual utterance" mark the center of my considerations about sign language poetry. To chart these considerations I will illustrate how sign language poetry intersects with the Western rhetorical tradition.

But first, I need to briefly chart a history of rhetoric and poetics. The history of rhetoric and poetics go back a long way together. Plato had to ban not only rhetoric but also poetics from his ideal republic, since they both were only cheap imitators of the Truth; of even greater concern to him, they were often deliberate falsifiers—arts of appearances only. Aristotle wrote treatises both on the art of rhetoric and on poetics, and issues of one come up in treating the other. In the mid–sixteenth century, Peter Ramus rather infamously truncated the venerable five-part canon of rhetoric (invention, arrangement, style, memory, delivery) and placed sole importance on style alone. Poetics was, to be sure, part of this "style." In fact, its identification with rhetorical style increased in the seventeenth century when Francis Bacon divided the human intellect into the five "faculties" of memory, imagination, reason, will, and intellect. While experimental science and inductive reasoning, which became all the rage, largely occupied the faculties of reason and intellect, rhetoric cast its lot more and more with the burgeoning tradition of belles lettres, becoming closely associated with the genres of history, poetry and literary criticism. As Patricia Bizzell and Bruce Herzberg tell us in their commentary in *The Rhetorical Tradition,* by the end of the seventeenth century, "the art of persuasion was thus perfectly consonant with the art of poetry."[4]

By the time Enlightenment philosophers such as the Abbé de Condillac and John Locke finish their quest for the origins of human understanding and a universal grammar—and by the time associational and faculty psychology makes its indelible mark on the rhetorical theories of the eighteenth- and nineteenth-century heavyweights Hugh Blair, George Campbell, and Richard Whately—these two, poetry and persuasion, are so consonant as to be practically interchangeable. In rhetorical theory at the turn of this century, metaphor and the art of making associations ruled the day—we could look to Alexander Bain, Friedrich Nietzsche, and Gertrude Buck for examples of this. And if we look on into the twentieth century, we would be allowed to conflate poetry and persuasion even further. We might find them joined, for example, in Kenneth Burke's concepts of *consubstantiality* and *identification;* empowered in Chaim Perelman's establishment of *presence* as the central act of persuasion; haunting Jacques Derrida's theoretical *metaphysics of presence* and its deferral of meaning; swinging with Henry Louis Gates's trope-toting trickster of the (human) jungle, the "signifyin[g] monkey"; or embodied in Hélène Cixous's woman writing her own body and "invent[ing] the impregnable language that will wreck partitions, classes, and rhetoric, regulations and codes."[5]

Poetry has almost always maintained, even as it has often tried to refrain from, an element of politics and rhetoric. Though Keats might have voiced the ideal (spoken through the Grecian urn, no less) that " 'Beauty is truth, truth beauty,'—that is all / Ye know on earth, and all ye need to know," the truth is that poetry has a long rhetorical tradition that intersects with and indeed sometimes overpowers its aesthetic one. Nor is this just a postmodern phenomenon. Critical scholarship conducted on nearly every period and school of poetry includes discussion of poetics, the aesthetic appeal of language poetically represented, *and* consideration of the period's politics as it plays out, sometimes not only in the subject of the poems but in their very style (meter, metaphor, symbolism, line scansion, etc.) as well.[6]

Even among the sign language poetry I feature throughout this chapter—the work of Ella Mae Lentz, Clayton Valli, and Flying Words Project—the strains of rhetoric and aesthetics variously intertwine, supersede, circumvent, and complement each other. To be sure, the five poems on which I focus are quite rhetorical, putting the politics of deafness at their center. But they are also aesthetic—crafted carefully, they appeal strongly to our intellect, senses, and emotions. And sometimes, too, as we will see, their aesthetic appeals are enhanced, if not indeed governed, by their political points. It is not easy to separate out rhetoric and aesthetics in this poetry, or in the poetry of any other period, language, or school. Moreover, I do not know why it would be necessary to make such a separation, even if it could be neatly done.

Still. Never standing still, I would mention a few of the more "aesthetic" pieces by these authors, if only to also make the point that their work is not entirely, overtly rhetorical. Lentz, for example, opens *The Treasure* with two renditions of an early poem, "Travels with Malz." The poem in itself is hardly political. It recounts the magic of an inspiring teacher (Malz) weaving a spell, as it were, on his student (the young Lentz). Metaphors of space travel through language are created visually. The tone is one of joy, fascination, elation that approaches exhaustion. The political side of this poem really only enters, for me, when the two versions of it are set side by side: first Lentz performs the poem in its earliest created version—in Signed English—and then she turns to another version in ASL, created later when she "fell in love with sign language" (a crush brought on, in fact, by Malz himself). The differences are stunning. And even the hearing students I have shown these two poems in various of my creative writing classes understand the rhetoric, get the political point being made with the performance of these two versions, side by side. What's more, those hearing students far prefer the ASL version, in which they find the poet far more "engaged, energized, expressive," noting that the craft seems more careful there and that the "stiffness and solemnity" of the Signed English version have been worked out.

Lentz has other more purely though not solely aesthetic poems on this video: her celebratory poem created for her brother's wedding, "Circle of Life," is arguably one of those, where the circular movement in many signs is featured as the trope that moves the poem; so, too, is "Silence, Oh Painful," a poem about the end of one of her own relationships, where space creates the sense of silence, perhaps more aesthetic than it is political. (But presenting an alternative view of what "silence" is is arguably a rhetorically motivated deaf world trope, too.) Even the poem I have chosen to feature in this chapter, "Eye Music," might be placed somewhere on the more aesthetic end of the rhetoric-aesthetic continuum—though of course any such a binary formulation only binds and poorly represents the full range of what poetry can be, can do, *is*. Every hearing student I have shown this poem to—and well over 200 hundred students have seen it thus far, in five different courses of mine—is enraptured with the simplicity, the lyrical unity, the flow and rhythm, the body metaphors, the expressions that occur all in this one-minute performance. It is as if Keats's words, his poetic ideal, are being represented yet another way: an other way that is part of the rhetoric of the poem as well. Other poems on this video are clearly more purely political, though not necessarily any less aesthetic. For example, we might look to "The Dogs," a poem in which Lentz treats the cultural infighting among d/Deaf persons through metaphor, or "The Children's Garden," in which the richness of a kindergarten experience—even for a deaf child—becomes the point.

I could make these same observations about Clayton Valli and Flying Words Project; I could, argue, too, that in general I find Valli's poetry less political than Lentz's and both of those less political than the works of

Flying Words Project. But again, I'm not convinced that such simple comparisons—more or less, A or B—in discussing the richness of their performances would do any of them (or myself, either) justice. More fruitful, more "truthful," would be to write about the interplay of rhetoric and aesthetics in sign language poetry. I could easily complete an entire book on that subject.[7] In what follows here, I am concerned with the case of poetry not as a purely rhetorical or aesthetic enterprise, but as both at once. Rhetoric's rule has always been, from at least Aristotle forward, as an "art" aimed at both convincing and pleasing, involved in both an intellectual and imaginative venture.[8] That is the rule I follow.

EMPOWERING PRESENCE

Instructing and pleasing, convincing and enchanting, reaching for both intellect and imagination—all are ways, Chaim Perelman would argue, that a rhetor might seek to create *presence,* perhaps the foremost goal of any rhetorical act. Sign language poetry (called "sign poetry" hereafter) maintains a presence—an emphasis on immanence, audience participation, and embodied performance—recalling the days of Greek and Roman rhetoric and oratorical arts; this is a presence that postmodern poetry often aches for but cannot achieve. In one of his many lists from the 1970s of features of modernist and postmodernist art, Ihab Hassan discusses how it is that to be *present* as a postmodern poet is to participate communally in "antielitism, antiauthoritarianism," to become "anarchic."[9] We see these anarchic acts in both the Flying Words Project poem "I Am Ordered Now to Talk" and the Clayton Valli rendition of "Deaf World": the authority of the hearing word is defied, as the elitism of hearing aids and speech training is overthrown, literally pushed aside in the closing signs of "Deaf World" and mocked in the inarticulate voice of the arduously speech-trained "victim" in "I Am Ordered Now to Talk."

In fact, so strong is the antiauthority of deaf poet Peter Cook in "I Am Ordered Now to Talk" that his collaborator-interpreter, Kenny Lerner, claims: "Really that piece is all Peter. I didn't have much to do with it." Lerner goes on to explain the anarchic effect of the poem:

> There is the obvious and eerie feeling you get when you see this incredible performer swim in his own language like a fish through water. In "I

am Ordered . . . " he is beached! I think that piece is a good example of form = content. He is saying, you're making me talk and I don't do it well. Again, we try to show things in this case with Peter's voice [which is nearly unintelligible here]. But he also literally says it too. I think this piece exposes a great deal of cruelty that people can inflict on others without really trying. Peter helped me create the signed interpretation and I always thought it was interesting because I can't sign like he can . . . and he can't voice like I can.[10]

Thus both poets—deaf Peter Cook and hearing Kenny Lerner—take stances counter to their "true" selves in order to take a stance on language oppression.[11] Similarly, the narrator in Valli's "Deaf World" rejects both deaf and hearing worldviews and sways between them, finally taking a stance that is both and neither of the rejected ones—becoming, in the end, the "me" in the center that pushes aside those other two (partial) views. To be present in postmodern poetry is also, according to Hassan's dated but still remarkably relevant dictum, to take such a performative stance while also being steeped in "simultaneism, now, the impermanence of art."[12] We have just such a sense of that both/and positioning, present but impermanent, in these two poems.

To be both present but impermanent requires what Hassan and Charles Altieri call *immanence,* the state, according to Altieri, "in which man is as much object as he is agent of creativity," present both in his own ongoing performance and in his audience's participation of/in his work.[13] We see the double stance of artist as object and agent in both "I Am Ordered Now to Talk" and "Deaf World"; additionally, it appears in Flying Words Project's "Poetry around the World" and Claudia Jimenez's version of Clayton Valli's "Hands." In all sign poetry or performances, presence and impermanence stand side by side as embodied language presents itself even as it is "erased" in its oral-like, nonprinted tracings. What distinguishes one sign from another in sign language is the place where it is made (location), the distinct configuration of the hands in making the sign (handshape), and the action of the hands, face, and body (movement direction and expression).[14] As Oliver Sacks has made impressionistically clear in his best-selling book *Seeing Voices: A Journey into the World of the Deaf,* Sign—his term for all sign languages—is the only language that incorporates "the unique linguistic use of space[,] . . . a use that is amazingly complex, for much of what occurs linearly, sequentially, temporally in speech [and, of course, in writing], becomes simultaneous, concurrent, multileveled in Sign."[15] It is this complex and unique use of space in sign language—of participatory, performative presence communicated silently and predominantly through images that are "simultaneous, concurrent, multileveled"—that makes sign poetry so powerfully and particularly present.

Much postmodern poetry privileges *place* and *presence,* repeatedly "calls for participation far more than for interpretation," and persistently values "creative activity," "creative energy," and the "embodied process of the energies of recognition."[16] This emphasis on presence, participation, performance, immanence, activity, embodied energy, and creation, juxtaposed against sheer objectification, arises in large part from poet-critic Charles Olson's well-known essay *Projective Verse.* Olson begins that essay lamenting the dominance of " 'closed' verse, that verse which print bred and which is pretty much what we have had, in English and American poetry, and have still got, despite the work of Pound and Williams." Olson offers instead something he calls "projective verse"—poetry centered "on the *kinetics* of the thing" (his emphasis), poetry that is "a high-energy construct and, at all points, an energy-discharge."[17]

His vision of such projective, process-oriented, energized poetry essentially takes form in sign poetry. A d/Deaf poet—always present, performing, participating with his audience (i.e., always immanent)—becomes both the object and agent of creation; the d/Deaf poet, in using uniquely spatial sign language, always occupies an embodied space and place in the permanent, but yet impermanent, present-tense here-and-now; the d/Deaf poet always embodies her language, her culture, and her self. "One can have or imagine disembodied speech," writes Sacks, "but one cannot have disembodied Sign."[18]

In the first two poems already discussed—"I Am Ordered Now to Talk" and "Deaf World"—presence and impermanence exist simultaneously in the taking of sociopolitical stances about matters that matter for Deaf culture (issues of hearing aids and intensive oral training in place of sign language immersion and instruction), even as those two concepts literally occupy two spaces/places. This double occupation occurs, for example, when the singular poet switches angles and body positions three times over (in Valli's "Deaf World"); more obviously, it occurs in the interplay of the dual poets of Flying Words Project. As already described above, in "I Am Ordered" they first stand in separate spotlights as the deaf one voices (rather ineffectively) and the hearing one signs (also rather ineffectively); then they momentarily merge in an act of deaf ventriloquism, as one becomes the arms of the other; then they split again into separate, linguistically differing entities.[19]

The play of presence and impermanence as the poet-performer melds roles of object and agent comes in numerous places in the transformational extravaganza that is Flying Words Project's "Poetry around the World." But perhaps most remarkable to me are the scenes when the poet is both "the painter and the portrait," painting (and transforming) both the canvas, then self, then self into canvas, canvas into self, canvas into object drawn, self into that object, object back to canvas . . . a breathtaking whirl of being and becoming where indeed, as Plato so feared, "the poet is like a painter." More subtly, though certainly not less dramatically, the hands at the center of Clayton Valli's poem "Hands" are doubly the object of the poem (the things that can represent and be represented in the seasons and circle of life) and the agent (in the "giving" of feeling that marks the last "utterance" of the poem). Here the hands offer a presence that often eludes words.

For twentieth-century rhetorician and legal philosopher Chaim Perelman, *presence* foregrounds any argument, opens up the space for persuasion to take place. Adherence to any argument, he argues, is won by creating "presence." Even in contemporary legal argument, Perelman discovered, this is done principally by relying on most of the common Aristotelian topoi (commonplaces) for the invention of all the available means of persuasion. The goal of establishing presence—indeed the goal of argument itself—is "a meeting of minds: the will on the part of the orator to persuade and not to compel or command, and a disposition on the part of the audience to listen. Such mutual goodwill must not only be general but must also apply to the particular question at issue."[20]

Sign poetry, as a developing genre in a culture just "coming out," needed to engage just such goodwill—and to do so generally while also making particular applications to deafness and Deaf culture. That is, it needed to make itself familiar enough to be accepted in the dominant Hearing culture, but strange enough to be interesting and attended to. It began and has continued this presence making—creating strange familiarity and familiar strangeness—by grounding itself in conventional poetic techniques even as it has played with and sometimes defied them. For sign poetry has all the "usual" poetic trappings: rhyme, rhythm, repetition, line breaks, common words/themes, sensual imagery, persona, tone, careful diction, metaphor, symbolism, wordplay, and surely more.

But it often employs these differently. Rhyme and repetition, for example, are often completed by using handshapes that are similar: the handshapes for the numbers 1 to 5 make up most of Lentz's "Eye Music" (and note that five lines compose a musical staff), and the number 5 handshape alone dominates Valli's "Hands"—a poem that also comprises essentially five image patterns (stanzas?). In Valli's "Deaf World" the rhyme and refrain come in the raised arms sequence in which each encountered "deaf world" image rises higher as the boy grows up, uplifted through visual images he can relate to. The whole poem, as we have seen, takes the form of a kind of sonnet.

Rhythm, as any good poet will tell you, comes from our bodies (consider the heartbeat of the iamb); in sign poetry, it is returned to the body. Here the sinuous slow S curves repeated (refrainlike) in "Hands" come to mind, as do the changing paces of the signs in "Poetry around the World"—from the gentle drift and flit of a butterfly to the fluttering, fast flames and popcorn. More examples of embodied rhythm come at the end of this dramatic poem, too, when the sequence in black light focusing on Lerner and Cook's four arms and hands alone takes place: couplets of arms revolving in parallel circles, four-line stanzas of arms all related to each other, punctuation marks with arms and hands.

In this eerie but fascinating closing sequence with the audience in the dark, the arms of Flying Words Project form faces, eyeballs, and eyebrows. Such conventional figures as image, metaphor, symbol, and synecdoche fly throughout sign poetry: the hands themselves, for example, standing in for so much in "Hands"; the raised-arms sequence in "Deaf World" representing growing up, celebration, wonder; the image of "nailing" and of one person becoming the voice or body of another in "I Am Ordered Now to Talk"; the drumbeat of telephone poles in "Eye Music."

Irony, tone, and personas abound in this poetry, too. They live and breathe, embodied as they are in the inarticulate articulations of Peter Cook ordered to talk; in a young deaf girl choosing telephone wires as her "Eye Music" (if only A. G. Bell could see this); and in a young deaf child turning from the aided hearing world, away from music and movies, to the awe of a more "natural" deaf world, where the images are indeed of nature—rocks, trees, mountains, sky. I could go on; for practically every element that we know "makes" a poem, sign poetry offers an analog, an interface, a parallel.

These parallels have carried sign poetry a long way toward the *presence* it needed to establish itself as a viable literary form in both Deaf and Hearing worlds. The three d/Deaf poets I focus on in this chapter—Clayton Valli, Ella Mae Lentz, and Peter Cook—have themselves all explained the existence and effect of these conventional poetic elements and techniques in sign language poetry. They do this often when they perform, in between the actual poem-performances. Valli, in fact, has devoted his entire doctoral dissertation to such explanations. More recently, he helped develop an authoritative instructional videotape that features several dozen of his own poems; signed often by others, of all ages and races, they are then explicated by a narrator (whose signing is voice-interpreted) and repeated again in slow-motion sequences with directional captioning to point out the various poetic and visual features of the poems.[21]

But what carries the presence of sign poetry even further and more strongly, I believe, is its unique presence—particularly how it adds the dimension of space and the embodiment of language—among literatures at large. Space is everything in a sign poem. It is the spatial dimension of sign language that allows Flying Words Project to *enact* couplets, stanzas, punctuation, and varying rhythms and to overlay both bodies and "voices" in a visual ventriloquism of other speaking for other. It is space that brings to life the symphony of telephone wires and punctuating poles "heard" simultaneously in "Eye Music." And space creates the stage for Flying Words Project's technique of "transformations"—one sign-metaphor-symbol literally metamorphosing into another, in a way that would be confusing, if not unintelligible, if it were tried with printed or spoken words. And it is space that spins the sinuous flow from season to season in the hands of Valli's "Hands" poem. In signing space, images come to life—and not just figuratively.

The "Voice" of "Vision"

While the rhetorical tradition, from at least Plato forward, has had to deal with the problem of disembodied voices in both oral and written expression, sign language asks us to consider the tradition from a quite different angle—that of de-voiced bodies. Here, I will use that approach to extend the reach of Paul Zumthor's *Oral Poetry,* which begins, ironically enough for my purposes, with a consideration of the "presence of voice." Sign language—and thus sign poetry, too—complicates this presence. For while sign language has often been paradoxically designated as an "oral" language—because it has no written form, because it takes place in the present-tense interaction of two or more bodies face-to-face—it is also recognized as anti-oral (or beyond oral?) in its visual nature. Oliver Sacks is again useful here: "The distinctiveness of the language [ASL], its 'character,' is biological as well, for it is rooted in gesture, in iconicity, in a radical visuality, which sets it apart from any spoken tongue."[22]

For deaf people and their sign poetry, then, vision *is* voice: without image, without iconicity, the Deaf might have no language; in a saying popular in Deaf culture, the sign for "listen" is placed in front of the eyes to signify "I listen with my eyes." And image and iconicity, perhaps best known to those of us who use the English language through William Carlos Williams's dictum "No ideas but in things," stands central to most twentieth-century poetry as well. Finally and certainly, the image occupies significant space in the rhetorical tradition: Aristotle himself names "bringing before the eyes" as a very important rhetorical skill for an orator, and this evocation of metaphor and image courses vibrantly through the tradition thereafter; Chaim Perelman's establishment of *presence* is simply one tributary.

Marie Harris and Kathleen Aguero, in the preface to their collection *A Gift of Tongues: Critical Challenges in Contemporary American Poetry*, claim that "it is the poet's gift to communicate across boundaries created by class and culture."[23] The image offers that gift: the image, as Allen Ginsberg claimed in a 1984 visit to the National Technical Institute for the Deaf (NTID) in Rochester, is what can be translated across time and cultures.[24] Furthermore, according again to critic Charles Altieri, the translation of images is "the most important way in which the postmoderns try to capture the prehensive energy of other cultures."[25] In these views, then, the image opens up translation and communication between cultures.

Image works much the same way in sign poetry, constituting what I call "the voice of vision." Ella Mae Lentz foregrounds this potential of the visual image to open up when she prefaces the poems on *The Treasure* with this invitation: "My comments [between poem-performances] will be interpreted; however, the poems will not. Most of the following poems were created in ASL, and do not even have English translations. I want you to experience my poems visually, without sound. Watch. Whether initially you understand them or not, the more you watch them, the more you will understand." And certainly, a poem like her "Eye Music" translates easily even to those whose linguistic world is not predominantly visually processed—we can *see* and understand those telephone wires whizzing, wheeling, and surging by us, punctuated by the drumbeat of telephone poles, building to a crescendo with gathering speed and urban density, slowing and simplifying a bit at stoplights or countryside.

We can also access and understand many of the images kaleidoscoped in Flying Words Project's "Poetry around the World"—a poem that presents a visual cornucopia of sensual images that are indeed translatable across all cultures. Guns firing, planets orbiting, explosions, windows opening, smoke, flames and fire, popcorn popping, painters painting (and being painted), butterflies, candles flickering, leaves falling from trees, rivers flowing, atomic mushroom clouds, nuclear winds, darkness, and hands and arms that *create*—paralleling and punctuating each other, performing in couplets, rhyme, rhythms, making faces, gazing at you, slapping and flying, growing things. In these transformations, one sign flows into and helps create the next. Strange but familiar—the rhetorical power of the image, the solidity and magic of bringing ideas before the eyes is unharnessed in "Poetry around the World."

More simply, though not less effectively, in Claudia Jimenez's performance of Clayton Valli's "Hands" the hands present the seasons, symbolizing experiences and images familiar to many people in many languages; the elements of the poem—water, wind, a tree, a leaf falling—are familiar across cultures: even in places where there is little water or trees, these elements are known. Developing from one basic handshape, for the number 5, the poem begins with the caressing of hands in the center space in front of the poet's body, then transfers into a series of flowing images for each season—water/rain falling in S curves down and then flowers growing up (spring); wind blowing in S curves sideways and wheat waving in the wind (summer); a leaf falling gently, again in S curves, down from a tree (autumn); and the final well-understood gesture of "giving," signed in a large movement out from the heart and leaving the hands open, ready to receive. Whether Deaf world or Hearing world—we understand these signs.

For the poets that participated in the first-ever official sign poetry workshop at the NTID in 1984, the poetics of space, the solidity of the image, and the image's ability to "interface" self and society, culture and culture, stood at the center of the event.[26] The deaf poets there suggested that the visual image builds a more concrete bridge between a general "audience" and the poet's particular "voice" or style. (And again, building such bridges to an audience through one's style is at the heart of rhetorical theory and practice.) Those bridges were built primarily through sign language's iconicity. As Jim Cohn, a poet and researcher studying Native American sign languages and poetry, claims in his article summarizing the 1984 workshops at NTID, "universality was the heart of the issue." One poet at the workshop, in fact, expressed the desire "to show something visually so that everyone could understand me, whether or not they were deaf. I can tell you through my performance, my actions, what's in my heart, my mind . . . that's international, anyone will understand that."[27]

The power of the image—the voice of vision—stands behind the success of Ella Mae Lentz, Clayton Valli, and Flying Words Project; they have all sought, in their live performances and published videos, to make their work accessible to both deaf and hearing worldviews and cultures. Sign poetry has a remarkable capacity to be both universal and particular—largely because of its use of imagery represented by the human body, its derivation from bodily experience, and its incorporation of facial expressions.[28] In simultaneously occupying particulars and universals it rhetorically instructs and yet aesthetically pleases both deaf and hearing audiences, and everyone in between. Again universally and particularly, it dabbles in at least three "arts": mime, as a performative act without words; "oral" performance, in that it occupies the present tense and takes a stance; and "written" poetry, since it plays with language in many of the same ways and with traditional poetic devices. In taking such a triple stance—as mime, oral performance, and poetry per se—sign poetry further blends aesthetics with rhetoric, universal with particular, mind with body.

Take one stunning example: the image's potential to be both mime and language, to universalize even as it particularizes, stands behind Kenny Lerner's chosen style of "interpreting" Peter Cook's performance. Cook tells me he began doing ASL poems with "The Birdbrain Society"—an "underground group at NTID" that "did not know that was a form of literature at that time." His initial solo performances were mostly, he claims, "signed translation of other people's works such as Ginsberg," and they tended to "focus on the Beat Generation poets because of [their] flexibility with hard and clear pictures."[29] Later, when Jim Cohn linked Peter Cook up with Kenny Lerner, Lerner developed a style of interpreting—in conjunction with Cook—that foregrounds the visual image over the sound (or "voice") of the poem or poet. This is a strategy that would surely shock critics like Sven Birkerts, for whom the two elements "indissolubly bound" in language—though pulled apart in poetry—are sound and sense. It is also an interpreting strategy that still sometimes gets Lerner into trouble as a violation of "the interpreter's code of ethics":

> I did not want to distract the hearing audience with my voice. So if there was an obvious picture presented, if I thought the hearing audience could understand something without me saying a word, I shut up. In fact, it became my goal to shut up as much as possible and let the audience see the art for themselves. I didn't want them relying so much on my voice that they would miss the pictures Peter created. I caught a lot of flack from the interpreter community here in Rochester [at NTID]. They were trained to voice everything in a normal setting, and so they expected me to voice everything in this performance setting.[30]

The particular brand of performance-interpretation developed by Flying Words Project sets the image flying free, quite dissolubly unbound by voice or sound. Perhaps turning our Western rhetorical notions of poetic images supporting the words we say or write on its head, Lerner claims that "the point of voicing for me is to support the image," because "Peter is awesome at what he does. I simply want the hearing audience to see the images for themselves. If I voice too much, the audience will rely on me and not see the images [so strong is the attraction between sound and sense]. Yet if I don't voice enough, they get lost. So my goal is to voice just enough so that they will see the image for themselves."[31] Lerner also articulates how important it is that his "voice matches the rhythm of Peter's signing." Thus, again, the concepts and practice of *voice* and *vision* are joined even in rhythm.

As a rhetorician who has lately, primarily because of work with sign language poetry, taken a strong interest in the elocutionary movement in rhetoric that sought to again make gestures, body positions, and voice qualities prominent in rhetorical theory in the seventeenth and eighteenth centuries, I find this reversed and revisionary relationship between sound/voice and vision/image, in which the two are overlaid and interplayed, most interesting. I think of how three of these sign poems—"I Am Ordered Now to Talk," "Deaf World," and "Eye Music"—all turn on the concept of "voice" and hearing even as they rivet us with visual and other sensory images and a sense of bodily comfort and space. In all three, the issue of one's comfort with self, position, and language is crucial.

For example, in Flying Words Project's "I Am Ordered Now to Talk" we have the image of two bodies working separately, then as one, then separately again—bodies blended then sifted, overlaid and interplayed—and we have, among others, the strong and uncomfortable images of being "nailed" (Christ-like) and of "talk" as something exaggerated, even ridiculously distorted. In Valli's "Deaf World" the frustration, told on the face, of trying to "hear" the world is juxtaposed (by switching body directions and orientation in space) with the wonder, again told on the face, of discovering "deaf water," "deaf forest," "deaf mountains," "deaf sky," even as the raising of the arms during these discoveries multiply conveys growing up, coming of age, and a sort of exaltation, as well as a fair amount of discomfort.[32] And finally, Lentz's "Eye Music" parallels a powerful hearing-world experience—that of music—with the visual attentiveness of a young deaf girl (even though the experience of being mesmerized by telephone wires is, as Lentz suggests, quite common for many of us around the world).

Lentz prefaces this provocative but simple poem with this analogy:

> Many of you probably share this experience. My family liked to take long trips by car. I loved to curl up in my mother's lap, look out the window, and see the telephone wires go by. I enjoyed watching the wires rise and fall. This was my music. Some years later, I came across the phrase "eye music." I liked it. It reminded me of the telephone wires; they were like lines on music sheets. The way the wires moved past me, I imagined them to be like the high notes of the flute. And the telephone poles punctuated the movement like the constant beat of drums.[33]

Yet a cross-cultural experience such as this also manifests the power of the image—as every rhetorician knows—to do more than translate across cultures: it also helps achieve solidarity within a culture, as Paul Lauter argues in "Class, Caste, and Canon." Even as the voice of the image helps make possible international communication, it also further invigorates and binds members of the home culture. Thus, "hands" portraying the seasons, telephone wires becoming music, hearing aids, careful (and painfully hard) pronunciation lessons, hearing someone speak but not quite getting what they are saying, and a poem as a nuclear bomb or a butterfly are all familiar enough to approach the "universal"; but even more than their universalizing possibilities, the image-experiences of these poems, in their very visual saturation, are markedly Deaf world ones. In their particularity, they create solidarity between the deaf poet and his or her deaf audience; and then, by extension, they increase the reach of solidarity between deaf members of that audience.

Community forms, and with it, pride. And with that pride comes more creativity and desire to play with one's language, to cultivate one's culture. Peter Cook of Flying Words Project explains that process and his role in it:

> Most of my works are not related to Deaf culture or deafness[;] . . . the works can be easily symbolized for any cultural group that experiences paternalistic oppression. The audience can decide for themselves. I do not force them to focus on my issues. I rather let them think about it and compare with their experiences. When I work with Kenny, our main subject isn't about Deafness. We want to go beyond that. *I believe that myself as a Deaf person who is playing with the language is a good example for the Deaf community. Deaf person who can create stories or poetry holds a powerful place—a powerful voice. The Deaf community looks at them highly because they use ASL (the strongest product of Deaf culture) as a weapon or tool for building self-esteem, pride, strengths, and independence in the community.*[34] (my emphasis)

The deaf poet creating and performing sign poetry is not just the "voice" of his or her own deafness or Deaf community, but the "vision" of it as well. And because of how these poets overlay voice and vision through the image, they can also provide the vision of communities and cultures beyond Deaf ones. They refreshingly revise the traditional Western wedding of sound and sense in their embodied, multisensory performances.

The Signification of "Silence"

Sign poetry and deaf poets also revise our traditional signification for silence. A deaf scholar, Carol Padden, explains that "to hearing people the metaphor of silence portrays what they believe to be the dark side of Deaf people, not only an inability to use sound for human communication, but a failure to know the world directly."[35] This is the "inkling of the sound / of death; not the mere / being without, but the not / knowing, at all" that the contemporary poet Richard Ryan recently has pathologized in "Deafness," dedicated to his deaf sister (quoted as one of the epigraphs for chapter 4).[36] Silence, in Deaf worldview, however, need hardly be the "sound of death" or "being without" or "not knowing at all"; Ella Mae Lentz makes this point in the introduction to one of her poems on *The Treasure.* "Silence, oh painful" is about a failed relationship; Lentz explains the nature of the silence she performs in that poem:

> The world "silence," when associated with deaf people, is interpreted by many as a world absent of sound, a world of loneliness. For me, however, silence means a world absent of communication. We were both fluent signers, we had no problem communicating. Our lives were full of "sound." When our relationship broke off, we were stuck in the same place together for several days, refusing to talk. That was very painful. During that silence, I began to create a poem about our situation. I used space to show the distance between us.

Here space becomes silence; the two are provocatively overlaid and interplayed, like the concepts of voice and vision I have already discussed.

To be sure, the history of rhetoric has long been one of anxiety over silence. Rhetoric has been predicated on the will to speech, as I have repeatedly asserted throughout this book, and it has often been both aware and suspicious of the muteness and mutability of language. Why else would Plato ban poets and rhetoric from his republic? Postmodernism, too, concerns itself with silence—even with the rhetoric of silence. "The art of our time is noisy with appeals for silence," writes Susan Sontag in "The Aesthetics of Silence."[37] And "the poet seeks refuge in muteness," echoes George Steiner in his essay "Silence and the Poet." Drawing (perhaps signing?) on Wittgenstein, Dante, Rimbaud, Keats, and Rilke, Steiner outlines the significant and signifying possibilities for silence in poetry:

1. silence as transcendence;
2. silence as an alternative ("when the words in the city are full of savagery and lies, nothing speaks louder than the unwritten poem");
3. silence as rhetoric, a choice left to the writer "who feels that the condition of language is in question, that the word may be losing something of its humane genius"; and finally, my personal favorite,
4. silence as a rhetorical, alternative transcendence to match our own deafness: "I am asking whether they are not writing too much, whether the deluge of print in which we seek our *deafened* way is not itself a subversion of meaning."[38] (my emphasis).

In her essay on silence, Sontag furthers the possibilities for silence, too. Silence, she argues, may also be transcendence and freedom—the "artist's ultimate otherwordly *gesture* [whereby] he freed himself from servile bondage to the world," or it may propose "termination . . . a zone of meditation, preparation for spiritual ripening, an ordeal that ends in gaining the right to speak" (my emphasis).[39] Thus, silence may lead to speech, that which it has just come out of or turned away from. This collapse of the difference between speech and silence, as speech *is* silence and silence *is* speech, only accentuates the problems of referentiality and signification. For if silence, the absence of speech, can be "a full void, an enriching emptiness, resonating and eloquent," then "silence remains inescapably, a form of speech . . . and an element in a dialogue." "Speech," Sontag makes clear, "can silence, too"; language can both express and create muteness, just as muteness can create and express language.[40]

This muteness and mutability of language characterize some of the work and writing by transnational feminists such as Michele Cliff (on whom I have dwelled as a model in chapter 1), Gloria Anzaldúa, Audre Lorde, and Adrienne Rich. Attention to the slippery and silent, as well as the silencing, potential of language also pervades much postmodern art and criticism (especially postmodern performance art, as I will elucidate shortly). And nowhere is this proverbially postmodern both/and nature regarding the signification of silence more evident than among deaf people—particularly in the hearing world's perception of the deaf and their language (as Padden, Ryan, Lentz, Preston, and Davis helped me illustrate above). But of course, for postmodern and poststructuralist artists and critics, no such direct line between signifier and signified necessarily exists. And thus, the power of silence possibly connects to knowing, to establishing a line between signifier and signified. For both a postmodern and a deaf perspective, then, language exists not only *in* silence, but *with* silence and even *beyond* silence. Sign poetry offers just such a rhetorical, alternative transcendence of the "deluge of print" and, yes, of even our own "deafness" that Steiner describes. Silence—not as the absence of voice but more as the foregrounded presence of body and image—signifies meaningfully, powerfully, uniquely in sign language poetry.

Consider, for example, how silence signifies in the five poems I have focused on in this chapter. Peter Cook points to his own "well-trained" voice that is not exactly "pleasing" to our ears, matched (or not) with Kenny Lerner's less-than-fluid or -aesthetic signing as the two of them, deaf and hearing, switch linguistic and cultural roles. In addition, both voiced and signed versions of the poem somehow fail to match the printed version also provided to the audience—the three versions tend to leave audiences pondering the price of silence, the potential of "voice," the gift of language. And still, the mystery of meaning eludes them as a silence runs steadily through all the cacophonous options offered here in the performance of "I Am Ordered Now to Talk." Those in the audience *hear* but do not catch the full meaning of the poem, struggling to understand the oddity of Cook's wooden and monotone voice; they *see* but likewise do not catch the full effect of Lerner's stiff, signing hands; finally, they *read* the printed version offered them and find that it, too, manages to escape them. The room is filled with the meaning of missed communication, missed oppportunities.

In the other poems, silence— a world beyond the glorified audiocentric one—appears as the preferred option. Thus, silence signifies a *choice*, not a default. In "Deaf World," for example, the poet's face crumples first in pain, then disgust, as he attempts to adjust to the sounds often deemed so "precious" in the hearing world—movies and music only boom annoyingly, even painfully, in the ears of the aided. The hands in "Hands" make the seasonal images full and satisfying enough without sounds; similarly, the young child's vision in Lentz's "Eye Music" finds plenty of comfort in the visual patterns of those telephone wires and the mother's lap. These things—silent in the predominant auditory frame—fill her up quite pleasurably. In the frame of sign poetry, silence seems secure; silence signifies enough.

THE POLITICS OF (SIGNED) PERFORMANCE

In many critical minds (and perhaps artistic ones as well), "performance," politics, and postmodernism function as three interdependent arenas.[41] They certainly do so in sign poetry. Yet even more functionally, even more powerfully, even more significantly, sign poetry—in part because of its empowered presence, overlay of "voice" and "vision," and silent signification—expands the boundaries of each of those three circles even as it reanimates the interactions between them. Sign poetry, like the technique so provocatively perfected by Flying Words Project, *transforms*

1. understandings of what deaf people can do, what deafness can be (individual and cultural identities)
2. limits of what language can do (linguistic parameters)
3. possibilities for what poetry can do and be (artistic/aesthetic genres)
4. potentials for persuasion (rhetorical traditions)

What is more, it effects these four kinds of transformations in two equally important ways: by changing *hearing* (dominant culture) notions of deafness, language, poetry, persuasion and by also changing, among *deaf* persons themselves, the notions of what deafness, language, poetry, and persuasion are, can be and do.

When hearing audiences encounter sign poetry, as often as not their attitudes and ideas about deafness are called into question. This questioning, for example, resonates throughout "I Am Ordered Now to Talk," as the success of oralist practices is mocked with both form and content—Cook, the product of one of the country's premier oral schools for the deaf, the Clarke School, recites his anguish over being "ordered now to talk" as audience members literally strain, on the edge of their seats, to understand his nearly unintelligible voice. In stark contrast, the other poem-performances of the set treat the audience to the sight of Cook—an "incredible performer," in Lerner's words—swimming fluently and fluidly in ASL "like a fish through water." The praise by (hearing) reviewers has been lavish: Cook and Lerner together "dance up there," perform "a theatre held aloft by Language," execute a "high-wire literary act [with] . . . lyricism," and offer "a revelation for both the deaf and hearing members of your audience."[42] Deafness here hardly seems a condition of disability or a pathologized "other" to oral/aural ways of encountering and experiencing the world.

These ascriptions of disability and pathology, common among hearing audiences, are called into question in the works of Clayton Valli and Ella Mae Lentz as well. Again, the child in Lentz's "Eye Music" hardly seems sensorially or linguistically impoverished by her deafness; indeed, she appears gifted with her abilities to experience this "eye music." So, too, the young adult of Valli's "Deaf World" obviously does not enjoy the aided cacophony of music, movies, conversations in the hearing world placed on him; he is just as obviously enthralled—made peaceful and engaged—by the visual deaf world around him. A world of the hands—the one in Valli's "Hands" and Flying Words Project's "Poetry around the World"—also seems complete and articulate enough, if not in fact even fuller than what orality/aurality can offer.

And these dominant hearing worldviews—deafness as disability or pathology—also become visible and questioned when critical reviews of such poetry are attempted. Cook has written of the critical problem of reviewing sign language poetry (like that of Flying Words Project), expressing his frustration with the disabling limits of many hearing reviewers' thinking:

> Often paternalism has influenced the reviewer's perception on Deaf artists. They often praise Deaf artists because of their "disability." They tend to downplay their talents by patronizing their handicap. Often disability is an issue in the reviews, rather than a focus on the talents or the materials. I haven't seen a review that discusses Deaf theater or Deaf artists without emphasizing their Deafness. Newspaper reporters often ask me how I overcome my Deafness to be a successful poet. My Deafness has nothing to do with my success. I love ASL literature, and I work hard to achieve in this field like other artists who want to succeed in their career.[43]

One way that artists like Flying Words Project, Clayton Valli, and Ella Mae Lentz have sought to redress the disability issue of their work—to "educate" hearing audiences about what deafness is or isn't even as they entertain and aesthetically captivate those audiences—is simply by performing with minimal or entirely without voice translations of their work. In this way, those whose ears are attuned to "hearing" language must attune themselves differently, must enter into another sensory channel for language. And the entry is possible, the door wide open, I believe, because many of us do, after all, always already process the world, even the linguistic one, through our eyes.[44]

Because of the visual processing required of sign poetry interpreted minimally or not at all, linguistic parameters held tight by a Western (hearing) rhetoric obsessed with the will to speech are removed and reconstructed. In this poetry, a tradition that allowed delivery, *actio,* initially into the rhetorical canon—but then spent 2,500 years ensuring that this canon would be constantly held in check or erased entirely—replaces and restores delivery as part of the utterance, part of the meaning. You see, hearing audiences do get this poetry—certainly not all its intricate nuances, but enough understanding, in both quantity and quality, for it to make linguistic sense even as our sense of *linguistic* is expanded. Words fly; that is the project.

Flying, too, are the boundaries of poetry. While conventions of rhyme, rhythm, line length, line breaks, stanza, and wordplay find a counterpart in sign poetry, we must reconceive the oral/aural ring of these conventions. We must turn off the lights and watch those flying arms in black light measure out a beat, perform a couplet or a four-line stanza, punctuate variously, grow seeds, form faces, become eyes staring back at us.

This was my experience: I had only glimpsed a signed poem once when I first tried to write about sign poetry as a graduate student, some ten years ago. It was the final paper in my final course, and my professor—leery of my interest in approaching something he knew nothing of, but apparently trusting my abilities—gave me the green light. I could find no critical literature at the time, save for one essay by Jim Cohn, a poet and scholar of Native American poetry who happened to be at that first-ever NTID deaf poetry workshop in 1984 and who, as already described, planted the seeds of Flying Words Project. I turned instead to criticism about postmodern and "multicultural" poetry at large. When the paper was done, and the professor had read it, he called me into his office. He had only one comment, one question: "Is this poetry written somewhere? Can I see a copy of it?" I don't remember my exact answer, but I know that I stuttered, shuffled feet, squirmed in my seat. Then a ray of realization hit me: how powerful were our notions of poetry as a verbal art—written or orally performed; how closely tied we were to the idea that a word, a meaning, must be represented in some sanctified alphabetic script. While that paper received an A—with hardly a comment—I had failed to open the understanding that I had desired. Or perhaps I hadn't. For it was in my professor's misunderstanding that I came myself to realize how "outlaw" the ontology of deafness truly was—and how in riding with that outlaw, sign poetry might powerfully further the issues that concerned postmodernism, poststructuralist art, and contemporary poetry.

This move to further, to *possibilize,* to persuade one to see and understand and believe in the ways of another, pushes into rhetoric, of course.[45] Sign poetry possibilizes Western rhetoric precisely in how it calls into question dominant (disabling, pathologizing) ideas about deafness, about the limits of language, and about the potential of poetry. In its creation and performance, a sign poem is a rhetorical act—a discursive moment when "all the available means of persuasion" are considered further, and individual and cultural identities formed by those available means are put into question (i.e., are argued over). If we are hearing and among the audience of a sign poem-performance, we come to question the will to speech we have always thought mattered most in our culture; we witness the long-dormant canon of delivery come alive—and become strong; we participate in the power of *presence,* the very embodiment of language right there before us.

Moreover, if we are deaf and among that audience, we also are likely to undergo the four conceptual transformations described above via the hands of the sign language poet. The potential (the possibilizing power) of the sign language poet and his or her poem in changing deaf persons' *own* ideas about what they can do, what their (sign) language can do, what poetry can be, and how persuasive they can be is anything but slight. Peter Cook, as we have already noted, knows how the Deaf community "will look to him [the Deaf poet] strongly because they use ASL (the strongest product of Deaf culture) as a weapon or tool [here rhetoric enters] for building self-esteem, pride, strengths, and independence in the community." What the Deaf poet takes to share with the hearing world at large, she also gives back, twofold, to her own community.

Perhaps the largest part of this giving grows from the circular, self-nurturing connection between a culture and its art: a culture grows, its art flourishes; its art flourishes, the culture grows. Little surprise then that most Deaf poets I know (Valli, Lentz, and Cook among them) have stories of beginning their artistic work principally in creating or translating English poetry into sign language—and then, at some near-epiphanic moment, realizing that sign language is a language in and of itself, capable of fashioning a literature and a poetry for itself. Ella Mae Lentz even chronicles the development among Deaf poets at large of a native, culturally self-designed sign for "poetry":

> Deaf poets who play creatively with their language, who explore and expand their language' capabilities, and who use ASL to share their poems view the traditional sign for poetry [she gives the "English" sign here, which is a version of the sign for MUSIC done with a *p* handshape] as an inappropriate sign when referring to this new body of work. This group of poets selected a new sign [which she gives here: the hand placed on the chest area, then opening and moving out from there, as if throwing out feelings, from the heart] because the sign is indicative of the expression of

feelings and experiences that come from within. The traditional sign for poetry now refers to English poetry, and the new sign to ASL poetry.[46]

What sign poetry does for deaf people and Deaf culture differs little from what any poetry or literature or art generally is capable of doing for and within its culture, for and with its individuals: sign poetry strengthens Deaf community, articulates and advances Deaf culture, makes deafness less alien and other (even among its own), reconfirms values, offers pride in identity, encourages linguistic play, wields persuasive power. In *Spreading the Word: Poetry and the Survival of Community in America,* Ross Talarico takes up some of these same community-forming powers for poetry as he strives "once and for all, to take poetry out of the hands of elitists and into the working vocabularies of the social arts."[47]

In just such a working vocabulary, a "deaf poetics"—for sign poetry— raises provocative possibilities, especially from a postmodern and rhetorical perspective. Sign language poetry not only can develop a further sense of cultural and cognitive solidarity among deaf people through its emphasis on the image but can also transcend print- and speech-centered notions of language and rhetoric, transcend (instead of filling up or battling) silence, and restore the sense of an artist's presence in the creation of a piece: these are but a few of its more potent possibilities. And maybe, too, through the embodied, present-tense images offered by sign poetry, the "energy of American poetry," which contemporary poet-critic Dana Gioia laments "was once directed outward, [but] is now increasingly focused inward," can be redirected.[48] But this time, that energy might be redirected inward *and* outward simultaneously, becoming both universal and particular, both political and aesthetic as it reaches toward audiences of both dominant hearing culture and "home" Deaf culture. In this double but not necessarily deceptive stance, sign poetry directs not only that poetry can again matter but that rhetoric—the art of both producing and receiving discourse, the art of audiences and "speakers" interacting in both civic and private spaces—might matter, really matter, again too.

Coda

And as we ride with the outlaw ontology of deafness on a saddle like sign poetry, Plato's ideal republic fades far into the sunset, disappearing in the dust. Now the poet (and the rhetorician with her)—yes, like a painter, and yes, as "the imitator or maker of the image"—knows not *nothing,* but nearly *everything.* In her acts and arts of approaching both intellect and imagination, of instructing even as she pleases, of studying the appearances of things, of discovering all the available means, of attending to the art of listening as carefully as to that of speaking even as she turns away from them both, of communicating across cultures, of using language and persuasion beyond speech and beyond writing, too, she might show those truthsayers, the critics and philosophers, a thing or two. She might show them how to lend (and bend) an ear, how to wield words another way.

NOTES

1. It is with a bit of reluctance and a lot of humility that I attempt to create written versions of these five poem-performances. In doing so I am struck, once again, by the vastly differing modalities between English—oral/aural even when it is written—and visual, embodied American Sign Language and by the cognitive and cultural leap it takes to cross between them adequately, to translate sensitively. I felt most keenly at a loss to put Flying Words Project's "Poetry around the World" to words in the way we "normally" think of words. That poem represents especially well what I mean by "words another way."

    My attempts to represent these five poems in written English also vary. That is, I could not represent these works consistently (using the same kind of language, sentence structure, diction, or even visual or emotive approach) across all five poems. Though the reasons may be obvious—the poems are radically different—I know it may make the task of understanding these poems all the more difficult as they are sit, static, here on the page.

    Some of the poems I will feature throughout this chapter are commercially available: Ella Mae Lentz's collection, *The Treasure,* is published by In Motion Press; Clayton Valli's *ASL Poetry: Selected works of Clayton Valli,* by Dawn Sign Press. Flying Words Project has yet to produce a commercial collection of their work on videotape; I own tapes of two different performances, donated by the artists themselves. Peter Cook and Kenny Lerner have expressed interest in producing a video of their work in the near future.

    I could not have completed these descriptions without the eye and attention of my colleague and friend Susan Burch, who is as excited as I am by the possibilities for sign poetry and who first introduced me to the work of Flying Words Project.

2. Cook, *Reach of Poetry,* p. 1.

3. Ibid., p. 26.

4. Bizzell and Herzberg, *The Rhetorical Tradition,* p. 638.

5. Cixous, "Laugh of the Medusa," pp. 1239–40. See also Burke, "From *Rhetoric of Motives*," esp. 1020; Perelman and Olbrechts-Tyteca, "*The New Rhetoric*"; Derrida, "Structure, Sign, and Play"; and Gates, "Signifying Monkey."

6. A sampling of scholarly work on the intersections of poetry and politics, spanning many eras and schools of poetry might include Barrell, *Poetry, Language, and Politics;* Blasing, *Politics and Form in Postmodern Poetry;* Bowra, *Poetry and Politics;* Day and Docherty, *British Poetry from the 1950s to the 1990s;* Edwards, *Imagination and Power;* Erskine-Hill, *Poetry and the Realm of Politics;* Flint, *Poetry and Politics;* Fulford, *Landscape, Liberty, and Authority;* Gass and Cuoco, *Writer in Politics;* Hogue, *Scheming Women;* Richard Jones, *Poetry and Politics;* Nelson, *Our First Last Poets;* Norbrook, *Poetry and Politics in the English Renaissance;* M. North, *Political Aesthetic of Yeats, Eliot, and Pound;* Parini, *Some Necessary Angels;* Scully, *Line Break;* Summers and Pebworth, "*The Muses common-weale*"; and Watkins, *Keats's Poetry and the Politics of the Imagination.*

7. Indeed, I hope to undertake such a book-length project on sign language poetry in the future.

8. Two of the rhetorical tradition's strongest instances of the wedding of argument and aesthetics, imagination and intellect, entertainment and instruction are provided by Francis Bacon, who defined "the duty and office of Rhetoric" in *The Advancement of Learning* (1605) as "*to apply Reason to Imagination* for the better moving of the will" (p. 629), and by George Campbell, who wrote in *The Philosophy of Rhetoric* (1776) that rhetoric is most broadly defined as "eloquence" which is "that art or talent by which the discourse is adapted to its end" and which involves understanding, imagination, and passion all three (pp. 749–53).

9. Hassan, *Contemporary American Literature,* p. 41.

10. Kenny Lerner, personal correspondence, 11 September 1996.

11. Most of the poems on *The Treasure* also take stances on the issue of language and culture oppression for deaf people. As already noted, Lentz begins the video by offering us an early Signed English poem-tribute to a high school teacher who first taught her the beauty of sign language, and then presenting the same poem, sans voiced interpretation, in ASL. "To a Hearing Mother" addresses the way that "hearing parents, after finding out the child is deaf, go into shock," and answers that shock poetically with a message that "things will be fine. Accept the deaf child; use sign language rather than spoken language." Likewise, "The Dogs" visually "describes two groups within the deaf community," a community she calls "very cohesive, but it too has its own internal struggles and conflicts." Here the internal cultural conflicts and linguistic oppressions that both groups impose on each other are portrayed. The closing three poems—"The Door," "The Children's Garden," and "The Treasure"—all address the historical educational oppression and repeated efforts at the

eradication of sign language and attempts by "hearing educators [to] try to change our culture and weaken the vitality of our people." (All quotations are taken from the signed and voice-interpreted discussions, by Lentz herself, between the ten poems; except for the Signed English version of the first poem, "Travels with Malz," all poems are performed in ASL *without* any voiced interpretation.)

12. Hassan, *Contemporary American Literature,* p. 42.

13. Altieri, "From Symbolist Thought to Immanence," p. 608.

14. These are the defining characteristics used to organize William Stokoe's landmark dictionary (Stokoe, Casterline, and Croneberg, *A Dictionary of American Sign Language on Linguistic Principles*), and they are referred to throughout Ursula Bellugi's pioneering work on the linguistic structures of sign languages.

15. Sacks, *Seeing Voices,* p. 87.

16. Altieri, "From Symbolist Thought to Immanence," pp. 605, 626.

17. C. Olson, *Projective Verse,* pp. 15, 16–17.

18. Sacks, *Seeing Voices,* p. 119.

19. In personal correspondence, both Kenny Lerner and Peter Cook explain their use of a "traditional technique that Deaf people tend to play with." As Cook remarks: "A person is in front of the audience and the other person hides behind the front person. The front person cannot use his arms. The back person will do it. The front must use facial expression to match the signs [of the back person's arms]. This is a classical example of Deaf literature" (June 1996).

20. Perelman and Olbrechts-Tyteca, "*The New Rhetoric,*" p. 1084.

21. Valli's dissertation, "Poetics of American Sign Language Poetry," was written as he completed a Ph.D. in linguistics and ASL poetics from the Union Institute Graduate School.

22. Sacks, *Seeing Voices,* p. 22.

23. Harris and Aguero, preface to *Gift of Tongues,* p. ix.

24. Cohn, "The New Deaf Poetics," p. 264.

25. Altieri, "From Symbolist Thought to Immanence," p. 630.

26. This workshop is one that Allen Ginsberg and the young Peter Cook participated in; at the time, Cook would have himself been fairly new to sign language and sign poetry, since, as already noted, he did not learn sign language until he was nineteen years old.

27. Cohn, "The New Deaf Poetics," pp. 268–69. This is the same Jim Cohn that Peter Cook and Kenny Lerner dedicate "Poetry around the World" to; it was Cohn, reports Kenny Lerner, who saw the "diamond in the rough" in Peter's

potential as a poet: "The work Peter did back then was very raw, especially considering the fact that he was relatively new to the language of ASL himself. But Jim Cohn saw the power in Peter's performance and he also saw the *imagery* that Peter presented" (personal correspondence, 11 September 1996; my emphasis). Cohn convinced Peter to perform and set him up with Kenny Lerner, whom Cohn mistakenly thought a skilled interpreter although, as Kenny claims, he "was just learning sign at the time. I'll never know why Jim told Peter to call me, but this advice changed both of our lives."

28. In sign language and Deaf culture, facial expressions are often referred to as the "grammar" of the language. Much as deaf people (and other ESL users) tend to struggle with the grammatical nuances of standard English, hearing people who learn sign language reportedly often do not "get" the intricacies of sign language grammar, expressed on the face. "They have stone faces," one Gallaudet student and sign language instructor told me (Charlie, 9 May 1996).

29. Peter Cook, personal correspondence, June 1996. Though a native user of sign language, Ella Mae Lentz tells us at the beginning of *The Treasure* that, like Cook, her experience with poetry began in English and in creating translations: "I started writing poems in the fifth grade. I was taught, just like all children, that there are four lines to a verse, and that they must rhyme. I asked my teacher, who could hear, how to do this. She would give me a list of words which rhymed, and I would arrange them into a poem. I had no idea that English and American Sign Language were different languages. I though that poems must be written—in English. It never then occurred to me that a poem could be created in sign."

30. Kenny Lerner, personal correspondence, 11 September 1996.

31. Ibid.

32. When I have viewed this poem with hearing students in my introduction to poetry classes, they have surmised that the lifting of arms is generally an act of exaltation, a lifting of spirits and consciousness. But then, when we have all tried out the move ourselves, they have quickly remarked that the act is tiring, that gravity (reality?) pulls hard and fast on the uplifting and uplifted.

33. Lentz, *The Treasure*.

34. Peter Cook, personal correspondence, 15 August 1996.

35. Padden, "The Deaf Community and the Culture of Deaf People," pp. 91–92.

36. Two CODAs and academic scholars, Lennard Davis and Paul Preston, also write pointedly and provocatively about our cultural perceptions of silence in general, and the (imagined) silences of deafness more particularly. See Davis's *Enforcing Normalcy* and Preston's *Mother Father Deaf.*

37. Sontag, "The Aesthetics of Silence," p. 181.

38. Steiner, "Silence and the Poet," pp. 57–76.

39. Sontag, "The Aesthetics of Silence," p. 183.

40. Ibid., pp. 187, 194.

41. In *Performance: A Critical Introduction,* for example, Marvin Carlson begins by "dealing with the relationships between 'performance' and 'postmodernism,' terms often rather casually linked in critical discourse, but in fact related to each other in very complex and occasionally quite contradictory ways" (p. 8). Other illuminations of the intersecting but contentious and tangled relations between these concepts can be found in Diamond's collection *Performance and Cultural Politics;* Stern and Henderson's *Performance;* Phelan's *Unmarked;* Erickson's "Appropriation and Trangression in Contemporary American Performance"; and Felshin's collection, *But Is It Art?*

42. Robert Koehler, review of Flying Words Project, *L.A. Times,* 24 February 1989, p. 4; Janice Arkatov, "With 'Flying Words,' Performance Duo Takes Wing," *L.A. Times,* 15 March 1989, p. 3; Mike Steele, "A Helping Hand Makes 'Flying Words Project' Work for Audience," *Minneapolis Star Tribune,* 23 December 1991, p. 3E.

43. Peter Cook, personal correspondence, 15 August 1996.

44. To be sure, this statement of how we process the world is not particularly sensitive to blindness or visual impairment. But perhaps, ironically, it is even *more* sensitive than most descriptions to those "conditions" because it recognizes the prominence of visual processing in our culture.

45. My use of the term *possibilize* comes from Mike Rose's use in his book about "the promise of public education in America," *Possible Lives.* Rose himself borrows the term from the coinage by philosopher Maxine Greene (in *Landscapes of Learning*); they both define *possibilizing* as an ability to imagine a better state of things, to live with "a consciousness of possibility" (*Possible Lives,* p. 428).

46. Lentz, *The Treasure.*

47. Talarico, *Spreading the Word,* p. xi.

48. Gioia, *Can Poetry Matter?* p. 2.

Interlude 3

Are You Deaf or Hearing?

This question confronted me every day during my five-month-long stay at Gallaudet University in 1991. And although it no longer confronts, it continues to haunt. It was the question I had begun asking myself late in my twenties, years before Gallaudet—the very question that had sent me, searching for answers, to Gallaudet in the first place. But at that time, I still did not know the nature or power of that unidentified identity question. And so, when I found myself just turned thirty, newly arrived at Gallaudet—the core of Deaf culture—and handed that question not only daily but many times daily, my hands went numb. I stood, trying to locate the signs for my answer, in a place where speech would not go.

This was a different kind of speechless. The question "Are you Deaf or Hearing?" greets nearly everyone on Gallaudet's campus, asked often before name signs are exchanged. It comes abruptly, squarely, so in-your-face matter-of-factly. It directly assaults the usual spoken convention of beginning with polite, purely informational, and often inconsequential exchanges and putting identity questions far, far later in social conversations—if, in fact, they ever arise at all. There it is: now tell it true—are you Deaf or Hearing?

And if one does not know this truth? Then not only does the *manner* of the question asking throw one off guard and tether the tongue, but the *content* of it unhinges as well. While this question appeared on the hands easily enough from most I encountered at Gallaudet, it was not one I had encountered before and also not one for which I had a sense of the available answers. I suspected my options were far more complex and multiple than

237

the two poles offered in the question itself; as a rhetorician, I never lose the sense of "all the available means." So it was that I found myself stuck against the rock of the question's unsettling directness and the hard place of its predetermined responses.

I had certainly never thought of myself as "hearing." That was something that people who heard crickets, birds, school bells, phones ringing, lover's whispers, and children's voices were. But I had also quite surely never thought of myself as "deaf"—as those with wooden voices, fluttering handtalk, isolated lives, and monstrous hearing aids were. Thus my own limited views of the terms limited me. I knew how to answer, "Are you German? British?" These were questions, ironically enough, that had often been posed to me as people puzzled over my odd "accent." While my accent was "deaf"—the residue of hardly hearing most consonants or the tonal felicities of others' speech, let alone my own—I always chose to answer "German," a comfortable but close lie since I was born in Germany as an army brat and had grandparents on both sides of my family who hailed from there.

But at Gallaudet the "German" would not pass ("Are you Deaf or Hearing?" "No, German . . ."). I was stuck. Stuttering. No, speechless. Hands pinned to my side, brow furrowed, identity crashing fast, fast, faster. I tried to pull up the nose, looked my interlocutor in the eye, signed "hard-of-hearing." Boom. Flames all around. Wreckage. Smoke billowing up.

Not the right answer—as when someone asks if you are male or female and you answer, "Native American." There is some residue of identity there but the answer wanders far from the playing field. I was in the ballpark, but some umpire—one I could barely hear myself—was yelling "Foul!" The trouble was, it took a long time before I could understand why this one kept going foul, why I kept getting put back up to bat, what I would need to do to hit the ball right, or why they were even letting me play in the first place. It took me ten years (and the process is ongoing) to learn the diamond of "deafness," to see the many facets—bright, yet often hard and cold—of Deaf culture. It took me ten years to come back home—to understand that my inability to answer that question would remain an inability to put the ball into play by those rules—and to settle for "hard-of-hearing": if not happily, at least convincingly and with comfort.

I am not Deaf. I am not Hearing. I am neither. But I am both. I am . . . well, let me cover the bases here.

EDUCATION AND THE LEAST RESTRICTIVE ENVIRONMENT

By some accounts—principally, by those of the dominant Hearing world, those that count the most—I was "lucky": I was mainstreamed. I went to a "regular" school, a public school—and a small one at that. I blended in. I passed. By all accounts (both dominant Hearing and nondominant Deaf ones), I was the model mainstreamed child. For not only did I do well in school—graduating at the top of my class, gaining a scholarship to college, becoming the apple of both my math and English teachers' eyes, graduating nearly a year early—but I survived, even thrived, socially as well, with friends and even boyfriends for all the requisite occasions. I was even so blissfully "ordinary" as to have friends and boyfriends that my parents didn't always approve of.

To be sure, I spent a little more time "alone" than becomes the average, decently popular schoolchild. I was comfortable that way. At my choosing (a deaf choice—although I did not know it then), I shied away from the mass parking lot, lunchroom, and gymnasium crowds that gathered to socialize over the lunch periods and after school. Literally and figuratively, I always took the path least traveled. Track was my best sport and I did well enough at running the long distances. The longer I ran, the more comfortable I got—a built-in buffer against the teamwork and chatter of volleyball and basketball. (If there had been a swim team at Greeley County High School in Tribune, Kansas, I'm sure that's where I would have been, as I was when I went to college and found the "perfect" social life in the university natatorium—immersed underwater until my eyes burned, my palms and soles wrinkled, and the smell of chlorine would never come out of skin and hair.)

At my own choosing, I was somewhat famous for keeping my boyfriends at bay. Among my mid-seventies high school small-town-on-the-plains crowd, CB radios were all the rage and "Tough Luck" became my CB call name, a tag gained from my reluctance to ever take the dating thing too seriously. I would only see my boyfriends on weekend nights, saving my social energy—my ability to attend, listen, and interact—for the job of "doing school" during the week. Instead, after school I ran when I could, read when I couldn't. So, for example, it was of my own choosing that one afternoon after I had finished a full day of attending school and then cheerleading a junior high school football game afterward, I faked being grounded to avoid the victory celebration at the drugstore scene—to avoid Cokes and ice cream with ten other eighth-graders crammed into a tiny booth, quipping and joking as I faked interest and understanding, laughing on cue when others did. I grounded myself, by preference; I went home and read (and oh, I remember it well) Thomas Hardy's *Far from the Madding Crowd* and got caught by my seventh-grade sister, who let some of my friends in the back door after telling them the truth—no, I wasn't grounded. But I might as well have been, for all the social damage that one caused me. Not grounded, just a deaf dork.

But I wasn't deaf, of course. No one thought of me that way—least of all myself. And I wasn't really mainstreamed either. I grew up in the Land Before Mainstreaming. Public Law 94-142, the Education for All Handicapped Children Act, which eventually radicalized deaf education in the United States and began the slow demise of state deaf residential institutions, did not go into effect until 1975. I graduated a year after that.

Mostly, I believe, I was mainstreamed by virtue of my living so very far from "mainstream" American life. My roots come from Tribune, Kansas—a town of 900 people, the only one in the county; the closest neighboring town is twenty-one miles away, and the total population of the county (one of the largest in the state) was only 1,800. This is one of the few places left in the lower forty-eight that claims less than twenty-five people per square mile. We have wheat. We have cows. We have good schools.

Or at least, it was a good school for me. With twenty-six in my graduating class (barely over a hundred in my entire high school), I could always sit front row and center and get all the individual attention I might need. I don't remember needing it much, since I took, even then, almost everything I knew from books and nothing from talk and classroom interactions. But still, it was there for the taking. And everyone knew me. Everyone had known that Brenda "had a hearing problem" for so long (it was discovered "officially" with a screening done in second grade) that we all had just adapted to and with it. I was never singled out, never given special treatment that would have marked me as different, let alone incompetent, in any way. Instead, my individual way of learning was encouraged: when I had made my way through all the math courses and textbooks my school had to offer (which were severely limited, to be honest—we didn't go beyond algebra, trigonometry, geometry, calculus I) by the end of my junior year, my math teacher dug out an old probability textbook he had from his own college days and set me to it. Then he brought in the school's first-ever computer and assigned me the task of programming it for some algebraic equations that I might then teach to the freshman algebra students.

My English teacher, too, challenged me on my own individual grounds—not only putting up with but carefully reading the ridiculously overdone reading response journals I would produce, making me revise poems I would scrawl in them, and calling me at home to make sure I met the deadlines for several scholarship-awarding essay contests he had found for me to enter. My psychology teacher gave me her own college Psych 101 textbook and even designed "tests" and writing prompts for me around it after I achieved perfect scores on each and every "health" test I took in her required freshman course. When I showed interest, perhaps even aptitude, for things psychological, my English, psychology, and math teachers pushed me toward an individual curriculum that would feed that interest—a dose of probability and statistics here, a copy of Sylvia Plath's *Bell Jar* there, a dictionary of psychological terms in between.

My handicap, defined within this educational context, never was one. I was simply told, from second grade on, to sit where I could best hear the teacher, to pay careful attention, and not to be afraid to ask questions about what I didn't "understand" (they meant "hear," of course). I don't remember that I was told to read a lot. I figured that one out for myself—behavior modeled, no doubt, on a mother who had a habit of picking up a book after her three children went to bed and not putting it down until she was finished with it and the night had really become morning.

I now know that I was not so much mainstreamed as jet-streamed—pushed along in a powerful current of educational excellence, immersed in the ultimate "least restrictive environment," that merged my own strong, self-motivated independence with the care of an individualized, flexible, "let's-make-the most-of-what-we-have-available" kind of curriculum. I now know, after almost two decades teaching in public schools myself, that I was damn lucky—regardless of whether I was hearing or deaf. And as is so often the way with luck, I mostly took my fortunes for granted.

It wasn't until college—when the radically unindividualized nature of most undergraduate education scared me squarely—that I understood how lucky I had been. What's more, in college I began to suspect liminality at my core. Before college, I had not sensed that the question "Are you Deaf or Hearing?" even existed in relation to myself. I was still a long way from being consciously aware of it, but the question was there, like the ghostly annoying tinnitus—the bells and buzzes in my ears from time to time—that plagued me without warning or pattern. Like my tinnitus, the source of my identity was unknown and so the appearance of the question was anything but comfortable.

SUFFERING LOSSES: OF dB AND Hz

The terrain is tricky here, the road not well-paved, the turns and switchbacks many and confusing. It's hard to get a good view. Audiologists measure hearing in decibel loss (dB), at levels typically from -10 to 120 dB (as a jet engine roars), across a range of frequencies, running generally from 125 hertz (Hz) to 8,000 Hz, from low to high. They are testing their client's hearing primarily in pure-tone frequencies—something we rarely hear in most of our "real-world" interactions. Beyond that they also usually test for "test reliability" itself, repeating some of the frequencies out of the usual pattern, looping back, to make sure clients aren't faking them out or "malingering." Speech discrimination skills, in isolated ears and then in tandem, and loudness discomfort levels are also assessed as a way of helping determine their client's potential "fit" with a hearing aid. And finally, "masking," a technique to identify overdependency on one ear when the hearing loss is thought to be nonparallel, might well be performed. Then all these results are plotted on an audiogram.

Once audiologists are past the pure-tone frequencies part of the audiological assessment that forms their baseline, most of the testing aims at peeling back what they call "the speech banana." This banana, for the signifying monkeys that we are, represents the focus of all involved in making an audiological assessment; how well one functions in the speech banana matters greatly—signifies most of all—to the client him- or herself, to those he or she interacts with, to the audiologist. For it is here, in this rather narrow, banana-like shaded area near the top of the audiogram, that push comes to shove regarding functioning well in the jungle we call the "normal" (i.e., "hearing") world. Once clients wanders outside the speech banana—regardless of their ability to still hear trucks bearing down on them, jet engines flying over them, the bass of their boom box beating—their humanity comes under question as their ability to work, interact socially with humans, survive our educational system, hear speech, and perform speech is stripped away.

From that point on, the goal is to get the banana back. But therein lies the problem—the audiologists can't just put the peel back on that banana and restore it. Human speech is more complicated than just a pure-tone frequency at a fixed decibel level. To be sure, some generalizations are possible: most consonants, especially the sibilants and such (*s, z, th*), occupy the higher frequencies, while long *o, a,* and *u* throb down lower. This is true of practically any voice. But it takes only a moment to realize how vast is the range of human variety—in inflection, pitch, enunciation, and loudness of voice (not to mention facial hair)—and to recognize how quickly something like pure-tone frequencies delivered at predetermined decibel levels falls away from what human speech actually is and can be.

Now add to this slippage even more oil: human hearing loss
that occurs neatly, in equal decibel loss across all frequencies, is
far more the exception than the rule. In fact, hearing loss in the
higher frequencies is more common and generally more severe.
We generally lose the sounds of phones ringing, birds, and the
dryer bell dinging before we lose the hum of the dryer running
itself and the actual voices on the phone. And there is a complication, already alluded to: consonants occupy the higher frequencies, while vowels hang lower (save for high *e* and *i*
sounds). And consonants comprise the bulk, the skeleton, of
most spoken languages: words tend to begin and end there.
Hence, people with high-frequency hearing loss often may *hear*
your voice (and numerous other sounds), but they may not be
able to discriminate your speech. Shifting in and out of those frequency patterns, the human voice comes and goes, like a radio
whose battery is nearly gone or whose signal fades, marking too
great a distance from the station or an interruption by some substantial object. So it is that when trapped in the audiologist's
soundproof booth and given single words to "repeat after me"
by the audiologist who purposefully hides her mouth—"No
cheating here," she jokes, as if my ability to lipread, the only
thing that now secures my survival in human interactions, were
somehow suspect—I fail miserably. On average, I cannot discriminate better than 40 percent of those single words when delivered at 50 dB, a good 20 dB above "normal" speech levels. It
does not matter how loud the words up are cranked up, the
consonants—key markers in single, uncontextualized words—
elude me, hidden in those higher frequencies that I cannot hear
even at 120 dB.

I need to see those lips, though they too can fool me; for example, *b* looks much like *p* when spoken. I need a frame—a sentence,
some body language, a facial expression, a contextual marker—to
put that word in. And a hearing aid won't give me this.

HOPING FOR GAINS: OF HEARING AIDS

So, add yet another complication, another treacherous twist in
the road here: hearing aids by and large boost hearing uniformly
across all frequencies. And in doing so, they often *add* to the

problem as much as—or more than—they address it. If, say, I need to hear that dryer go "ding" at the end of the cycle, the amount of amplification I require will bring the dryer itself to a dangerously deafening 100 decibels. To amplify the higher frequencies I so completely lack is also to risk eardrum destruction and total hearing loss. A friend of mine with a similar hearing loss calls this the Hearing Aid Catch-22.

My latest audiology report, in its tidy, clinical, objectifying way, masks this situation in medical mumbo-jumbo (very hard to lipread) as it "interprets [my] test results": "conventional pure tone audiometry revealed normal hearing acuity through 750 Hz [the lowest measured frequency that humans can hear is 250 Hz] steeply sloping to a profound sensorineural hearing loss bilaterally, with two frequency pure tone averages of 30 dB for the right ear and 40 dB for the left." On the chart accompanying the written report, my audiologist has drawn arrows: past 1,500 Hz, the arrows squiggle off the edges of the audiogram and dive straight for the bottom of the page, heading right beyond 120dB where danger to the human ear is definite. This frequency, 1,500 Hz, is still a long way away from 8,000 Hz; there, on the audiogram horizon, at 8,000 Hz the audiologists' measuring and human hearing itself tend to "normally" end.

Their solution to this problem of the steep drop-off has become as predictable as my results have become after decades of testing, especially since I have become a professional, working person who relies on her hearing daily and also since hearing aid technologies have, by their accounts, "advanced" considerably: "Ms. Brueggemann," they report, "would be a good hearing aid candidate due to her poor word discrimination ability, and also due to her report of feeling handicapped by her hearing impairment."

Lately my audiologists have been placing a great deal of faith in their new hearing aid technology, revived by new lines of remarkably small, discreet in-the-ear (ITE) aids and sophisticated (i.e., expensive) digital, computer-programmed aids, which are typically still behind-the-ear products. And since my audiologists have, it is true, watched my growing frustration with my own ability to function adequately at my job, which I happen to love, I too have become attached to their faith. And although I'm still some way from making it my own faith, I now own—and even sometimes wear—a very expensive pair of digitally programmable aids.

To understand my life with my hearing aids, consider one day as an example. I recently helped interview candidates to be crowned at my university's football homecoming. Now, this is no small deal at Ohio State, where football, for better or worse, is the glue that binds some 55,000 students and 4,500 faculty together at one of the largest universities in the country. Four faculty members interviewed four student candidates in forty-minute shifts on the "preliminaries" night. We interviewed in a series of rooms separated by heavy, accordion-like curtains. And since the student candidates sat right in front of those curtains, my hearing aids picked up their voices *along with* the ones of the faculty interviewers in the next room, on the other side of the curtain. One of the interviewers beyond the curtain, male, had a booming voice and a tendency to laugh loudly and often—usually at himself. My hearing aids clung to him.

It drove me nearly crazy for the first set of forty-minute interviews. I surfed all the channels on my digitally programmable hearing aids, which, thanks to the wonders of microchip computer technologies, do now offer me some degree of flexibility in enhancing higher frequencies without drastically (and dangerously) boosting the lower ones. But still, the boost is there. I tried all my eight available options—two different "programs" with four volume levels. But that voice on the other side of the curtain stayed with me. Finally, I gave up: I pulled out my little plastic storage box, put my aids away, and turned to the sign language interpreters I had (thank God) had the foresight to request for this event.

This move, however, unhinged the other three faculty members who saw me do it. Their eyes began to dart nervously back and forth between me, the two interpreters, and the box I was putting back in my bag. Given my array of actions in that one-hour period—from tinkering with my hearing aids, conversing "naturally" with the students and the other interviewers, and responding to all of them—I had been marked as "hearing," though "hard of." Now they were witnessing this deaf and foreign act of turning to break eye contact with them in favor of the sign language interpreters. And this had left them quite unsure: was I deaf or hearing?

My attempt to answer this question, albeit evasively and partially (like that radio that brings the tune in intermittently), illustrates another layer of complications here. In Deaf culture, audiograms, degrees of dB loss, and frequency variations are simply not spoken about. The issue is supposedly moot, the discussion mute. If you have to mention your audiogram, you aren't really Deaf. Perhaps deaf, audiologically; but culturally, the acknowledgment of an audiogram, ironically, decertifies you.

Yet another catch-22. For while Deaf culture chooses to ignore, in one frequency, the audiological moment and the audiogram that medically marks any individual, as part of their way of "proving" that deafness is more cultural than medical, admissions to the cultural hot spots of big D "Deafness" are still tracked through an audiogram. The fact remains: entry into Gallaudet University, or any state residential institution, for that matter, is largely determined by being able to offer up an audiogram that certifies one as "deaf," having an average decibel loss of x. There are cutoffs, and this x is slippery. It changes—from institution to institution, state to state, year to year.

People don't talk about their audiograms at Gallaudet, and generally they don't wear their hearing aids, either. But they are there because of that chart. So the question "Are you deaf or hearing?" trips you up at every turn: you can't mention your audiogram in answering it, but really, that audiogram has brought you here in the first place. And everyone, deaf and Deaf alike, knows that. It's like trying to talk about your birth and pretending you don't have a mother. The question of origins is denied even as it is called forth.

PHONE TALK

When people ask me questions on the telephone, I am utterly lost. Questions generally come uncontextualized, dropped in as a change in conversation. I am talking, for example, about how poorly I did on the chemistry test yesterday and then my friend says, "So, what are you doing Saturday?" I flush a little on the other end, feel my pulse quicken and try, ever so quickly, to figure out what something-something-day has to do with my chemistry test yesterday. Did my friend ask what we are doing in chemistry on . . . Monday? Did she ask me the day of the next chemistry test? I might as well tell her I'm German. . . .

I consider myself far more deaf on the phone than in other places and scenes. I will generally go to great extremes to avoid the phone. I talk with my family on the phone (sadly, a conversation with my mother-in-law, whose own ears don't work so well anymore, is out of the question these days), I conduct business if I must (but am still a near-genius at circumventing even these necessities), and I have a lot of fun with telemarketers. I let them ramble, uncontextualized and therefore meaninglessly to me—oh, for far too long—and can sense their mounting excitement as they grow sure that they've got one hooked. Then I let the axe fall: "I'm sorry, but I have quite a substantial hearing loss. I really haven't understand anything you said." That pretty much shuts them up. I am no doubt one of the few people in the country who routinely gets telemarketers to hang up on her first.

They hang up because most people are generally puzzled by someone "with substantial hearing loss" talking on the phone in the first place. Paradoxically, their confusion cuts both ways. The phone, at this stage in our cultural-technological game, is so naturalized as to seem accessible to all: even when someone knows you are deaf he might still call you. Countless times I have seen the flush of both embarrassment and bemusement when I've had to remind a hearing person that he can't call a deaf person we might both know without using a TDD or the deaf relay service. What's worse, that first flush will often bloom into impatience mixed with indignation, perhaps peppered with disbelief, as if the burden of being so technologically inconvenienced is beyond him.

But the perspective in the phone game can flip. While hearing people often insultingly forget that the phone is not natural for some, they can just as easily also jump to conclusions in the other direction. Because I am hard-of-hearing, people are surprised—no, make that shocked—when I can and do talk on the phone. "How do you do that?" they ask, as if I had just given birth to triplets right there on the floor. It is an irony unbounded: they call me on the phone and then at some point in the conversation express utter amazement that I can talk with them in the first place. If they didn't think I could talk on the phone, why did they call?

And my phone talking is often, in and of itself, deceptive. I am not a good listener on the phone. In fact, I avoid it at all costs. When forced, on occasions, to call for a pizza, I state my name, address, phone number, pizza choice. The end. Any variation on that theme by the employees on the other end—who frequently speak over a background of clanging, banging, and boom box blaring and without parting their lips, the mouthpiece no doubt hanging below their chin as they toss dough or sprinkle pepperoni with phone-free hands—any variation, and I am clueless. Like a rewound tape, I will repeat my information sequence once more. If my tidy repetition is met with irritation, an exaggerated emphasis on some statement they make, or the puzzling pause that is usually followed by a tentative rising tone in their voice, indicating a question following something they did not well understand—I hang up. Ask me no questions, I will tell you no lies. Back to the yellow pages.

When the conversation needs to be a little more social than pizza delivery operators generally crave, I do my part well. A little too well. I talk. And talk. Push the play button and I'm off and running, a one-woman show of verbal gymnastics. You won't get a word in edgewise. I won't need to listen if I just keep talking. I'll hang up and feel bad about that; I always do. But I'm willing to make the trade-off—that guilt for gaining the immediate comfort of saving my face, and, too, for keeping my conversation partner comfortable. Better to seem a bit of a flapjaw and self-centered than, lordy, deaf and dumb. That would embarrass us both.

FAMILY, VERSION ONE

My husband and children are never, I think, embarrassed by my hearing loss. Frustrated, yes, but ashamed, no. Yet, to be fair, I know that their reactions are likely but a reflection of my own. The phone itself again provides the best example here.

My husband and I fight about the phone with frightful—and fruitless—regularity. He is, by nature, not a phone talker. I knew this when I married him. In fact, it was one of his better qualities when we were dating—enchanted, as I was, by his preference for letter and note writing over phone contact, which was difficult for me to begin with. But like most spells, the enchantment dulls a little with time, and a catch usually comes with the deal. Once we became a couple, and especially when our professional and social lives took off and children came into the picture as well, the phone became more necessary. There were medical appointments to make, transactions to complete, social obligations to meet, colleagues and students to respond to, messages to take and leave.

My husband, I sometimes think, would and could live happily in a world without phones. I could count on one hand the times I know that he has picked up the phone, of his own accord (without my nagging), to call anyone about anything. Once people get him on the phone (they have called him) he can and will talk well, engagingly, at length. But he will not himself "reach out and touch someone."

I don't do phones either. But still, it seems, we need that thing to survive in our daily lives as academics, teachers, parents, neighbors. And so, we are at phone war most of the time. I don't want to make the calls to secure the doctor's appointment with a receptionist who won't articulate her words and who will be very impatient, if not insulted, when I ask her to. I don't want to call the neighbor back and get stuck in small-talk chat that I will mostly fail to comprehend. I don't want to call in the catalog order for the kids' Halloween costumes and suffer through the strange-sounding and downright rude New Yorker on the other end who literally snorts when I ask him to repeat his question slowly and with careful pronunciation. I don't want to check the voice mail and miss half the message (especially those left by unfamiliar female voices) and all the phone numbers given.

But he doesn't want to, either. I wheedle, demand, implore, cry, sigh, stomp and shout, beg pitifully and passionately for him to help me with this phone business. And each and every approach I use works—this time. But next week, I'll be doing it again. It's a dance we've somehow mastered, much as we both hate it. The phone is a sticking point, for better or worse, in our marriage.

And it sticks so much because for me, at least, it so sticks out. Almost everything else about our interactions, communications, day-to-day lives as hard-of-hearing woman and hearing man works well. We are comfortable with each other, understanding now nearly without speaking of it when I need help with hearing (in restaurants, with strangers, at ticket counters, at parties, when my three-year-old talks) and when I prefer to try stumbling through it myself (with my students, at an academic conference, when company is over). Still, I know that he is not sure—ever—just when I am "hearing" and when I am "deaf." Nor is he ever really sure when I am happy in whatever state I currently am. Our comfort as a couple is always clouded by my shifting identity. And what most controls the weather patterns here is that he knew me first—as a graduate student and before I began coming out with my hearing loss—as "hearing." First impressions matter.

My children, however, have an entirely different first impression. For them I have always been "hard-of-hearing"; "My Mom's ears don't work very well," I hear my son tell one of his new kindergarten friends. In fact, in many ways five-year-old Karl seems more comfortable with my shifting, multiply-hyphenated identity than his father is. But this is only, I know, because he has grown up with it. It has been a part of his life since the days before he knew how carefully I would watch the little red light on the receiver end of my monitor into his room, not trusting my ability to hear his breathing, his waking, his voice crying out.

Karl, and his three-year-old sister Esther, too, have come to language with their ABCs always fingerspelled even as they were voiced or sung, and with signs always in the conversational picture, particularly at mealtimes. At age three, Esther recognizes sign language ABCs—on her own pudgy fingers and my own—far better than she can yet recognize the English alphabet in print. And both my children mastered their first sign—"finished"—around the age of ten months, long before they could speak a word. Esther especially is a miniature master at executing signs, her fine motor control, strong body awareness, and willingness to try anything without fear guiding her prodigious skills in this regard. In some ways, then, my children are growing up more "Deaf" than I ever did.

They certainly have the awareness in ways it has taken me over thirty years to acquire myself. They have always known, for example—even if they didn't always act in complete understanding—that I can't process background noise at all while I'm on the phone, that I need to have absolute silence in the room. Now I watch them leave the room immediately and instinctively anytime *anyone* picks up the phone at our house. Karl also tells me when the phone rings, just in case I miss the blinking light, and reminds me to wear my hearing aids if I am to take him to the latest animated film or to one of his favorite places, the aviary at the local zoo. Karl knows the words at the bottom of the TV screen are the way I "hear" his videos with him. And Karl often translates the less articulate, more high-pitched words of his three-year-old sister for me. He is learning the responsibility of deafness, the responsiveness of hearing. He listens remarkably well and responds to others with a stunning sensitivity, qualities noted by our friends and his teachers as well. And he is only five.

FAMILY, VERSION TWO

My other family, the one I was born into, has little problem dealing with the question "Is Brenda Deaf or Hearing?" They simply do not answer it; they do not hear it. Thirty-plus years of silence over the matter—broken by little more than my mother's occasional quip about "Brenda's Selective Hearing" or my sister's reference to "Brenda's La-La Land," the place I have supposedly gone to when my hearing is being "selective"—has powerfully constructed yet another vacillating position for me in relation to this question.

Sometimes I am quite comfortable with the notion of my "selective hearing," but other times it prickles. My mother makes it poke the most. And when she gets under my skin in this way, as she often does, I try hard to get out of my own skin, to project, to imagine myself as her. I try to imagine what it must have been like to have been so young and in a strange land, having a new-born and then a young child that you sensed "something was different" about—as my mother has said she always knew about me—but being unable to place precisely what that difference was. Then to have the school nurse, and later an audiologist, tell you that your seven-year-old daughter had substantial hearing loss—possibly, although not definitively, since birth. And then to be asked by them hundreds of questions that might well hint at your incompetence as a mother: Were you ever significantly ill during the pregnancy—and not seen by a doctor? Was your daughter significantly ill early in her childhood—and not seen by a doctor? Did your daughter ever suffer any blow or trauma to the head? Didn't you notice your daughter's inattentiveness to conversations and unresponsiveness to certain noises?

> No, no, no, no—and my daughter is not deaf, either. You see, she has selective hearing and she chooses to hear me and others when she wants to. Nothing is wrong with her. She is only a bit willful, even stubborn, a private kind of child who immerses herself in whatever task is at hand. Nothing is wrong with me. When I speak, she doesn't listen. It is that way with mothers and daughters, you know. We are no different. Nothing is wrong with us.

Those are the conversations and scenes I hear in my head when I am selectively trying to imagine life as my mother, in her mid-twenties during the mid-sixties with a child whose hearing loss reaches into the "profound" on over half the measured frequencies. At other times, I select differently: I flare back in anger, especially since I have been trying to claim some of the "deaf-ened" parts of myself left mute for over thirty years. In these angry, nonempathetic, hey what about me, me, me moments, I charge at her with claims of "selective ignorance," matching wound for wound.

The scar that remains is that she is right, you know. I do have selective hearing. A look at my audiogram proves that—here I have only moderate loss, there I slope ("precipitously") into profound losses. I hear this consonant, but not that one. I follow this voice, but not that one well. When I am tired, or not devoting undivided attention to the listening, things get even more selective. And over the years, I have learned quite automatically but thoroughly, as a coping strategy, to develop increased selectivity, shutting off some things in order to save energy and attention for other things.

When I read, for example, or work at the computer, or cook. I turn my back; I tune out. My officemates in my years since I entered the academy have been all but amazed at my ability to complete enormous amounts of work at the computer, in my office, grading papers, reading while the hubbub of the university day whirls around me. "I can't think when I'm up here," said one recent officemate. "I can't write at all with the commotion in the halls and the students coming and going. And yet, even when I have students sitting right here, two feet away from you, for conferences, sobbing over their midterm grade, you go right on working, pounding on those keys, oblivious, productive."

I smile. "It's my selective hearing," I quip. The medicine is not so bitter when you prescribe it yourself.

THE SOCIAL OWL AND THE BUZZ OF CONVERSATION

Another of my self-inflicted quips occurs when I explain to committees I work with or partygoers I am trying to socialize with that I will be the "owl" in the group. "And not the wise owl, either," I continue joking. Because context changes suddenly and often in these social situations, and because the conversation at parties and academic committee meetings is almost invariably about people, I hoot often, "Who? Who?" In such settings, I always feel one step behind, lurching along, grabbing for ropes, stumbling often.

Still, I'm a people person. I've tried giving up these social scenes, bowing out of parties among colleagues, friends, neighbors. I've even explained to them why I won't be there. So, I'll miss a gathering once. But the next time the contact-carrot is dangled my way, I'm grabbing and going. I just like people. And oh, I like talking too. So, I've learned to adjust my strategies so as to avoid hooting too much. When I'm talking with someone at a party, for instance, and another person joins us, I flinch a little, but continue the conversation. When the circle goes wider than those three mouths, though, I'm gone—flying away to find another soul, another sole voice that I can follow well enough. It is hard to lipread and follow the bouncing verbal ball when the players multiply.

Still, if I play too hard at this social game—an interminable afternoon with lines of students out my door, a committee meeting too intense, or all day with my five-year-old who never shuts up—I defeat myself. Tinnitus sets in. The ringing, buzzing, and auditory blacking out that sometimes plagues my ears deafens me in ways that my audiogram cannot even begin to represent. Mysterious in origin, vastly varying in quality and quantity, strangely sparked and just as oddly silenced, the ringing that some people experience—most of them with auditory nerve deafness like mine—knows no cure or clear medical cause. An ultimate enigma—even beyond speech and writing: tinnitus, the affliction of hearing sounds in one's ears that are not sounds from the environment, was long thought to be a sure sign of madness. While it is no longer recognized as necessarily indicative of mental instability, it is definitely known to affect one's stability. There is no doubt about it: the ringing in my ears is near-maddening.

Once it starts, I cannot turn it off, turn away, or control it in any way. It will stop me in midsentence, obliterate my thought in process, destroy my sleep, render me socially incapable, intellectually unproductive. And the cycle of tinnitus dangerously feeds itself: if I can't sleep for the ringing in my ears, I face the next day and its attendant stresses on my listening and interacting abilities with my strategies and stamina already weakened. It is when I am tired and stressed that tinnitus strikes most often; then, too, it is my tinnitus that renders me tired and stressed.

A few years ago, with a one-year-old in the house who had her own problems sleeping and with an insanely intense academic schedule, it nearly got the better of me. My ears drilled out a high-pitched, warbling bell-like sound when I lay down to sleep; and when I finally did fall to sleep—brow furrowed, fists clenched, teeth grinding, angry and hating myself and my ears—I was wakened by my baby daughter. The cycle repeated itself throughout the night. At work, I carried a full teaching load, then shared an office with an officemate who every day had as many students in as I did. Always there was noise in that office. I came home to a preschooler who was, as others were quick to note, the ultimate verbal machine, a nonstop talker, charming but relentlessly engaging in his desire to talk about the world, his world.

Soon, the tinnitus began to creep into all corners of my day—stopping me short, my train of thought derailed, in the middle of something I was saying in class. My voice would trail away, the students would all lean forward, their own brows now furrowed when they tried to catch what I was saying as I dived down many decibels, as if that diving would rescue the ringing that had begun in my ears. Several times I remember that I even gasped in the middle of something I was saying when the ringing began, as it always did, abruptly—and my students jumped back, waiting to hear what had alarmed me so. (And no, I would not tell them, "Hey, I hear bells ringing in my ears.") But a few of them wrote about these strange things in their course evaluations.

I faded away from committee meetings entirely, one of my closest colleague-friends often waving me to attention and then asking, concerned, after the meeting, "Are you okay?" (And no, I would not tell her, "Hey, I hear bells ringing in my ears.") I met with my department chair to beg for a one-course release in the following quarter, afraid already that I would soon also have to tell him that I'd be quitting this job altogether. (And no, I did not tell him, "Hey, I hear bells ringing in my ears"—but I did allude to "medical reasons.") I became nearly hostile, often impatient, when my husband would try to have conversations with me at the end of our full days. (And yes, I finally did begin to tell him, "Hey, I hear bells ringing in my ears.")

But most of all, I began to dislike myself—grouchy toward my children, scared to teach my classes, tired of talking with students, crying nearly every night at both the sleep I wasn't getting and my fear of having to give up a career I loved and had worked so hard in and for. My whole social sphere seemed to be collapsing fast and I felt suffocated under it. Then one day, while I was waiting in the medical clinic to get my annual flu shot, I caught a flyer about tinnitus. Just waiting there for me. In it were addresses of the National Tinnitus Association—an association devoted entirely to the study and dissemination of information about ears ringing for no known medical reason, particularly among people with hearing loss—and a subscription form for their newsletter. I signed on.

The first thing I learned is that some success in treating tinnitus had been reported when the sufferer wore hearing aids as a way to mask the tinnitus itself—to create a white-noise background that somehow, mysteriously and magically, erased the other maddening noises. I went directly to "Go" (taking my $200 with me for deposit) and wound up back at my audiologist. "Hearing aids," I said. "I want them."

And I got them. But not, of course, until we also had long conversations about how I might also change my life to help alleviate some of the listening stress my job and family life had begun to hand me. Armed with these strategies, backed up by an official letter from my audiologist, sporting several thousand dollars' worth of the latest technology in hearing aids, I went back to my department chair and negotiated some things that might help me continue to do my job, do it well, and not go mad in the bargain. And although it did not take the courage lent by an official audiology letter to do so, my husband and I had a similar conversation about reconceiving our home life in some little, but important, ways.

And so it was that I was born again, as a social and nearly sane being once more. The tinnitus still comes and goes. When it is there, I have but another reminder of my deafness. When I wear my hearing aids—in large part to help ward off the evil ringing—my identity shifts again, dancing on and hopping between the several hyphens of "hard-of-hearing." But there are days, too—whole days and nights—when no bells ring and I have no meetings, no student appointments, no social obligations; the kids are in school, and I am just simply, unaided, "hearing." It makes me want to hoot and holler.

CHOOSING AND USING (A) LANGUAGE

One of the most popular misconceptions about deaf people is that they are silent. I myself nearly shouted for joy when I first came to Gallaudet and discovered so much about deafness—both its cultural and individual forms—and about myself as well. The utter noisiness of the place stunned me—boom boxes, bass cranked up, blaring out, together with deaf voices shouting with incredible volume in the halls, since deaf bodies do often catch the tactile vibrations of sound where deaf ears can't. But even more stunning was the cacophony of deafness represented in individuals there and the way I saw myself, both fascinated and frightened, reflected in so many of the young, deaf students now attending Gallaudet.

These students, by and large, are not native signers. In fact, many of them are quite new to sign language and are enrolled in a "new signers" program, much as a native Chinese speaker might take a crash course in English on entering an American university. They struggle hard with identity, trying to locate themselves in an answer to "Are you Deaf or Hearing?," trying to learn sign language, trying to adjust to a social environment that is now so rich as to nearly induce overload as, for the first time in their eighteen-plus years, they meet with others who are like them—more like them than they could have ever imagined possible in those endless, isolated days as the phenomenal (and often singular) mainstreamed deaf student in an all-hearing educational environment. And yes, too, they are trying to pass their classes and even do well in their schoolwork, to find a major and career that will suit them for life.

But the identity thing—answering "Are you Deaf or Hearing?"—and learning the language, whether English or ASL, that will certify and cinch their answer to that question seem to concern them most. Their use of and skills with ASL signify most strongly here. In a move that is constructively empowering, linguistically sensible, and also, sadly, a bit bitterly lashing back (and therein backpedaling) against the countless years of hearing oppression and sign language eradication, the core of Deaf culture at Gallaudet University now places a high premium on the purity of sign language. In the backlash, some of these deaf students fall between the cracks—unable to conquer sign language overnight and still stuck, after years of mostly inadequate mainstreamed education in which they really could not participate "equally" in the classroom, with poor English skills as well. And that identity question "Are you Deaf or Hearing?" is not well-equipped to withstand, let alone welcome, such cracks.

In the six months I was at Gallaudet, I too nearly cracked under this linguistic pressure, wanting desperately to learn sign language and to learn it well, wanting desperately to be accepted, even wanting to answer that question simply and surely. But I kept slipping up, finding both my hands and tongue initially tied when it came time to answer my inquisitors. Eventually my hands and mouth would doom me as, almost of their own will, they uttered—together—the double-*h* handshape and the hyphenated adjective "hard-of-hearing."

I grew up a poet—or thinking myself one—rising to the challenge of my fifth-grade teacher's assignment to write a poem and then recite it in class with a four-stanza ode to the glorious western Kansas harvest moon that had my classmates envious and my teacher suspicious (of plagiarism). To defy her charges and put her suspicions to rest, I went on a poem-writing frenzy for the rest of the year, gluing each and every carefully copied one onto differently colored sheets of construction paper and presenting them as a book, to my doubter, at the end of the year. Later, I came to know that Helen Keller had gone here before me. As an eleven-year-old at the Perkins Institute for the Blind, Helen had been accused of plagiarizing, in her case a short story; much as I, at the age of ten, was hauled to the principal's office by my fifth-grade teacher, who called my parents in as well, she too "stood trial" for her imagined crime, without Anne Sullivan by her side to aid her defense.

Helen and I, both exonerated, also obviously shared a love of the English language. And although I could not be conscious of it then, I know now that I claimed my "home" in English with those early poems that later blossomed to short stories, letter writing, essays, biographies, newspaper reporting—a garden of language. Helen grew one, too.

I also loved sign language; in fact, I am, in general, a lover of all languages. In many ways it felt as natural as, perhaps even more natural than, a spoken tongue I could never quite catch. I had always been a "hand-talker," always been a physical person, a performer, too. In these ways, sign language felt like home. But it was not native. My nine years of life in Kentucky and Ohio now let me comfortably call this part of the country "home," but I still speak—with comfort—of Kansas as "Home," with the capital claim.

And so, a decade after my first sign language class in the basement of a Louisville Baptist church, I finally composed my first sign language poem last year. It is a simple thing—and crudely delivered, no doubt. But it shines, like a harvest moon, golden and full of promise, signifying bounty and a new season, in my soul. It comforts. And ironically enough, it is a poem about discomfort, about being "stuck between" being Deaf and Hearing. When I finish it, I sign the unique version of "finally" that ASL users know. This "finally" is not the one that indicates "final, as in finished"—the first sign my children learned, using it to signal that they were done with their meal—but the "finally, success!" version that became so popular in Deaf culture after the Deaf President Now protest.

Yes, *finally*, I am just me. Stuck between. And feeling successful there.

ℬibliography

Published Sources

Altieri, Charles. "From Symbolist Thought to Immanence: The Ground of Postmodern American Poetics." *Boundary 2* 1 (1973): 605–41.

Anderson, Benedict R. *Imagined Communities: Reflections on the Origin and Spread of Nationalism.* London: Verso, 1983.

Anzaldúa, Gloria. "The Path of the Red and Black Ink." *The Graywolf Annual Five: Multicultural Literacy.* Ed. Rick Simonson and Scott Walker. St. Paul: Graywolf, 1988. 13–29.

Aristotle. *On Rhetoric.* Trans. and ed. George Kennedy. New York: Oxford University Press, 1991.

Aronowitz, Stanley, Barbara Martinsons, and Michael Menser, eds. *Technoscience and Cyberculture.* New York: Routledge, 1996.

Astell, Mary. *The First English Feminist: Reflections upon Marriage and Other Writings.* Ed. Bridget Hall. Aldershot: Gower/Maurice Temple Smith, 1986.

Augustine. *On Christian Doctrine.* Trans. D. W. Robertson Jr. Indianapolis: Bobbs-Merrill, 1958.

Austin, Gilbert. *Chironomia; or, A Treatise on Rhetorical Delivery . . .* (1806). Ed. Mary Margaret Robb and Lester Thonssen. Carbondale: Southern Illinois University Press, 1966.

Bacon, Francis. "From *The Advancement of Learning.*" Bizzell and Herzberg, *The Rhetorical Tradition* 625–31.

Baker, Charlotte, and Robin Battison, eds. *Sign Language and the Deaf Community: Essays in Honor of William Stokoe.* [Silver Spring, Md.]: National Association of the Deaf, 1980.

Balsamo, Anne. *Technologies of the Gendered Body; Reading Cyborg Women.* Durham, N.C.: Duke University Press, 1996.

Barrell, John. *Poetry, Language, and Politics.* Manchester: Manchester University Press, 1988.

Bauman, H. Dirksen. "'Voicing' Deaf Identity: Through the 'I's' and Ears of an Other." *Getting a Life: Everyday Uses of Autobiography.* Ed. Sidonie Smith and Julia Watson. Minneapolis: University of Minnesota Press, 1996. 47–62.

Baynton, Douglas C. *Forbidden Signs: American Culture and the Campaign against Sign Language.* Chicago: University of Chicago Press, 1996.

Beaman, C. M. "The Holy Cross Integration Project: Successful Mainstreaming of the Hearing Impaired." *ACEHI Journal* 13.1 (1987): 40–46.

Bell, Alexander G. "How to Improve the Race." *Journal of Heredity* 5 (1914): 1–7.

———. *Memoir upon the Formation of a Deaf Variety of the Human Race.* 1884. Washington, D.C.: Alexander Graham Bell Association for the Deaf, 1969.

Bellugi, Ursula. "The Acquisition of a Spatial Language." *The Development of Language and Language Researchers: Essays in Honor of Roger Brown.* Ed. F. Kessell. Hillsdale, N.J.: Erlbaum, 1988. 153–85.

———. "How Signs Express Complex Meanings." Baker and Battison, *Sign Language and the Deaf Community* 53–73.

———. "The Link between Hand and Brain: Implications from a Visual Language." D. Martin, *Advances in Cognition, Education, and Deafness* 11–35.

Berlin, James. "Revisionary History: The Dialectical Method." *Pre/Text* 8.1–2 (1987): 47–61.

Bertling, Tom. *A Child Sacrificed: To the Deaf Culture.* Wilsonville, Ore.: Kodiak Media Group, 1994.

———. *No Dignity for Joshua: More Vital Insight into Deaf Children, Deaf Education, and Deaf Culture.* Wilsonville, Ore.: Kodiak Media Group, 1997.

Bess, Fred H., and Larry E. Humes. *Audiology: The Fundamentals.* Baltimore: Williams and Wilkins, 1995.

———. 2nd ed. *Audiology: The Fundamentals.* Baltimore: Williams and Wilkins, 1995.

Bhabha, Homi K. *The Location of Culture.* London: Routledge, 1994.

Birkerts, Sven. "Hamann's Bone: A Note on the Language of Modern Poetry." *The Electric Life: Essays on Modern Poetry.* New York: Morrow, 1989. 19–27.

Bitzer, Lloyd F. "The Rhetorical Situation." *Rhetoric: Concepts, Definitions, Boundaries.* Ed. William A. Covino and David A. Jolliffe. Boston: Allyn and Bacon, 1995. 300–310.

Bizzell, Patricia, and Bruce Herzberg, eds. *The Rhetorical Tradition: Readings from Classical Times to the Present.* Boston: Bedford/St. Martin's Press, 1990.

Blasing, Mutlu Konuk. *Politics and Form in Postmodern Poetry: O'Hara, Bishop, Ashbery and Merrill.* Cambridge: Cambridge University Press, 1995.

Boothroyd, Arthur. "Speech Perception Tests and Hearing-impaired Children." Plant and Spens, *Profound Deafness and Speech Communication* 345–71.

Bowra, Cecil Maurice. *Poetry and Politics, 1900–1960.* Cambridge: Cambridge University Press, 1966.

Brand, Alice G. "The Why of Cognition: Emotion and the Writing Process." *College Composition and Communication* 42 (1991): 436–43.

Brandt, Deborah. *Literacy as Involvement: The Acts of Writers, Readers, and Texts.* Carbondale: Southern Illinois University Press, 1990.

———. "Literacy as Knowledge." *The Right to Literacy.* Ed. Andrea Lunsford, Helene Moglen, and James Slevin. New York: MLA, 1990. 189–96.

Brereton, John C., ed. *The Origins of Composition Studies in the American College, 1875–1925: A Documentary History.* Pittsburgh: University of Pittsburgh Press, 1995.

Brill, Richard G., Barbara MacNeil, and Lawrence R. Newman. "Framework for Appropriate Programs for Deaf Children." *American Annals of the Deaf,* April 1996, 65–76.

Brodkey, Linda. "On the Subjects of Class and Gender in 'The Literacy Letters.'" *College English* 51 (1989): 125–41.

———. "Tropics of Literacy." *Journal of Education* 168 (1986): 47–54.

———. "Writing Ethnographic Narratives." *Written Communication* 4 (1987): 25–50.

Brooke, Robert. "Control in Writing: Flower, Derrida, and Images of the Writer." *College English* 51 (1989): 405–17.

Brueggemann, Brenda Jo. "The Coming Out of Deaf Culture and American Sign Language: An Exploration into Visual Rhetoric and Literacy." *Rhetoric Review* 13 (1995): 409–20.

———. "Context and Cognition in the Composing Processes of Deaf Student Writers." Ph.D. diss., University of Louisville, 1992.

———. "Still-Life: Representations and Silences in the Participant-Observer Role." *Ethics and Representation in Qualitative Studies of Literacy.* Ed. Gesa Kirsch and Peter Mortensen. Urbana, Ill.: National Council of Teachers of English, 1996. 17–34.

———. "'They've Got Power—They're Hearing': Case Studies of Deaf Student Writers at Gallaudet University." *Situated Stories: Valuing Diversity in Composition Research.* Ed. Emily Decker and Kathleen Geissler. Portsmouth, N.H.: Boynton/Cook, 1998. 31–43.

Bruffee, Kenneth. "Social Construction, Language, and the Authority of Knowledge: A Biographical Essay." *College English* 48 (1986): 773–90.

Bulwer, John. *Chirologia: Or, the Naturall Language of the Hand . . .* (1644). New York: AMS Press, 1975.

Burke, Kenneth. *Counter-Statement.* [2nd ed.] Los Altos, Calif.: Hermes, 1953.

———. "From *A Rhetoric of Motives.*" Bizzell and Herzberg, *The Rhetorical Tradition* 1018–34.

———. *A Grammar of Motives.* Berkeley: University of California Press, 1969.

———. *Language as Symbolic Action: Essays on Life, Literature, and Method.* Berkeley: University of California Press, 1966.

Calkins, Lucy M. "Forming Research Communities among Naturalistic Researchers." *Perspectives on Research and Scholarship in Composition.* Ed. B. W. McClelland and T. R. Donovan. New York: MLA, 1985.

Campbell, George. "From *The Philosophy of Rhetoric.*" Bizzell and Herzberg, *The Rhetorical Tradition* 749–97.

Carlson, Marvin. *Performance: A Critical Introduction.* London: Routledge, 1996.

Caroom, Ilene C. "Like Love, This Choice of Language." *Deafness: Life and Culture.* Ed. Mervin D. Garretson. Silver Spring, Md.: National Association of the Deaf, 1994. 8–9.

Cereta, Laura. "Letter to Augustinus Aemilius, Curse against the Ornamentation of Women and Letter to Bibulus Sempronius, Defense of the Liberal Instruction of Women." Bizzell and Herzberg, *The Rhetorical Tradition* 492–98.

Certeau, Michel de. *The Writing of History.* Trans. Tom Conley. New York: Columbia University Press, 1988.

Christiansen, John B., and Sharon N. Barnartt. *Deaf President Now! The 1988 Revolution at Gallaudet University.* Washington, D.C.: Gallaudet University Press, 1995.

Cicero. *De Inventione. De Optimo Genere Oratorum. Topica.* Trans. H. M. Hubbell. Loeb Classical Library. Cambridge: Harvard University Press, 1960.

Cixous, Hélène. "The Laugh of the Medusa." Bizzell and Herzberg, *The Rhetorical Tradition* 1232–45.

Clark, Graeme M. "Cochlear Implants: Historical Perspectives." Plant and Spens, *Profound Deafness and Speech Communication* 165–217.

Cliff, Michelle. "Journey into Speech" and "If I Could Write This in Fire I Would Write This in Fire." *Multi-Cultural Literacy.* Ed. Rick Simonson and Scott Walker. St. Paul: Graywolf, 1988. 53–82.

Clifford, James, and George E. Marcus, eds. *Writing Culture: The Poetics and Politics of Ethnography.* Berkeley: University of California Press, 1986.

Clifton, Lucille. *Quilting: Poems, 1987–1990.* Brockport, N.Y.: Boa Editions, 1991.

Cohen, Leah Hager. *Train Go Sorry: Inside a Deaf World.* Boston: Houghton Mifflin, 1994.

Cohn, Jim. "The New Deaf Poetics: Visible Poetry." *Sign Language Studies,* no. 52 (fall 1986): 263–77.

Connolly, William E. *Identity/Difference.* Ithaca, N.Y.: Cornell University Press, 1991.

Cook, Albert. *The Reach of Poetry.* West Lafayette, Ind.: Purdue University Press, 1995.

Cook-Gumperz, Jenny, ed. *The Social Construction of Literacy.* Cambridge: Cambridge University Press, 1986.

Corbett, Edward P. J. *Classical Rhetoric for the Modern Student.* 3rd ed. New York: Oxford University Press, 1990. [A 4th ed. is forthcoming in 1999.]

Cranny-Francis, Anne. *The Body in the Text.* Carlton South, Vic.: Melbourne University Press, 1995.

Daly, Mary. *Gyn/Ecology: The Metaethics of Radical Feminism.* Boston: Beacon, 1978.

———. *Outercourse: The Be-Dazzling Voyage . . .* San Francisco: Harper, 1992.

———. *Pure Lust: Elemental Feminist Philosophy.* Boston: Beacon, 1984.

———. *Webster's First New Intergalactic Wickedary of the English Language.* Boston: Beacon, 1987.

Davis, Lennard J. *Enforcing Normalcy: Disability, Deafness, and the Body.* London: Verso, 1995.

———. "The Prisoner of Silence: Deaf Prisoners." *Nation,* 4 October 1993, 354.

Davis, Townsend. "Hearing Aid." *New Republic,* 12 September 1988, 20–22.

Day, Gary, and Brian Docherty, eds. *British Poetry from the 1590s to the 1990s: Politics and Art.* New York: St. Martin's Press, 1997.

"Deaf Studies Mission Statement." American Sign Language and Deaf Studies Task Report. Gallaudet University, Washington, D.C. 31 August 1992.

de Castell, Suzanne, Allan Luke, and Kieran Egan, eds. *Literacy, Society, and Schooling.* Cambridge: Cambridge University Press, 1986.

Decker, Emily, and Kathleen Geissler, eds. *Situated Stories: Valuing Diversity in Composition Research.* Portsmouth, N.H.: Boynton/Cook, 1998.

Delpit, Lisa. *Other People's Children: Cultural Conflict in the Classroom.* New York: New Press, 1995.

Derrida, Jacques. "Structure, Sign and Play in the Discourse of the Human Sciences." *Modern Criticism and Theory.* Ed. David Lodge. New York: Longman, 1988. 108–23.

Denzin, Norman K. *Interpretive Interactionism.* Newbury Park, Calif.: Sage, 1989.

Denzin, Norman K., and Yvonna S. Lincoln, eds. *Handbook of Qualitative Research.* Thousand Oaks, Calif.: Sage, 1994.

Diamond, Elin, ed. *Performance and Cultural Politics.* London: Routledge, 1996.

Dillon, George. *Constructing Texts.* Bloomington: Indiana University Press, 1981.

Dillon, Harvey, and Teresa Ching. "What Makes a Good Speech Test?" Plant and Spens, *Profound Deafness and Speech Communication* 305–29.

Dolnick, Edward. "Deafness as Culture." *Atlantic Monthly,* September 1993, 37–51.

Edwards, Thomas R. *Imagination and Power: A Study of Poetry on Public Themes.* New York: Oxford University Press, 1971.

Epstein, June. *The Story of the Bionic Ear.* Melbourne: Hyland House, 1989.

Erickson, Jon. "The Body as the Object of Modern Performance." *Journal of Dramatic Theory and Criticism* 5.1 (1990): 231–43.

———. "The Language of Presence: Sound Poetry and Artaud." *Boundary 2* 14.1–2 (1985–86): 279–90.

Erskine-Hill, Howard. *Poetry and the Realm of Politics: Shakespeare to Dryden.* New York: Oxford University Press, 1996.

Ewoldt, Carolyn. "The Early Literacy Development of Deaf Children." Moores and Meadows-Orlan, *Educational and Developmental Aspects of Deafness* 85–114.

Fairclough, Norman. *Language and Power.* New York: Longman, 1989.

Fant, Gunnar. "Speech Related to Pure Tone Audiograms." Plant and Spens, *Profound Deafness and Speech Communication* 299–304.

Farrell, Thomas. "Knowledge, Consensus, and Rhetorical Theory." *Quarterly Journal of Speech* 62 (1976): 1–5.

———. *Norms of Rhetorical Culture.* New Haven: Yale University Press, 1993.

Featherstone, Mike, and Roger Burrows, eds. *Cyberspace/Cyberbodies/Cyberpunk: Cultures of Technological Embodiment.* London: Sage, 1995.

Fell, Margaret. "Women's Speaking Justified, Proved, and Allowed by the Scriptures." Bizzell and Herzberg, *The Rhetorical Tradition* 677–86.

Felshin, Nina, ed. *But Is It Art? The Spirit of Art as Activism.* Seattle: Bay, 1995.

Fetterman, David M. *Ethnography: Step by Step.* Newbury Park, Calif.: Sage, 1989.

Fine, Michelle. "Working the Hyphens: Reinventing Self and Other in Qualitative Research." *Handbook of Qualitative Research.* Ed. Norman K. Denzin and Yvonna S. Lincoln. Thousand Oaks, Calif.: Sage, 1994. 70–82.

Finger, Anne. "And the Greatest of These Is Charity." *The Ragged Edge: The Disability Experience from the Pages of the First Fifteen Years of the Disability Rag.* Ed. Barrett Shaw. Louisville, Ky.: Avocado, 1994. 115–19.

Fish, Stanley. *Anti-Foundationalism, Theory Hope, and the Teaching of Composition: Doing What Comes Naturally.* Durham, N.C.: Duke University Press, 1989.

Flint, Kate, ed. *Poetry and Politics.* Cambridge: Brewer, 1996.

Flower, Linda, and John Hayes. "A Cognitive Process Theory of Writing." *College Composition and Communication* 32 (1981): 365–87.

Foss, Sonja K. "The Construction of Appeal in Visual Images." *Rhetorical Movement: Essays in Honor of Leland M. Griffin.* Ed. David Zarefsky. Evanston, Ill.: Northwestern University Press, 1993. 210–24.

———. "Judy Chicago's *The Dinner Party:* Empowering of Women's Voice in Visual Art." *Women Communicating: Studies of Women's Talk.* Ed. Barbara Bate and Anita Taylor. Norwood, N.J.: Ablex, 1988. 9–26.

Foss, Sonja K, and Karen A. Foss. *Women Speak: The Eloquence of Women's Lives.* Prospect Heights, Ill.: Waveland, 1991.

Foss, Sonja K., Karen A. Foss, and Robert Trapp. *Contemporary Perspectives on Rhetoric.* 2nd ed. Prospect Heights, Ill.: Waveland, 1991.

Foss, Sonja K., and Cindy L. Griffin. "A Feminist Perspective on Rhetorical Theory: Toward a Clarification of Boundaries." *Western Journal of Communication* 56 (1992): 330–49.

Foster, Susan. "Examining the Fit." Paper presented at the Society for Disability Studies Annual Meeting, Washington, D.C., 22 June 1996.

———. *The Impact and Outcome of Mainstreamed and Residential School Programs.* Rochester, N.Y.: NTID/RIT, 1987.

———. "Life in the Mainstream: Deaf College Freshmen and Their Experiences in the Mainstreamed High School." *Journal of the American Deafness and Rehabilitation Association* 22 (1988): 27–35.

———. "Reflections of a Group of Deaf Adults on Their Experiences in Mainstream and Residential School Programs in the United States." *Disability, Handicap, and Society* 4.1 (1989): 37–56.

Foster, Susan, and Paula B. Brown. *Academic and Social Mainstreaming: Deaf Students' Perspectives on Their College Experience.* Rochester, N.Y.: NTID/RIT, 1988.

Foster, Susan, and Lisa Elliot. *Alternatives in Mainstreaming: A "Range of Options" Model for the Postsecondary Hearing-Impaired Student.* Rochester, N.Y.: NTID/RIT, 1986.

Foster, Susan, and Patricia Mudgett-DeCaro. "Mainstreaming Hearing-Impaired Students within a Postsecondary Educational Setting: An Ecological Model of Social Interaction." Paper presented at the American Education Research Association, Boston, Mass., 18 April 1990. 1990, ERIC ED 322 699.

Foucault, Michel. *The History of Sexuality.* Trans. Robert Hurley. New York: Vintage, 1990.

———. "Nietzsche, Genealogy, History." *The Foucault Reader.* Ed. and trans. Paul Rabinow. New York: Pantheon, 1984. 76–100.

————. *The Order of Things: An Archaeology of the Human Sciences.* New York: Pantheon, 1971.

Fredal, James. "Diffidence and the Will to Speech." Paper presented at the MLA Convention, Washington, D.C., 30 December 1996.

Freire, Paulo. *Pedagogy of the Oppressed.* Trans. Myra Bergman Ramos. New York: Continuum, 1970.

Fulford, Tim. *Landscape, Liberty, and Authority: Poetry, Criticism, and Politics from Thomson to Wordsworth.* Cambridge: Cambridge University Press, 1996.

Furth, Hans. "Research with the Deaf: Implications for Language and Cognition." *Psychological Bulletin* 62 (1964): 145–64.

————. *Thinking without Language: Psychological Implications of Deafness.* New York: Free Press, 1966.

Gallagher, Hugh Gregory. *FDR's Splendid Deception.* New York: Dodd, Mead, 1985.

Gallaudet, Edward Miner. *History of the College for the Deaf, 1857–1907.* Ed. Lance J. Fischer and David L. de Lorenzo. Washington, D.C.: Gallaudet College Press, 1983.

"Gallaudet: A Legacy and a Promise: A Brief History of Gallaudet University." Washington, D.C.: Gallaudet University, National Information Center on Deafness, 1990.

Gannon, Jack R. *Deaf Heritage: A Narrative History of Deaf America.* Silver Spring, Md.: National Association of the Deaf, 1991.

————. *The Week the World Heard Gallaudet.* Washington, D.C.: Gallaudet University Press, 1989.

Garbe, V., and M. Rodda. "Growing in Silence—the Deaf Adolescent." *ACEHI Journal* 14.2 (1988): 59–69.

Garretson, Merv. *Deafness: Life and Culture II.* Silver Spring, Md.: National Association of the Deaf, 1995.

Gass, William H., and Lorin Cuoco, eds. *The Writer in Politics.* Carbondale: Southern Illinois University Press, 1996.

Gates, Henry Louis, Jr. "The Signifying Monkey and the Language of Signifyin(g): Rhetorical Difference and the Orders of Meaning." Bizzell and Herzberg, *The Rhetorical Tradition* 1193–223.

Gee, J. P., and W. Goodhart. "American Sign Language and the Human Biological Capacity for Language." *Language Learning and Deafness.* Ed. Michael Strong. Cambridge: Cambridge University Press, 1988. 49–74.

Geertz, Clifford. *The Interpretation of Cultures: Selected Essays.* New York: Basic Books, 1973.

————. *Local Knowledge: Further Essays in Interpretive Anthropology.* New York: Basic Books, 1983.

————. *Works and Lives: The Anthropologist as Author.* Stanford: Stanford University Press, 1988.

"General Description of the English Language Program." *Gallaudet University English Department Handbook.* Washington, D.C., 1990.

Gioia, Dana. *Can Poetry Matter? Essays on Poetry and Culture.* St. Paul: Graywolf, 1992.

Giroux, Henry A. "Literacy and the Pedagogy of Political Empowerment." *Literacy: Reading the Word and the World.* Ed. Paulo Freire and Donald Macedo. South Hadley, Mass.: Bergin, 1986. 1–27.

————. "Literacy and the Politics of Difference." *Critical Literacy: Politics, Praxis, and the Postmodern.* Ed. Colin Lankshear and Peter McLaren. Albany: State University of New York Press, 1993. 367–77.

————. "Literacy, Ideology, and the Politics of Schooling." *Theory and Resistance in Education: A Pedagogy for the Opposition.* Ed. Henry A. Giroux. South Hadley, Mass.: Bergin, 1986. 205–32.

————. *Schooling and the Struggle for Public Life: Critical Pedagogy in the Modern Age.* Minneapolis: University of Minnesota Press, 1988.

Glickman, Ken. *Deafinitions for Signlets.* Silver Spring, Md.: DiKen Products, 1986.

————. *More Deafinitions for Signlets.* Silver Spring, Md.: DiKen Products, 1989.

Goetz, Judith Preissle, and Margaret D. LeCompte. *Ethnography and Qualitative Design in Educational Research.* Orlando, Fla.: Academic Press, 1984.

Goffman, Erving. *Stigma: Notes on the Management of a Spoiled Identity.* New York: Simon and Schuster, 1963.

Goody, Jack. *The Interface between the Written and the Oral.* Cambridge: Cambridge University Press, 1987.

————. *Literacy in Traditional Societies.* Cambridge: Cambridge University Press, 1968.

————. *The Logic of Writing and the Organization of Society.* Cambridge: Cambridge University Press, 1986.

Goody, Jack, and Ian Watt. "The Consequences of Literacy." Kintgen, Kroll, and Rose, *Perspectives on Literacy* 3–27.

Gould, Stephen J. *The Mismeasure of Man.* New York: Norton, 1981.

Gray, Chris Hables, ed. *The Cyborg Handbook.* New York: Routledge, 1995.

Greene, Maxine. *Landscapes of Learning.* New York: Teachers College Press, 1978.

Grimké, Sarah. "Letters on the Equality of the Sexes and the Condition of Woman, Letters, III, IV, and XIV." Bizzell and Herzberg, *The Rhetorical Tradition* 685–96.

Gross, Alan. *The Rhetoric of Science.* Cambridge, Mass.: Harvard University Press, 1990.

Gumperz, John J., ed. *Language and Social Identity.* New York: Cambridge University Press, 1982.

Hahn, Harlan. "The Politics of Physical Differences: Disability and Discrimination." *Journal of Social Issues* 4.1 (1988): 38–47.

———. "Toward a Politics of Disability: Definitions, Disciplines, and Policies." *Social Science Journal* 22 (1985): 87–106.

Hall, Stephanie. "Train-Gone-Sorry: The Etiquette of Social Conversations in American Sign Language." Wilcox, *American Deaf Culture* 89–102.

Hammersley, Martin, and Paul Atkinson. *Ethnography: Principles in Practice.* New York: Tavistock, 1983.

Haraway, Donna J. "Cyborgs and Symbionts: Living Together in the New World Order." *The Cyborg Handbook.* Ed. Chris Hables Gray. New York: Routledge, 1995. xi–xx.

———. *Simians, Cyborgs, and Women: The Reinvention of Nature.* New York: Routledge, 1991.

Harding, Sandra, ed. *The "Racial" Economy of Science.* Bloomington: Indiana University Press, 1993.

Harris, Marie, and Kathleen Aguero. *A Gift of Tongues: Critical Challenges in Contemporary American Poetry.* Athens: University of Georgia Press, 1987.

Harvey, J., and S. Siantz. "Public Education and the Handicapped." *Journal of Research and Development in Education* 12.1 (1979): 1–9.

Hassan, Ihab. *Contemporary American Literature, 1945–1972: An Introduction.* New York: Ungar, 1973.

Havelock, Eric A. *The Muse Learns to Write: Reflections on Orality and Literacy from Antiquity to the Present.* New Haven: Yale University Press, 1986.

Heath, Shirley Brice. "Protean Shapes in Literacy Events: Ever-Shifting Oral and Literate Traditions." Kintgen, Kroll, and Rose, *Perspectives on Literacy* 348–70.

———. *Ways with Words: Language, Life, and Work in Communities and Classrooms.* Cambridge: Cambridge University Press, 1983.

Hemwall, Margaret K. "Ethnography as Evaluation: Hearing-Impaired Students in the Mainstream." *Ethnography in Educational Evaluation.* Ed. D. M. Fetterman. Beverly Hills, Calif.: Sage, 1984.

Hill, Adams Sherman. "From *The Principles of Rhetoric.*" Bizzell and Herzberg, *The Rhetorical Tradition* 881–84.

Hirsch, E. D., Jr. *Cultural Literacy: What Every American Needs to Know.* Boston: Houghton Mifflin, 1987.

Hodgson, A. "How to Integrate the Hearing-Impaired." *Special Education: Forward Trends* 11.4 (1984): 27–29.

Hogue, Cynthia. *Scheming Women: Poetry, Privilege, and the Politics of Subjectivity.* Albany: State University of New York Press, 1995.

Horvath, Bruce K. "The Components of Written Response: A Practical Synthesis of Current Views." *Rhetoric Review* 2 (1985): 136–56.

Hosford-Dunn, Holly, Daniel R. Dunn, and Earl R. Harford. *Audiology Business and Practice Management.* San Diego: Singular, 1995.

Hull, Glynda, and Mike Rose. "Rethinking Remediation: Toward a Social-Cognitive Understanding of Problematic Reading and Writing." *Written Communication* 8 (1989): 139–54.

———. "'This Wooden Shack Place': The Logic of an Unconventional Reading." *College Composition and Communication* 41 (1990): 287–98.

Hull, Glynda, Mike Rose, Kay Lorey Fraser, and Marissa Castellano. "Remediation as a Social Construct: Perspectives from an Analysis of Classroom Discourse." *College Composition and Communication* 42 (1991): 299–29.

Isocrates. *Antidosis.* Trans. George Norlin. Loeb Classical Library. London: Heinemann; New York: Putnam's, 1929.

Jacobs, Leo. *A Deaf Adult Speaks Out.* Washington, D.C.: Gallaudet University Press, 1974.

Jankowski, Katherine A. *Deaf Empowerment: Emergence, Struggle, and Rhetoric.* Washington, D.C. Gallaudet University Press, 1997.

Jarratt, Susan. *Rereading the Sophists: Classical Rhetoric Refigured.* Carbondale: Southern Illinois University Press, 1991.

Jenks, Chris, ed. *Visual Culture.* London: Routledge, 1995.

Johnson, Nan. *Nineteenth-Century Rhetoric in North America.* Carbondale: Southern Illinois University Press, 1991.

Johnson, Robert E., S. K. Liddell, and Carol J. Erting. "Unlocking the Curriculum: Principles for Achieving Access in Deaf Education." Washington, D.C.: Gallaudet Research Institute Working Paper 89–3, 1989.

Jones, Richard, ed. *Poetry and Politics: An Anthology of Essays.* New York: Morrow, 1985.

Jones, Robert L. "Can Deaf Students Succeed in a Public University?" *ACEHI Journal* 12.1 (1986): 43–49.

Kannapell, Barbara. "Inside the Deaf Community." Wilcox, *American Deaf Culture* 21–28.

———. *Language Choice Reflects Identity Choice: A Sociolinguistic Study of Deaf College Students.* Ph.D. diss., Georgetown University, 1985. Ann Arbor: UMI, 1986.

———. "Personal Awareness and Advocacy in the Deaf Community." Baker and Battison, *Sign Language and the Deaf Community* 105–16.

Kantor, Kirby J., Dan R. Kirby, and Judith P Goetz. "Research in Context: Ethnographic Studies in English Education." *Research in the Teaching of English* 15 (1981): 293–309.

Katz, Jack, ed. *Handbook of Clinical Audiology.* 3rd ed. Baltimore: Williams and Wilkins, 1992.

Keller, Helen. *The Quiet Ear: Deafness in Literature.* Ed. Brian Grant. London: Deutsche, 1987.

Kelly, Ben R., Deborah Davis, and M. N. Hedge. *Clinical Methods and Practicum in Audiology.* San Diego: Singular, 1994.

Kelly, Leonard P. "Relative Automaticity without Mastery: The Grammatical Decision Making of Deaf Students." *Written Communication* 5 (1988): 325–51.

Kennedy, P., W. H. Northcott, R. W. McCauley, and S. M. Williams. "Longitudinal Sociometric and Cross-Sectional Data on Mainstreaming Hearing Impaired Children: Implications for Preschool Programming." *Volta Review* 78 (1976): 71–81.

Kintgen, Eugene R., Barry M. Kroll, and Mike Rose, eds. *Perspectives on Literacy.* Carbondale: Southern Illinois University Press, 1988.

Kirsch, Gesa, and Peter Mortensen. *Ethics and Representation in Qualitative Studies of Literacy.* Urbana, Ill.: National Council of Teachers of English, 1996.

Kozol, Jonathan. *Illiterate America.* New York: Anchor Press/Doubleday, 1965.

Kretschmer, Richard R., and Laura W. Kretschmer. *Language Development and Intervention with the Hearing Impaired.* Baltimore: University Park Press, 1978.

Kristeva, Julia. "Women's Time." Bizzell and Herzberg, *The Rhetorical Tradition* 1251 66.

Kroll, Barry M. "Writing for Readers: Three Perspectives on Audience." *College Composition and Communication* 35 (1984): 172–83.

Kroll, Barry M., and John C. Schafer. "Error-Analysis and the Teaching of Composition." *College Composition and Communication* 29 (1978): 242–48.

Kuhn, Thomas S. *The Structure of Scientific Revolutions.* 2nd ed. Chicago: University of Chicago Press, 1970. [1st ed. 1962]

Ladd, G. W., et al. "Social Integration of Deaf Adolescents in Secondary-Level Mainstreamed Programs." *Exceptional Children* 50 (1984): 420–28.

Lane, Harlan. "Constructions of Deafness." *Disability and Society* 10.2 (1995): 171–89.

———. "Is There a Psychology of Deafness: A Response." *BRIDGE: Bridging Research in Deafness and General Education* 15.1 (June 1996): 4–7.

————. *The Mask of Benevolence: Disabling the Deaf Community.* New York: Knopf, 1992.

————. "Reply to Peter Paul's Second Article." *BRIDGE: Bridging Research in Deafness and General Education* 15.3 (March 1997): 4–7.

————. *When the Mind Hears: A History of the Deaf.* New York: Random House, 1984.

Lanham, Richard. "The 'Q' Question." *South Atlantic Quarterly* 87 (1988): 653–700.

Lauer, Janice M., and John W. Asher. *Composition Research: Empirical Designs.* New York: Oxford University Press, 1988.

Lauter, Paul. "Class, Caste, and Canon." *A Gift of Tongues: Critical Challenges in Contemporary American Poetry.* Ed. Marie Harris and Kathleen Aguero. Athens: University of Georgia Press, 1987. 17–38.

Lentz, Ella Mae. *The Treasure.* Videocassette. Berkeley, Calif.: In Motion Press, 1995.

Libbey, S. S., and W. Pronovost. "Communication Patterns of Mainstreamed Hearing Impaired Adolescents." *Volta Review* 82 (1980): 197–213.

Lincoln, Yvonne, and E. G. Guba. *Naturalistic Inquiry.* Beverly Hills, Calif.: Sage, 1985.

Lorde, Audre. "The Master's Tools Will Never Dismantle the Master's House." *Sister Outsider: Essays and Speeches.* Trumansburg, N.Y.: Crossing, 1984. 110–13.

Lou, Mimi Whei-Ping, Michael Strong, and A. DeMatteo. "The Relationships of Educational Background to Cognitive and Language Development among Deaf Adolescents." D. Martin, *Advances in Cognition, Education, and Deafness* 118–26.

Lucas, Ceil. *Sign Language Research: Theoretical Issues.* Washington, D.C.: Gallaudet University Press, 1990.

————, ed. *Sociolinguistics in Deaf Communities.* Washington, D.C.: Gallaudet University Press, 1995.

Lunsford, Andrea. "Cognitive Studies and Teaching Writing." *Perspectives on Research and Scholarship in Composition.* Ed. Bruce W. McClellan and Timothy R. Donovan. New York: MLA, 1985. 145–61.

Lunsford, Andrea, Helene Moglen, and James R. Slevin, eds. *The Right to Literacy.* New York: MLA, 1990.

Marcus, George E., and Michael J. Fischer. *Anthropology as Cultural Critique: An Experimental Moment in the Human Sciences.* Chicago: University of Chicago Press, 1986.

Markowicz, Harry. *American Sign Language: Fact and Fancy.* Washington, D.C.: Gallaudet University Press, 1977.

Martin, David S., ed. *Advances in Cognition, Education, and Deafness.* Washington, D.C.: Gallaudet University Press, 1991.

Martin, Frederick N. *Introduction to Audiology.* 6th ed. Boston: Allyn and Bacon, 1997.

Matsuhashi, Ann. "Explorations in the Real-Time Production of Written Discourse." *What Writers Know: The Language, Process, and Structure of Written Discourse*. Ed. M. Nystrand. New York: Academic Press, 1983. 269–90.

Mayberry, R., and R. Wodlinger-Cohen. "After the Revolution: Educational Practice and the Deaf Child's Communication Skills." *They Grow in Silence: Understanding Deaf Children and Adults*. Ed. E. D. Mindel and McKay Vernon. Boston: College-Hill, 1987. 149–86.

McCarthy, Lucy P. "A Stranger in Strange Lands: A College Student Writing-Across-the-Curriculum." *Research in the Teaching of English* 21 (1987): 233–65.

McCollom, H. F., Jr., and J. M. Mynders. "How to Recognize (and Handle) the Troublesome Client." *Hearing Aid Dispensing Practice*. Danville, Ill.: Interstate Printers and Publishers, 1984. 115–31.

McLauchlin, Robert M., ed. *Speech-Language Pathology and Audiology: Issues and Management*. Orlando, Fla.: Grune and Stratton, 1986.

McLaughlin, Daniel, and William G. Terry. *Naming Silenced Lives: Personal Narratives and Processes of Educational Change*. New York: Routledge, 1993.

Merker, Hannah. *Listening*. New York: HarperCollins, 1995.

Mertens, David M. "Social Experiences of Hearing-Impaired High School Youth." *American Annals of the Deaf* 134 (1989): 15–19.

Miles, Michael B., and A. M. Huberman. *Quantitative Data Analysis: A Sourcebook of New Methods*. Beverly Hills: Sage, 1984.

Miller, Suzanne M., and Barbara McCaskill, eds. *Multicultural Literature and Literacies: Making Space for Difference*. Albany: State University of New York Press, 1993.

Mindel, Eugene D., and McKay Vernon, eds. *They Grow in Silence: Understanding Deaf Children and Adults*. 2nd ed. Boston: College-Hill, 1987.

Mittelman, L. J., and L. K. Quinsland. "A Paradigm for Teaching Written English to Deaf Students: A Cognitive Fluency Assessment Model." D. Martin, *Advances in Cognition, Education, and Deafness* 152–61.

Moores, Donald F. *Educating the Deaf: Psychology, Principles, and Practices*. Boston: Houghton Mifflin, 1978.

———. "Reactions from the Researcher's Point of View." D. Martin, *Advances in Cognition, Education, and Deafness* 224–28.

Moores, Donald F., and Kathryn P. Meadow-Orlans, eds. *Educational and Developmental Aspects of Deafness*. Washington, D.C.: Gallaudet University Press, 1990.

Moores, Donald F., and Catherine Sweet. "Factors Predictive of School Achievement." Moores and Meadow-Orlans, *Educational and Developmental Aspects of Deafness* 154–201.

Mow, Shanny. "How Do You Dance without Music?" Wilcox, *American Deaf Culture* 33–44.

Myklebust, Helmer R. *The Psychology of Deafness: Sensory Deprivation, Learning, and Adjustment.* New York: Grune, 1964.

National Information Center on Deafness. "Deafness: A Fact Sheet." Washington, D.C.: Gallaudet University, NICD, 1989.

———. "Educating Deaf Children: An Introduction." Washington, D.C.: Gallaudet University, NICD, 1987.

Neisser, Arden. *The Other Side of Silence: Sign Language and the Deaf Community in America.* New York: Knopf, 1983.

Nelson, Cary. *Our First Last Poets: Vision and History in Contemporary American Poetry.* Urbana: University of Illinois Press, 1981.

Neuleib, Janice. "The Friendly Stranger: Twenty-Five Years as 'Other.'" *College Composition and Communication* 43 (1992): 231–43.

Neuman, Tina. "Deaf Identify, Lesbian Identity: Intersections in a Life Narrative." *Queerly Phrased: Language, Gender, and Sexuality.* Ed. Anna Livia and Kira Hall. New York: Oxford University Press, 1997. 274–86.

Newby, Hayes A., and Gerald R. Popelka. *Audiology.* 6th ed. Englewood Cliffs, N.J.: Prentice Hall, 1992.

Norbrook, David. *Poetry and Politics in the English Renaissance.* Boston: Routledge and Kegal Paul, 1984.

North, Michael. *The Political Aesthetic of Yeats, Eliot, and Pound.* New York: Cambridge University Press, 1991.

North, Stephen. *The Making of Knowledge in Composition: Portrait of an Emerging Field.* Upper Montclair, N.J.: Boynton/Cook, 1987.

Oliver, Michael. *The Politics of Disablement: A Sociological Approach.* New York: St. Martin's Press, 1990.

———. *Understanding Disability: From Theory to Practice.* New York: St. Martin's Press, 1996.

Olson, Charles. *Projective Verse.* New York: Totem, 1959.

Olson, David. "From Utterance to Text: The Bias of Language in Speech and Writing." Kintgen, Kroll, and Rose, *Perspectives on Literacy* 175–89.

———. "The Language of Instruction: On the Literate Bias of Schooling." *Schooling and the Acquisition of Knowledge.* Ed. Richard Anderson, Randy Spiro, and William Montague. Hillsdale, N.J.: Erlbaum, 1977. 6–89.

Ong, Walter J. *Interfaces of the Word: Studies in the Evolution of Consciousness and Culture.* Ithaca, N.Y.: Cornell University Press, 1977.

———. *Orality and Literacy: The Technologizing of the Word.* New York: Methuen, 1982.

———. *The Presence of the Word: Some Prolegomena for Cultural and Religious History.* New Haven: Yale University Press, 1967.

———. *Why Talk? A Conversation about Language with Walter J. Ong conducted by Wayne Altree.* San Francisco: Chandler and Sharp, 1973.

Padden, Carol A. *Deaf Children and Literacy: Literacy Lessons.* Geneva: International Bureau of Education, 1990.

———. "The Deaf Community and the Culture of Deaf People." Baker and Battison, *Sign Language and the Deaf Community* 89–103.

Parini, Jay. *Some Necessary Angels: Essays on Writing and Politics.* New York: Columbia University Press, 1997.

Patton, Michael Q. *Qualitative Evaluation Methods.* Beverly Hills, Calif.: Sage, 1990.

Paul, Peter V. "A Final Reply to Harlan Lane." *BRIDGE: Bridging Research in Deafness and General Education* 15.3 (March 1997): 8–11.

———. "Is There a Psychology of Deafness? The Influence of Clinical and Cultural Perspectives." *BRIDGE: Bridging Research in Deafness and General Education* 14.3 (March 1996): 8–11.

Perelman, Chaim, and Lucie Olbrechts-Tyteca. "From *The New Rhetoric.*" Bizzell and Herzberg, *The Rhetorical Tradition* 1068–77.

Perl, Sondra. "Understanding Composing." *The Writer's Mind: Writing as a Mode of Thinking.* Ed. Janice N. Hays et al. Urbana, Ill.: National Council of Teachers of English, 1983. 43–51.

Phelan, Peggy. *Unmasked: The Politics of Performance.* New York: Routledge, 1993.

Philibert, Nicolas, dir. *In the Land of the Deaf,* prod. Les Films d'ici. New York: Kino on Video, 1994.

Pisan, Christine de. "From *The Treasure of the City of Ladies.*" Bizzell and Herzberg, *The Rhetorical Tradition* 488–92.

Plann, Susan. *The Silent Minority: Deaf Education in Spain, 1550–1835.* Berkeley: University of California Press, 1997.

Plant, Geoff, and Karl-Erik Spens, eds. *Profound Deafness and Speech Communication.* San Diego: Singular, 1995.

Plato. *Phaedrus.* Trans. Alexander Nehamas and Paul Woodruff. Indianapolis: Hackett, 1995.

———. *Republic.* Trans. Paul Shorey. 2 vols. Loeb Classical Library. Cambridge, Mass.: Harvard University Press, 1970.

Pratt, Mary Louise. "Arts of the Contact Zone." *Mass Culture and Everyday Life.* Ed. Peter Gibian. New York: Routledge, 1997.

Preston, Paul. *Mother Father Deaf.* Cambridge, Mass.: Harvard University Press, 1994.

Quintilian. *Institutio Oratoria.* Trans. H. E. Butler. 4 vols. Loeb Classical Library. Cambridge, Mass.: Harvard University Press, 1963.

Quigley, Stan P., and Peter V. Paul. *Language and Deafness.* San Diego: College-Hill, 1984.

Reagan, Timothy. "American Sign Language and Contemporary Deaf Studies in the United States." *Language Problems and Language Planning* 19 (1986): 282–89.

———. "Cultural Considerations in the Education of Deaf Children." Moores and Meadow-Orlans, *Educational and Developmental Aspects of Deafness* 73–84.

———. "The Deaf as a Linguistic Minority: Educational Considerations." *Harvard Educational Review* 55 (1985): 265–77.

———. "Multiculturalism and the Deaf: An Educational Manifesto." *Journal of Research and Development in Education* 22 (1988): 1–6.

———. "The Oral-Manual Debate in Deaf Education: Language Policies in Conflict." *Journal of the Midwest History of American Society* 16 (1988): 19–33.

Resnick, Daniel P., ed. *Literacy in Historical Perspective.* Washington, D.C.: Library of Congress, 1983.

Rich, Adrienne. *Blood, Bread, and Poetry: Selected Prose, 1979–1985.* New York: Norton, 1986.

Rodriguez, Richard. *Hunger of Memory: The Education of Richard Rodriguez.* Boston: Godine, 1982.

Rogerson, Charles W. "Clockwork Oranges: The Development of the Cyborg as Fictional Character." Ph.D. diss., Ohio State University, 1991.

Ronnberg, Jerker. "What Makes a Skilled Speechreader?" Plant and Spens, *Profound Deafness and Speech Communication* 393–415.

Roof, Judith, and Robyn Wiegman, eds. *Who Can Speak? Authority and Critical Identity.* Urbana: University of Illinois Press, 1995.

Rose, Mike. *Lives on the Boundary: The Struggles and Achievements of America's Underprepared.* New York: Free Press, 1989.

———. *Possible Lives: The Promise of Public Education in America.* Boston: Houghton Mifflin, 1995.

———. "Remedial Writing Courses: A Critique and a Proposal." *College English* 45 (1983): 109–28.

————. "Rigid Rules, Inflexible Plans, and the Stifling of Language: A Cognitivist's Analysis of Writer's Block." *College Composition and Communication* 31 (1980): 389–400.

————. *Writer's Block: The Cognitive Dimension.* Carbondale: Southern Illinois University Press, 1984.

Ross, Linda. "A Re-examination of Acculturation and Enculturation: Evidence from a Residential Deaf School." Paper presented at the 95th Annual Meeting of the American Anthropological Association, San Francisco, 20 November 1996.

Rush, Benjamin. *Essays: Literary, Moral, and Philosophical.* Ed. Michael Meranee. Schenectady, N.Y.: Union College Press, 1988.

Ryan, Richard. "Deafness." *Poetry,* October–November 1995, 30.

Rymer, Russ. "The Sounds of Silence: Review of Leah Hager Cohen's *Train Go Sorry.*" *New York Times Book Review,* 13 March 1994, 1.

Sacks, Oliver. *Seeing Voices: A Journey into the World of the Deaf.* Berkeley: University of California Press, 1989.

Said, Edward. *Orientalism.* New York: Random House, 1979.

Sandoval, Chela. "Dis-Illusionment and the Poetry of the Future: The Making of Oppositional Consciousness." Ph.D. qualifying essay, University of California, Santa Cruz, 1984.

Scheetz, Nanci A. *Orientation to Deafness.* Boston: Allyn and Bacon, 1993.

Schein, Jerome D., and Marcus T. Delk. *The Deaf Population of the United States.* Silver Spring, Md.: National Association of the Deaf, 1974.

Schein, Jerome D., and David A. Stewart. *Language in Motion: Exploring the Nature of Sign.* Washington, D.C.: Gallaudet University Press, 1995.

Schiebinger, Londa. *Nature's Body: Gender in the Making of Modern Science.* Boston: Beacon, 1993.

Schildroth, A. "Recent Changes in the Educational Placement of Deaf Students." *American Annals of the Deaf* 133.2 (1988): 61–67.

Scribner, Sylvia. "Literacy in Three Metaphors." Kintgen, Kroll, and Rose, *Perspectives on Literacy* 71–81.

Scribner, Sylvia, and Michael Cole. *The Psychology of Literacy.* Cambridge, Mass.: Harvard University Press, 1981.

Scully, James. *Line Break: Poetry as Social Practice.* Seattle: Bay, 1988.

Sedey-Roman, A., et al. "Enjoying Each Other's Company: Our Model of a Mainstream Classroom." *Perspectives for Teachers of the Hearing Impaired* 5.4 (1987): 8–10.

Sedgwick, Eve Kosofsky. *Epistemology of the Closet.* Berkeley: University of California Press, 1990.

Shakespeare, William. *Hamlet. The Complete Works of William Shakespeare.* Ed. Irving Ribner and George Lyman Kittredge. Waltham, Mass.: Ginn, 1971.

Shapiro, Joseph. *No Pity: People with Disabilities Forging a New Civil Rights Movement.* New York: Times Books, 1993.

Shaughnessy, Mina P. *Errors and Expectations: A Guide for the Teacher of Basic Writing.* New York: Oxford University Press, 1977.

Sheridan, Thomas. *A Course of Lectures on Elocution* (1796). Delmar, N.Y.: Scholar's Facsimiles Reprints, 1991.

Sidransky, Ruth. *In Silence: Growing Up Hearing in a Deaf World.* New York: St. Martin's Press, 1990.

Simon, Robert I., and Daniel Dippo. "On Critical Ethnographic Work." *Anthropology and Education Quarterly* 17.4 (1986): 195–202.

Simonson, Rick, and Scott Walker, eds. *The Graywolf Annual Five: Multi-Cultural Literacy.* St. Paul: Graywolf, 1988.

Sommers, Nancy. "Revision Strategies of Student Writers and Experienced Adult Writers." *College Composition and Communication* 31 (1980): 378–88.

Sontag, Susan. "The Aesthetics of Silence." *A Susan Sontag Reader.* New York: Farrar, Straus, and Giroux, 1982. 181–204.

Spivak, Gayatri. "The Politics of Translation." *Destabilizing Theory: Contemporary Feminist Debates.* Ed. Michèle Barrett and Anne Phillips. Stanford: Stanford University Press, 1992. 177–201.

Steele, Joshua. *An Essay towards Establishing the Melody and Measure of Speech, 1775.* Menston, Eng.: Scolar Press, 1969.

Steiner, George. "Silence and the Poet." *Language and Silence: Essays, 1958–1966.* Harmondsworth: Penguin, 1979. 57–76.

Stern, Carol Simpson, and Bruce Henderson. *Performance: Texts and Contexts.* New York: Longman, 1993.

Stewart, David A. "American Sign Language: A Forgotten Aspect of Total Communication." *ACEHI Journal* 8.3 (1982): 137–48.

Stokoe, William C. *Sign Language Structure.* Rev. ed. Silver Spring, Md.: Linstok, 1978.

———, ed. *Sign and Culture: A Reader for Students of American Sign Language.* Silver Spring, Md.: Linstok, 1980.

Stokoe, William C., Dorothy Casterline, and Carl G. Croneberg. *A Dictionary of American Sign Language on Linguistic Principles.* Silver Spring, Md.: Linstok, 1976.

Stone, Deborah. *The Disabled State.* Philadelphia: Temple University Press, 1982.

Strauss, Anselm L., and Juliet M. Corbin. *Basics of Qualitative Research: Grounded Theory Procedures and Techniques.* Newbury Park, Calif.: Sage, 1990.

Street, Brian, ed. *Cross-Cultural Approaches to Literacy.* Cambridge, Mass.: Harvard University Press, 1993.

Stromberg, Peter. *Language and Self-Transformation.* Cambridge: Cambridge University Press, 1993.

Strong, Michael. *Language Learning and Deafness.* Cambridge: Cambridge University Press, 1988.

Stuckey, J. Elspeth. *The Violence of Literacy.* Portsmouth, N.H.: Boynton/Cook, 1991.

Summers, Claude J., and Ted-Larry Pebworth, eds. *"The Muses Common-weale": Poetry and Politics in the Seventeenth Century.* Columbia: University of Missouri Press, 1988.

Talarico, Ross. *Spreading the Word: Poetry and the Survival of Community in America.* Durham, N.C.: Duke University Press, 1995.

Terry, Jennifer, and Melodie Calvert, eds. *Processed Lives: Gender and Technology in Everyday Life.* New York: Routledge, 1997.

Terry, Jennifer, and Jacqueline Urla, eds. *Deviant Bodies: Critical Perspectives on Difference in Science and Popular Culture.* Bloomington: Indiana University Press, 1995.

Treesberg, Judith. "The Death of a 'Strong Deaf.'" *Nation,* 11 February 1991, 155–58.

Trybus, Raymond. "Sign Language, Power, and Mental Health." Baker and Battison, *Sign Language and the Deaf Community* 201–17.

Tucker, Bonnie Poitras. *The Feel of Silence.* Philadelphia: Temple University Press, 1995.

Valli, Clayton. "Deaf World." *ASL Poetry: Selected Works of Clayton Valli.* Perf. Jed Galimore. Videocassette. San Diego: Dawn Sign Press, 1995.

———. "Hands." *ASL Poetry: Selected Works of Clayton Valli.* Perf. Claudia Jimenez. Videocassette. San Diego: Dawn Sign Press, 1995.

———. "Poetics of American Sign Language Poetry." Ph.D. diss., Union Institute Graduate School, 1993.

Valli, Clayton, and Ceil Lucas. *Linguistics of American Sign Language: A Resource Text for ASL Users.* Washington, D.C.: Gallaudet University Press, 1992.

Van Cleve, John V., ed. *Deaf History Unveiled: Interpretations from the New Scholarship.* Washington, D.C.: Gallaudet University Press, 1993.

Van Cleve, John V., and Barry A. Crouch. *A Place of Their Own: Creating the Deaf Community in America.* Washington, D.C.: Gallaudet University Press, 1988.

Vico, Giambattista. *On the Study Methods of Our Time* (1709). Trans. Elio Gianturco. Indianapolis: Bobbs-Merrill, 1965.

Vives, Juan Luis. *Selected Works of J. L. Vives.* Ed. C. Matheeussen. New York: Brill, 1987.

Walker, Lou Ann. "The Sounds of Silence: Review of Hannah Merker's *Listening.*" *New York Times Book Review* 13 March 1994, 1.

Wallin, Anita. "The Cochlear Implant: A Weapon to Destroy Deafness or a Support for Lipreading? A Personal View." Plant and Spens, *Profound Deafness and Speech Communication* 219–30.

Watkins, Daniel P. *Keats's Poetry and the Politics of the Imagination.* Rutherford, N.J.: Fairleigh Dickinson University Press, 1989.

Webster, Alex. *Deafness, Development, and Literacy.* New York: Methuen, 1986.

Weis, Louis, and Michelle Fine, eds. *Beyond Silenced Voices: Class, Race, and Gender in U.S. Schools.* Albany: State University of New York Press, 1993.

Weisel, Amatzia, ed. *Issues Unresolved: New Perspectives on Language and Deaf Education.* Washington, D.C.: Gallaudet University Press, 1998.

West, Robert. "The Mechanical Ear." *Volta Review* 35 (1936): 345–46.

Wheeler, David A. "Lessons in the Signs: Researchers Explore the World of the Deaf to Study the Evolution of Language." *Chronicle of Higher Education,* 9 November 1994, A2, A14.

Wick, Audrey. "The Feminist Sophistic Enterprise: From Euripides to the Vietnam War." *Rhetoric: Concepts, Definitions, Boundaries.* Ed. William A. Covino and David A. Jolliffe. Boston: Allyn and Bacon, 1995. 398–410.

Wilcox, Sherman, ed. *Academic Acceptance of American Sign Language.* Burtonsville, Md.: Linstok, 1992.

———. *American Deaf Culture: An Anthology.* Silver Spring, Md.: Linstok, 1989.

Wilson, Deborah S., and Christine Moneera Laennec, eds. *Bodily Discursions: Genders, Representations, Technologies.* Albany: State University of New York Press, 1997.

Winefield, Richard. *Never the Twain Shall Meet: Bell, Gallaudet, and the Communications Debate.* Washington, D.C.: Gallaudet University Press, 1987.

Winzer, Margret. *The History of Special Education: From Isolation to Integration.* Washington, D.C.: Gallaudet University Press, 1993.

Wolcott, H. "Criteria for an Ethnographic Approach to Research in Schools." *Human Organization* 34 (1975): 111–27.

Wollstonecraft, Mary. *Political Writings.* Ed. Janet Todd. London: Pickering, 1993.

Wood, Kathleen. "Coherent Identities amid Heterosexist Ideologies: Deaf and Hearing Lesbian Coming-Out Stories." *Reinventing Identities: From Category to Practice in Language and Gender.* Ed. Mary Bucholtz, A. C. Liang, and Laurel A. Sutton. New York: Oxford University Press, forthcoming.

Woodward, James. *How You Gonna Get to Heaven if You Can't Talk with Jesus? On Depathologizing Deafness.* Silver Spring, Md.: T.J. Publishers, 1982.

———. "Sociolinguistic Research on American Sign Language: An Historical Perspective." Baker and Battison, *Sign Language and the Deaf Community* 117–33.

Wright, David. *Deafness: A Personal Account.* New ed. London: Faber and Faber, 1990.

Wrigley, Owen. *The Politics of Deafness.* Washington, D.C.: Gallaudet University Press, 1996.

Zumthor, Paul. *Oral Poetry.* Trans. Kathryn Murphy-Judy. Minneapolis: University of Minnesota Press, 1990.

INTERVIEWS

Amy, second-year audiology student, Ohio State University, 2 October 1997.

Yerker Andersson, chair, Deaf Studies, Gallaudet University, 8 May 1996.

Anna, Gallaudet student, September–December 1991.

Bev, Gallaudet student, 5 September 1991.

Charlie, Gallaudet student, September–December 1991 and 9 May 1996.

Charlotte, deaf literacy researcher, 19 April 1996.

Christian, Ohio State University student, 5 June 1996.

Cynthia, ASL interpreter, 8 August 1996.

David, Gallaudet student, 7 May 1996.

Ellen, ASL teacher, Gallaudet graduate, 3 June 1996.

Gwen, audiologist, program director, Ohio State University, 13 March 1996.

Helen, audiologist, program director, Ohio State University, 2 October 1997.

Kate, second-year audiology student, Ohio State University, 2 October 1997.

Kathy, social worker, Gallaudet graduate, 20 June 1996.

Laura, second-year audiology student, Ohio State University, 2 October 1997.

Liz, second-year audiology student, Ohio State University, 2 October 1997.

Mike, Gallaudet student, 1 November 1991.

Ray, audiology Ph.D. student, Ohio State University, 16 October 1997.

Rick, Gallaudet history/government professor, 8 May 1996.

Scott, school/counseling psychologist, Gallaudet graduate (hearing), 9 May 1996.

Sharon, sign language interpreter, 8 May 1996 and 30 May 1998.

Stacy, second-year audiology student, Ohio State University, 2 October 1997.

Sue, assistive listening devices consultant, Columbus, Ohio, 11 April 1996.

CORRESPONDENCE

Peter Cook, Flying Words Project performer, June–August 1996.

Dale, Gallaudet English instructor, August 1998.

Ella, Gallaudet student, 10 September 1998.

Joe, Gallaudet English instructor, August 1998.

Karen, Gallaudet English instructor, March–September 1998.

Linda, Gallaudet student, 6 September 1998.

Kenny Lerner, Flying Words Project performer, June 1996–July 1998.

Sylvia, Gallaudet history instructor, 1996–98.

Terry, Gallaudet English instructor, March–July 1998.

INDEX